The French Revolution Debate in Britain

The Origins of Modern Politics

GREGORY CLAEYS

First published in 2007 by
PALGRAVE MACMILLAN
Houndmills, Basingstoke, Hampshire RG21 6XS and
175 Fifth Avenue, New York, N.Y. 10010
Companies and representatives throughout the world.

PALGRAVE MACMILLAN is the global academic imprint of the Palgrave
Macmillan division of St. Martin's Press, LLC and of Palgrave Macmillan Ltd.
Macmillan® is a registered trademark in the United States, United Kingdom
and other countries. Palgrave is a registered trademark in the European
Union and other countries.

ISBN-13: 978–0–333–62646–7 hardback
ISBN-10: 0–333–62646–X hardback
ISBN-13: 978–0–333–62647–4 paperback
ISBN-10: 0–333–62647–8 paperback

This book is printed on paper suitable for recycling and made from fully
managed and sustained forest sources.

A catalogue record for this book is available from the British Library.

A catalog record for this book is available from the Library of Congress.

10 9 8 7 6 5 4 3 2 1
16 15 14 13 12 11 10 09 08 07

Printed in China

British History in Perspective
General Editor: Jeremy Black

David Scott *Politics and War in the Three Stuart Kingdoms, 1637–49*
G.R. Searle *The Liberal Party: Triumph and Disintegration, 1886–1929 (2nd edn)*
John Stuart Shaw *The Political History of Eighteenth-Century Scotland*
W.M. Spellman *John Locke*
William Stafford *John Stuart Mill*
Robert Stewart *Party and Politics 1830–1852*
Alan Sykes *The Radical Right in Britain*
Bruce Webster *Medieval Scotland*
Ann Williams *Kingship and Government in Pre-Conquest England*
Ian S. Wood *Churchill*
John W. Young *Britain and European Unity, 1945–99 (2nd edn)*
Michael B. Young *Charles I*
Paul Ziegler *Palmerston*

Please note that a sister *series, Social History in Perspective*, is available
covering the key topics in social and cultural history.

British History in Perspective
Series Standing Order:
ISBN 0–333–71356–7 hardcover
ISBN 0–333–69331–0 paperback

You can receive future titles in this series as they are published by placing a standing
order. Please contact your bookseller or, in case of difficulty, write to the address
below with your name and address, the title of the series and the ISBN quoted above.

Customer Services Department, Macmillan Distribution Ltd
Houndmills, Basingstoke, Hampshire RG21 6XS, England

Contents

v

Acknowledgements

Portions of the argument presented here have previously appeared in *History of Political Thought*, the *Journal of Modern History*, *Political Theory*, the *Bulletin of the Society for the Study of Labour History*, the *Journal of the History of Philosophy* and in Gordon Schochet, ed. *Empire and Revolutions. Papers Presented at the Folger Institute Seminar 'Political Thought in the English-Speaking Atlantic, 1760–1800'* (Washington DC, The Folger Library, 1993), John Whale, ed. *Edmund Burke's Reflections on The Revolution in France* (Manchester, Manchester University Press, 2000) and Glenn Burgess, *English Radicalism 1550–1850* (Cambridge, Cambridge University Press, 2007). I am grateful to Cambridge University Press for permission to use some of the latter material here.

Amongst the many individuals I have benefited from discussing these issues over the years, I am especially grateful to John Barrell, Richard Bourke, Dawn Clively, J.E. Cookson, Iain Hampsher-Monk, Istvan Hont, Gareth Stedman Jones, Iain McCalman and J.G.A. Pocock.

Note on references: all books cited here were published in London unless otherwise noted.

Brief Chronology of Leading Events Connected with the French Revolution

1789

24 Jan.	States-General summoned by Louis XVI
15 June	Third Estate renamed the National Assembly
14 July	Fall of the Bastille
4 Aug.	Abolition of feudalism; Declaration of Rights
2 Nov.	Church property nationalised in France
4 Nov.	Revolution Society celebrates Glorious Revolution of 1688; Rev. Richard Price sermon, published as *A Discourse on the Love of Our Country*
12 Dec.	Assignats introduced

1790

19 June	Abolition of aristocratic titles in France
Nov.	Edmund Burke. *Reflections on the Revolution in France*

1791

Feb.	Thomas Paine. *Rights of Man*, Part One
20 June	Louis XVI's flight to Varennes
Sept.	French Constitution adopted

1792

Jan.	London Corresponding Society founded
16 Feb.	*Rights of Man*, Part the Second
11 April	Society of the Friends of the People founded
20 April	France declares war on Austria
21 May	Royal Proclamation against seditious writings
24 June	Prussia declares war on France
10 Aug.	Attack upon the Tuileries; Louis XVI imprisoned; monarchy suspended
2–3 Sept.	September Massacres of prisoners

20 Sept.	Second National Assembly dissolved; National Convention formed
20 Nov.	Association for the Protection of Liberty and Property against Republicans and Levellers founded
11–13 Dec.	Convention of the Scottish Friends of the People in Edinburgh
18 Dec.	Paine convicted of seditious libel for *Rights of Man*

1793

21 Jan.	Louis XVI executed
1 Feb.	France declares war on Britain and the United Netherlands
30 April	Second general Convention of Scottish reformers
31 May–2 June	Girondins overthrown in Paris
Oct.	Girondins executed
16 Oct.	Marie Antoinette executed
20 Oct.– 6 Nov.	Edinburgh Convention meets
5 Dec.	Maurice Margarot, Joseph Gerrald and William Skirving arrested
6 Dec.	Edinburgh Convention halted

1794

Jan.–March	Scottish reformers convicted of sedition and sentenced to transportation
1–5 Dec.	John Thelwall tried for treason and acquitted

1795

26 Oct.	Largest London Corresponding Society meeting
18 Dec.	Pitt and Grenville Acts on treason and sedition become law

1798

23–26 May	Irish rebellion begins
22 Aug.	French invasion of Ireland; surrender on 8 Sept.

1799

9 Nov.	Napoleon Bonaparte overthrows Directory and becomes First Consul

Later Events

25 March 1802	Peace of Amiens
18 May 1803	Britain declares war on France
18 May 1804	Napoleon becomes Emperor of France
July 1804	French invasion threat to Britain
21 Oct. 1805	British victory over French and Spanish fleets at Trafalgar
April 1814	Abdication of Napoleon
30 May 1814	Peace of Paris
20 March 1815	Restoration of Napoleon
18 June 1815	Napoleon defeated at Waterloo

Chapter One: Introduction
The Origins of Modern Political Discourse

THE revenue of France was near twenty million when Lewis XVI, finding it inadequate, called upon the nation for supply. In a single lifetime it rose to far more than one hundred million, while the national income grew still more rapidly; and this increase was wrought by a class to whom the ancient monarchy denied its best rewards, and whom it deprived of power in the country they enriched. As their industry effected change in the distribution of property, and wealth ceased to be the prerogative of a few, the excluded majority perceived that their disabilities rested on no foundation of right and justice, and were unsupported by reasons of State. They proposed that the prizes in the Government, the Army, and the Church should be given to merit among the active and necessary portion of the people, and that no privilege injurious to them should be reserved for the unprofitable minority. Being nearly a hundred to one, they deemed that they were virtually the substance of the nation, and they claimed to govern themselves with a power proportioned to their numbers. They demanded that the State should be reformed, that the ruler should be their agent, not their master.

That is the French Revolution ... [1]

While the apparent simplicity of such an explanation may seem questionable today, the French Revolution is incontrovertibly the defining act of modern politics. From it flowed the European upheavals of 1848, the Russian Revolution, and a goodly share of those urgent demands for democracy, liberty and equality, whose often contradictory fusion remains the unresolved problematic of our times. Yet the meaning of the Revolution has remained, from its inception, heavily contested. Some have hailed the events commencing on 14 July 1789 as the inexorable

1

progress of Enlightenment towards the eradication of aristocratic, monarchical and clerical tyranny, the downfall of superstition and exploitation, and an end to the enslavement of non-whites.[2] Others, however, date the origins of the colossal bloodbath of twentieth-century totalitarian tyranny in the degeneration of the Revolution into mob rule, the Terror of 1793–4, and the later Napoleonic dictatorship.[3] In the latter view, Robespierre begat Stalin, and the Enlightenment should be symbolised less by the incandescence of Reason than the ghastly illumination cast by the *lanterne* upon corpses suspended from it. Nor was there, even initially, agreement as to the causes of the Revolution. For the Abbé Barruel, Mounier and others, writing in the late 1790s, a conspiracy of freethinking anti-clerical philosophers had plotted to bring down the *ancien régime*.[4] But there were other plausible explanations. A later generation amongst the Whigs, the more liberal and reform-minded of the two main British political groupings, like Francis Jeffrey, would lay greater stress upon the chronic financial instability of the reign of Louis XVI.[5] That returning soldiers who had aided the American colonists' revolt against Britain circulated new ideas of liberty is undisputed. So too is the widespread resentment by the oppressed peasantry of the privileges of the 200,000 nobility, who had long since, in Carlyle's words, 'ceased either to guide or misguide',[6] and the clergy, who had substantial landholdings but were exempted from property tax.[7] The character of the king was weak; if (again Carlyle) 'French kingship had not, by course of Nature, long to live, he of all men was the man to accelerate Nature.'[8] And as the quote, above, from Lord Acton, indicates, the Revolution was widely perceived as the effort of the town-dwelling middle classes to achieve a social and political recognition commensurate with their wealth and importance to national vitality. (In Marxian terms, thus, this was a 'bourgeois' revolution.) But were the principles of 1789 those of 1776, or, searching still further back, those of Britain's 'Glorious Revolution' of 1688? If they were attempts at imitating either, could such principles simply be transplanted from one social milieu to another, without reference to the conditions which had fostered them? And even if they were transferable, how far did the desire for liberty mask a more deeply rooted quest for equality, a quest fuelled, perhaps, by a much deeper resentment of privilege than had prevailed in America, and one which might, accordingly, break out into licentiousness and bloodshed all too easily?

The complexity of such issues, and the volatility of the Revolution itself, ensured that in Britain the Revolution caused an 'irrepressible passion for discussion' of political principles on a scale not seen since the upheavals of the mid-seventeenth century.[9] 'Grown up people', one observer recalled, 'talked at this time of nothing but the French Revolution and its supposed consequences'.[10] The more enthusiastic contended that 'The late glorious revolution in France holds forth an example which sooner or later will be imitated by every nation in Europe'.[11] Some, intoxicated by a heady brew of liberty, equality and rights, and the sense of creating a world *de novo*, with a new calendar, clothing, forms of address, and a dictionary full of neologisms, would champion revolutionary principles for decades. Others would be first enthusiasts and then, in the grey aching morn of post-celebratory sobriety, vehement opponents of French developments. Some, initially suspicious, rapidly denounced the new ideals as heralding tyranny and conquest. Yet others, torn between optimism and pessimism, would resist the temptation to condemn the Revolution's failures as owing to inherent flaws in republicanism or democracy as such. Very quickly, the spectrum of interpreting French events would solidify into that basic, if complex and frequently shifting, set of positions, from 'right' to 'left', which has dominated subsequent modern politics.[12]

This book offers a very brief introduction to the leading strands of thought which evolved from this impassioned collision of ideas.[13] Commencing with an assessment of the leading themes of Edmund Burke's *Reflections on the Revolution in France* (1790), which began the British debate, it examines the development of radicalism through the works of Thomas Paine and his followers; the emergence of feminist argument in the works of Mary Wollstonecraft; the growth of a loyalist-radical confrontation in the early 1790s; divisions amongst the Whig party in the early years of the debate; the origins of philosophical anarchism in the writings of William Godwin; and the increasing focus upon property rights in the writings of John Thelwall. The range of positions established by these writers produced the starting point of socialist economic thought, of both radical and liberal conceptions of the welfare state originating in particular with Paineite republicanism; of modern conservatism, inspired by Burke's *Reflections on the Revolution in France* (1790); and, as Adam Smith's reputation grew rapidly, of subsequent theories of modern 'laissez-faire' commercial society.

Thereafter, nineteenth- and twentieth-century European politics would come to be defined by a grand conflict between liberal democracies based on free market economic ideals, and socialism, especially Marxism. The grand issue of modern times, whether private or public ownership and management of property would produce the greatest and most widespread prosperity; and beneath this, whether, in what degree, and how society should seek to maximise an equality of ranks and conditions, and whether this furthered or undermined the cause of liberty, were increasingly forced onto a public agenda after 1789. Such questions would come to be understood as an extension of the central language of 'rights' which lay at the core of Revolutionary discourse. But they did not yet produce fully fledged ideologies of the mid-nineteenth century variety, and we should beware of the anachronistic extension of later concepts back into this period. While 'radical' is used in the 1790s, 'radicalism' is not. 'Socialism' would not be coined until the mid-1820s. 'Feminism' appears only at the end of the nineteenth century. It is with the 'origins' of these modern ideals that we are concerned, not their maturation and more systematic expression, which occurred at varying rates of tempo across the following two centuries. And I have concentrated here primarily upon English, as opposed to Irish or Scottish, debates,[14] as well as upon more narrowly political discussions, thus excluding any consideration of poetry, literature, or symbolic expression.[15]

While every country in Europe experienced this controversy, Britain was, and remained acutely conscious of being different from other nations, and moreover considerably in advance of them. Britons had good cause to suppose they had already embraced modernity fairly comprehensively well before 1789, and thus disdained instruction in its principles from foreigners. The extensive growth of what was rapidly being termed 'commercial society', in the language of its chief Scottish theoreticians, such as David Hume and Adam Smith, had brought unprecedented wealth and refinement, a rapidly evolving division of labour, and an astonishing boom in technological innovation. Vanity, frivolity, and the constant emulative quest for fashionable novelty had long been accepted as definitive of commercial society, as had the increasing fusion of identity with the acquisition and consumption of commodities, even if they tended to obfuscate the differences between social ranks, even to hasten insubordination. Nonetheless qualms respecting the moral effects of widespread luxury, the chronic instability induced by relentless ambition, and the all-consuming greed fuelled by an incessant passion for money getting, upon both private morals and public virtue were rapidly being laid to rest.[16] Such forces and passions, it was contended, could be harnessed, harmonised and induced to serve the common weal. Other apparent evils, too, like expensive wars and imperial expansion, had necessitated new schemes of public finance to fund an enormous national debt. But these, too, paradoxically seemed to strengthen rather than weaken the state. And if Britons knew themselves to be the wealthiest nation in the world by 1789, they also fancied themselves, and with good reason, the freest: the constitutional settlement of the 'Glorious Revolution' of 1688 had fettered the hands of an overly ambitious monarch, and guaranteed a measure of civil liberty which was the envy of Britain's neighbours, including most of the chief perpetrators of the French Revolution itself. There was, admittedly, widespread political corruption, including the buying of votes and the advertisement of parliamentary seats for sale openly in newspapers, and considerable aristocratic and monarchic manipulation of the House of Commons. Nonetheless most observers agreed that it was not difficult to establish both 'the general satisfaction of the English people with their own constitution and Government' and the fact that:

> This was not the case in France. The people here were insulted, oppressed, and plundered. They had Bastilles to demolish and tyranny to resist; nor had they the means of restoring themselves to the indubitable 'Rights of Men' living in society except by the dreadful expedient of a revolution.[17]

Britain's prosperity and its possession of a substantial measure of civil and political liberty, we will see, were to remain central to the fierce controversies of the early 1790s. Other factors, too, inhibited greater public sympathy with 'French principles'. France was, after all, Britain's 'hereditary enemy', with whom, now in the shape of a 'Jacobin republic', she would be yet again at war from early 1793. The political degeneration of the Revolution into Jacobinical despotism in the same year, with the accompanying execution of the king and queen, and then the leading moderate Girondists, also explain why the Revolutionary debate did not ultimately pose a stronger challenge to the status quo. Despite naval mutinies and the Irish uprising of 1798, and a variety of closet conspiracies, no credible threat of revolution thus emerged in Britain itself throughout the 1790s and the lengthy Napoleonic period.[18]

Yet events might have indicated a different outcome. In the early 1790s a substantial number of Britons did come to believe that their own government and society were ruled by a small, rapacious aristocracy, that the established church was not representative of much of the population, that both were inordinately expensive, and that the lower orders were taxed disproportionately to support them. It was not necessary to embrace republican egalitarianism in order to perceive that these grievances demanded remedy; that more Britons, in other words, could be still freer than they already were, and the labouring poor might be considerably more affluent. In the measure in which such claims could be seen as a protest against existing corruption, the limited possession of the franchise, and the oppressiveness of an arrogant establishment, they were tied to earlier proposals for parliamentary reform by writers like Major John Cartwright, most recently in the early 1780s. As such they could appear not as 'French' or 'Jacobin' principles, but as a purification of the 'ancient constitution', a return to first principles, a cleansing of the parliamentary Augean stable, for which substantial support might be elicited from the propertied classes. Such had been the main strategy of those reformers who met to commemorate the Glorious Revolution of 1688, on 4 November 1789, and who heard the leading Protestant Dissenter (from the Thirty-Nine Article creed of the established Church of England), and pro-American minister Richard Price's sermon, published as *A Discourse on the Love of Our Country* (1789), which provoked Burke's famous riposte and commenced the debate which we will examine here. Particularly after war commenced in 1793, such reform proposals needed to be construed as 'British' as such, to have any chance of success. Ultimately, for large numbers of the middling orders, they did not, and this, too, accounts for the failure of the reform agenda in this period.

Yet this 'failure', too, needs to be weighed against the fact that the British constitution would become inexorably more democratic throughout the next century. Many of the key demands of reformers would reappear in the Chartist six points of 1836–50. Conservatives would deny that the 'rights of man' underpinned their efforts, even as they advanced the cause of democracy in mid-century.[19] Official rejection of the Revolution's principles was long lasting: the government would refuse to permit its ambassador to attend celebrations of the centenary of the Revolution in 1889.[20] But Britain would eventually expand and amend its constitution to encompass virtually all that most reformers in the 1790s had demanded, and for some later Victorian liberals – at any rate Francophile liberals – the Revolution could be seen indeed to herald 'a new phase of civilisation … a movement of the human race towards a completer humanity.'[21] Far from having failed, then, the much-castigated 'Jacobins' of the 1790s laid the foundations for that political and social democratisation of Britain, and the elimination of its feudal institutions, which continues through the present day, and in some instances, notably feminism, has scarcely yet achieved its egalitarian goals.

The account of these ideas presented in this book stresses the mounting importance of issues of property rights, and the impact of commerce and luxury in particular, in the political debates of this period. While the origins of nineteenth-century political and economic liberalism are well documented, few readings of the chief radical texts of this era have focussed closely on theories of property, especially in light of the now considerable and complex scholarship on late eighteenth-century republicanism.[22] A more careful reconstruction of the evolution of plebeian radicalism will show us, among other things, that the assumption of a central opposition of 'liberal' to 'republican' thought, or of Hume and Smith on the one hand to Rousseau and the English revolutionary republicans of the seventeenth century on the other, does not take us very far in explaining some of the crucial intellectual shifts of this period. As in the preceding century, there were many different types of 'republicans' writing in this period, and the more radical among them, in particular, freely mixed rights- and virtue-based theories in support of popular sovereignty. They also possessed many different conceptions of economic freedom and intervention. Moreover, the term 'liberal' had not yet achieved any recognisable political status, though many of the concepts we associate with it were in use. My aim here, then, besides presenting a general account of the revolutionary debates, is to explore how attitudes towards commerce, luxury and inequality of property, in particular, divided the radicals and revealed crucial differences in their republicanism. I want to show, too, that despite these disagreements, radicals came in this period to accept as increasingly central claims for the just reward of the labouring classes. (Such pleas on the basis of justice and humanity had been offered by writers like Adam Smith, however).[23] More innovatively, radicals linked such demands with an account of the poverty of the labouring classes. This in turn generated a strikingly new description of the relationship between wage-labourers and their employers which would become crucial for nineteenth-century radicalism and socialism.

This book thus plots a clear trajectory of development in the political debate of this period. By the mid-1790s much of the traditionally Whig discourse on natural rights and an original social contract was ceded by more moderate reformers, after considerable struggle, to the rhetoric of working class radicalism, which retained such themes until well into the nineteenth century. Middle class reformers instead quickly moved towards a new liberal ideal dominated by classical political economy (which had many Tory adherents by 1815 as well), and attended by several forms of utilitarianism.[24] The growing prominence of discussions of economic laws in liberal political thought was ensured by the end of the decade with the thorough-going assault on the poor's right to charity and rejection of 'speculative' social theory in Malthus' *Essay on Population*.

* * *

Such a scenario would have been difficult to anticipate in the early months of the Revolution. The initial British reaction to French developments was overwhelmingly positive. It seemed generally agreed that 'If there be any people to whose admiration [the Revolution] is particularly entitled', it was 'the English, who have known the value of liberty.'[25] There was much popular curiosity about events in France. Visitors to London reported that shops were full of prints of key figures and occurrences. Tracts like *Tyranny Annihilated: or, The Triumph of Freedom over Despotism ... With an Ample and Just Description of That Horrid State Prison, the Bastille* (1790) appeared. A performance entitled 'Taking the Bastille' played at no less than three theatres in 1790–1.[26] Sympathisers enthused over 'much the greatest event ... that ever happened in the world!' (Charles James Fox),[27] 'an event the most beneficial to humanity in all the records of mankind' (David Williams),[28] and 'the greatest Revolution ever recorded in the history of mankind' (Thomas Christie).[29] Some imagined such eruptions presaged 'the downfal, the total overthrow of despotism, and the extirpation of all hereditary Despots out of Europe'.[30] The religiously minded fancied 'that the Revolution is of God ... that the hand of God has very visibly appeared in it, and that this glorious event carries with it the most indubitable evidence of the Divine approbation'.[31] Philosophers heralded the culmination of Reason's conquests, and the prospect of heady, undiluted virtue supplanting the rancid corruption of the old regime. To its supporters the emotional euphoria generated by the Revolution was intoxicating: the pungent aroma of liberty provoked the reformer George Dyer to proclaim that 'in no period of my life have I felt stronger passions, or purer motives'.[32] The quintessential principle of the British constitution, liberty, no longer seemed the jealously guarded privilege of the few but the right of all; no longer the creation of 'Saxon, Danish, or Norman ancestors', as Thomas Christie averred, but (in James Mackintosh's words) 'the immortal daughter of Reason, of Justice, and of God'.[33] European enmity, fuelled by national chauvinism, seemed ready to succumb to cosmopolitanism, fraternity and universal benevolence.[34] Debt-ridden through past wars, Britons stood to gain not only peace with France, but the recognition that British principles of liberty were universally applicable. 'If it be asked', wrote Thomas Paine, 'what is the French Revolution to us? … We answer … It is much. Much to us as Men: Much to us as Englishmen'.[35]

Two groups in particular linked their own causes to this enthusiasm. Dissenters from the Established Church had long rattled the chains of civil and political disability clamped upon them after the Restoration in 1660, when they were punished for supporting the overthrow of Charles I.[36] They thus rapidly seized upon the issues of religious toleration and ecclesiastical reform lent prominence by events in France. Secondly, radical Whigs and political reformers, already inspired by the American Revolution, and alarmed by ministerial incompetence in the pursuit of a lengthy and unpopular war against the ex-colonists, welcomed French efforts to reduce arbitrary privileges and to extend the franchise. They did not, however, necessarily seek identical reforms in Britain, for conditions in the two nations were obviously dissimilar.[37] But they aimed, through newly revived organisations like the Revolution Society and the Society for Constitutional Information, to make parliament both less corrupt and more representative. They thus sought principally to curb the growing patronage of the government, and its subsequent ability, through 'borough-mongers', to muster large parliamentary majorities, and to reduce the alarming burden of taxation this 'corrupt' influence entailed.[38]

Few British admirers of the French Revolution, at least up to 1792, thus desired any fundamental alteration in the British Constitution. The more radical reformers, like Major John Cartwright and the Duke of Richmond, had proposed universal male suffrage in the 1780s.[39] But most, in the Whig tradition of Locke, Harrington and Sidney (but equally that of Washington and Jefferson), wanted the franchise limited to property-holders in some way, in the belief that they alone could wield the franchise responsibly, and to prevent the despoliation of the rich by the poor. Most embraced the staple doctrine of eighteenth-century

European liberalism, popularised in Britain by Blackstone and others, and on the Continent by Montesquieu and De Lolme, that Britain's tripartite constitutional balance between King, Lords and Commons guaranteed political stability and liberty alike more effectively than any other government. And many boasted that Britain's great opulence practically guaranteed popular satisfaction with these arrangements, even among the labouring poor.

The latter assumption in particular was subjected to a severe test during the next decade. British public opinion, as we will see, began to polarise in the autumn of 1790.[40] The occasion was a savage attack upon the enemies of the *ancien régime* from an unexpected quarter. On 1 November 1790 was published *Reflections on the Revolution in France*. Its author was a philosopher and leading Whig politician, Edmund Burke, renowned as an opponent of monarchical profligacy and jealous guardian of the privileges of the House of Commons against regal interference. Only recently, he had been a noted supporter of American independence. He might, accordingly, have been expected to welcome the overthrow of a despotic monarchy and the extension of 'British' ideas of liberty. His intervention, proposing exactly the opposite interpretation, provoked an explosive reaction across the entire spectrum of political opinion which essentially shaped the contours of the debate which this book explores.

Chapter Two: Edmund Burke
Reflections on the Revolution in France *(1790)* and the Origins of Conservatism

Background

Born in Dublin in 1729, of Catholic extraction on his mother's side, Edmund Burke studied law, wrote several philosophical works, notably *A Vindication of Natural Society* (1756), a satire on Bolingbroke, and *A Philosophical Inquiry into the Origin of our Ideas of the Sublime and Beautiful* (1756), and conceived and edited the *Annual Register*, a leading historical periodical. He became a Whig M.P. for Wendover from 1765–74, then for Bristol (1774–80) and Malton (1781–94). Renowned as an orator, he achieved acclaim as a financial reformer, and as the scourge of the East India Company's abuses of power through his prosecution of Warren Hastings' excesses in pursuing British conquests in India. A prominent defender of Catholic rights and leading advocate of the American colonists' claims, Burke had nonetheless failed to attain high office despite a distinguished career, and was disgruntled by the great Whig magnates' failure to appreciate his talents.[1] By 1789 he was still a leading political figure of considerable influence; he would soon be the most controversial politician of his age. He died in July 1797.

The Revolution Commences

Like most Whigs, Burke in the early months following the storming of the Bastille had some hopes for the events which followed, averring in November 1789 that 'I shall Rejoice in seeing such a happy order establish'd in France as much as I do in my consciousness, that an order of the same kind, or one not very Remote from it, has been long settled, and I hope on a firm foundation in England'.[2] He was even willing to concede that 'a positively vicious and abusive government ought to be chang'd, and if necessary, by Violence, if it cannot be (as is sometimes the case) Reformed'.[3] And he certainly considered the French 'deserving of liberty'.[4] But Burke also voiced private reservations about French developments in the early months of the Revolution.[5] The chief problem was that reckless Gallic reformers, 'instead of redressing grievances, and improving the fabrick of their state, to which they were called by their monarch',[6] were in his view galloping headlong towards an illusory democracy which would might disintegrate into 'the tyranny of a multitude'.[7] Soon, and in large measure as a consequence of British reaction to French events rather than those events themselves, Burke was condemning 'the deplorable view of the wreck of France'.[8]

The spark which ignited Burke's *Reflections* had been a highly political sermon preached by a leading Dissenter and pro-American, the Rev. Richard Price, on 4 November 1789, on the anniversary of the Revolution of 1688, which was published as *A Discourse on the Love of Our Country*.[9] This revived the question of how to interpret the 'Glorious Revolution'. In 1688–9, the second son of Charles I, King James II, had been deposed for pro-Catholic activities. The grandson of Charles II, the Dutch King William of Orange, was then invited by Parliament to ascend the throne with his wife Mary, James's daughter. This much was evident. But had William been 'elected' on the basis of some principle of popular sovereignty, or did he inherit the throne through pre-existing channels of succession? Price supported the former view. To him, the events of 1688 illustrated three leading principles of British contractual theory which would be referred to constantly over the next few years:

1. The people's right to choose its own governors;
2. The right to cashier the latter for misconduct; and
3. The right to frame a government 'for ourselves'.[10]

This construction of William's accession suggested, in particular, that any British monarch could be deposed for 'misconduct', and another installed in his place.[11] Price had waxed zealous in the cause of American liberty, and believed that the Revolutions of 1688, 1776, and 1789 were linked by a growing awareness of universal natural rights, notably to liberty and to resist oppression. Such rights had been modified for the common good by the contract which created civil society, but had been frequently usurped to support privilege and tyranny thereafter. Nonetheless they remained yardsticks for assessing social and political justice everywhere. If their original existence was not conceded, however, or their contemporary application was denied, precedent and prescriptive right, based upon actual possession, had a much stronger case to answer, and justifying dramatic constitutional alteration was that much more difficult.

Burke read Price's sermon in late January 1790. By mid-February, noting with alarm the Dissenters' activities in particular, he lamented the 'extraordinary things [that] have been said and done here, and published with great ostentation, in order to draw us into a connexion and concurrence with that nation upon the principles of its proceedings, and to lead us to an imitation of them'.[12] Doubtless still fresh in his mind was the memory of London's anti-Catholic riots of 1780, in which the prisons had been opened, a vast amount of property pillaged, and over 450 people killed. Though he had supported their claims in the 1770s, Burke was now ill disposed to agree with the Dissenters, who had been amongst the leading opponents of extending toleration to Catholics, a cause near to his own heart (his beloved son Richard was employed full time upon it in mid-1790). As he acknowledged privately, Burke was thus at least as interested – if not more so – in engaging with British reformers as he was in criticising the revolutionaries.[13] Nonetheless he insisted that the problem with France was that the Revolution posed the threat of a new form of tyranny, that of a democracy fuelled, like a new religion, by its own sense of infallibility: 'I hate it most of all where most are concerned in it. The tyranny of a multitude is a multiplied tyranny'.[14] With extraordinary swiftness he moved beyond the possibility of contemplating any compromise with the new regime. France had become like a neighbouring house on fire: we do not reason as to the causes, but extinguish the menace before the conflagration engulfs us as well. Likewise, he conceived of France as having removed itself from the international order of civilised states, hence liable to the same treatment as a barbarian power. In the debates on the Army Estimates in February 1790 Burke said that France should be 'considered as expunged out of the system of Europe … as not politically existing'.[15] The fervency of his opposition was focussed on the issue of religion, which in the view of a leading modern historian of his thought,

J.G.A. Pocock, was at 'the center of his vision',[16] and beyond this, upon Ireland.[17] (And for some Burke consequently remained 'essentially a religious thinker'.)[18] By March Burke had concluded 'That peoples (The French peoples) great Object seem'd to me to be, to destroy their Church – that is, to plunder it'.[19] Others agreed, too, as to the importance of the issue. At the famous meeting of the Revolution Society in which an argument erupted over the *Reflections*, the radical John Horne Tooke, taking a line favoured by many Dissenters, called it 'the tears of the Priesthood for the loss of their pudding'.[20] By July Burke was writing that 'instead of freedom, the french revolution is a usurpation obtain'd by fraud and sustain'd by force'.[21] Begun in late 1789, and completed by late the following August, puffed by rumour until it was eagerly awaited, the *Reflections* burst upon the world on 1 November 1790.

Burke's Main Arguments

From virtually the outset the *Reflections* argues that France in the hands of the revolutionaries was analogous to a madman or highwayman, lacking in government and possessing 'liberty' only in the wild and anarchic sense of the having power in the state of nature. The new *régime* was thus 'founded on principles of anarchy'.[22] France in 1790, Burke asserted, had no government: by analogy, it was not to be treated as a member of the civilised community of nations. It had exiled itself: Burke wished to transform this exile into formal ostracism. And yet to Burke the significance of the Revolution went still further; as Carlyle would later put it, he had eloquently demonstrated 'that the end of an Epoch is come, to all appearance the end of Civilised Time'.[23]

The *Reflections* is arranged around four themes: a denunciation of Richard Price's sermon lauding the French revolution; an attack on the character of the revolutionaries; an assessment of their principles, in which his denial of their conception of abstract natural rights is central; and a defence of the British constitution and of prescriptive right, grounded upon a conception of human nature.

Much of Burke's disagreement with Price stemmed from their differing interpretations of the events of 1688. The Catholic monarch James had violated his coronation oath to maintain a Protestant kingdom. Burke conceded that he had been legitimately deposed. But William and Mary's coronation demonstrated an orderly and historically grounded rule of succession in a Protestant kingdom, in which the next lineal (male) Protestant claimant inherited the throne without being freely chosen by Parliament, much less 'elected' by the 'people'. This involved no claim on behalf of popular sovereignty emanating from any 'abstract' or 'metaphysical' right. The 'Glorious Revolution' of 1688 was a slight deviation from constitutional practice to enforce a Protestant succession; it was not the norm against which current constitutional practice should be tested. Against Price, Burke thus contended that the king owed his crown to a fixed rule of succession, not the choice of his people, which form of election would always be unruly and destructive. The monarch could not be 'cashiered for misconduct', as Price insisted, because he did not serve the people like other members of government. As the crown was hereditary, so too was allegiance to it, and to its principle of succession. To argue the contrary was to invite a 'total contempt' for ancient institutions which could only terminate in social ruin. The root of Britain's liberties lay in its 'ancient constitution'; this too was the message of 1688. These liberties, the wise contrivance of our forefathers, were transmitted to posterity like any other inheritance, and wedded to 'an inheritable crown, an inheritable peerage, and a House of Commons and a people inheriting privileges, franchises and liberties from a long line of ancestors'. The wish to alter them was in itself, Burke asserted, suspect: 'A spirit of innovation is generally the result of a selfish temper and confined views.'[24] The tantalising allure of novelty, so central to the psychology of modernity, which would ultimately make tradition as such suspect, held no appeal to Burke.

So, too, no 'new government' could be created if constitutional liberties were inherited and defined historically rather than understood as abstract principles. Britain's constitution instead exhibited a 'manly, moral, regulated liberty'[25] rooted in prescriptive rights which, from Magna Charta onwards, had gradually limited the royal prerogative until an elaborate, finely tuned constitutional balance between King, Lords and Commons had been hammered out. Any changes in it should always be contemplated with a 'cautious and deliberate' spirit. By contrast, the principles of the French Revolution, the 'rights of man', had been conjured out of 'the nakedness and solitude of metaphysical abstraction'.[26] While admitting that the French revolution was 'the most astonishing that has hitherto happened in the world', Burke denied any parallel between 1789 and 1688. French principles lay closer to the intolerant puritan spirit of Britain's failed

republican revolution of 1649. Even more distantly, they recalled
the peasant uprising of 1381, in which Wat Tyler's ragged mob had
butchered indiscriminately anyone of social rank.[27] The result was
little less than catastrophic:

> Laws overturned; tribunals subverted; industry without vigor; com-
> merce expiring; the revenue unpaid, yet the people impoverished;
> a church pillaged, and a state not relieved; civil and military anar-
> chy made the constitution of the kingdom; everything human and
> divine sacrificed to the idol of public credit, and national bank-
> ruptcy the consequence; and, to crown all, the paper securities of
> new, precarious, tottering power, the discredited paper securities
> of impoverished fraud and beggared rapine, held out as a currency
> for the support of an empire.[28]

Burke then turned to the perpetrators of the revolution, chiefly the
leaders of the Third Estate. His collective portrayal of them is as a class of
self-seeking, mean-spirited, ignorant and power-hungry men who readily
turned their backs upon their own origins, affecting cosmopolitanism
while neglecting their own 'little platoon' in society, the 'first principle' of
public affection. These 'discontented men of quality', second-rate 'petty-
fogging' provincial lawyers and the like, were motivated by 'sinister ambition and a lust of meretricious glory'. Their eyes glimmered greedily at
the spoils within their reach, to the seizing of which they were willing to
unleash the fury of the mob. Ill equipped for the exercise of authority,
they grasped at any project of self-aggrandisement which came to hand.
'Unprepared greatness' upon the international stage beckoned as an
alternative to inferior, obscure provincial squabbling over insignificant
litigation: who could resist the alternative of ruling a glorious empire to
languishing in a dusty parish? Crucially, the revolutionaries had little
property of their own and thus remained undeterred by the instability
they had engineered. They had shed none of their own blood and were
not themselves the victims of their own cruelty and despoliation. By contrast, the landed possessions of the traditional ruling class represented a
stake in the country nearly identical to the national interest itself. But the
Revolution's attack on the nobility, and the daily growing prominence of
the Third Estate, ignored this interest deliberately. Despite Burke's pen-
chant for the landed aristocracy and Gothic *mores*, he was far from hostile
to commerce.[29] But he did harbour grave reservations about the speculative spirit surrounding the Revolution, and the government's power to

manipulate the money supply and thus the value of all other forms of wealth. Burke particularly condemned the printing of so-called assignats, or certificates, initially to the value of nationalised lands, for use as paper money, claiming that such actions would only result in a new nobility of moneylenders and stock speculators – 'Aristocracy of Feudal Parchment' being replaced by 'Aristocracy of the Money Bag … An infinitely baser; the basest yet known', in Carlyle's later phrase.[30]

Like the French revolutionaries, Burke asserted, Price and his associates harboured equally ambitious plans for dramatic constitutional alteration under the guise of parliamentary reform. Price implied, said Burke, that the entirety of the British government was 'absolutely *illegitimate*, and not at all better than a downright *usurpation*', whose overthrow could be justifiably effected by another revolution. The House of Lords was 'at one stroke, bastardized and corrupted in blood. That House is no representative of the people at all, even in "semblance" or in form' and 'The case of the crown' was 'altogether as bad'.[31] The motive, again, Burke asserted, was a purely wilful desire to pull down and destroy, to substitute novelty for antiquity, to induce any calamity necessary to engineer the downfall of Church and State. Being mere professors of abstract principle, Price and the members of the Revolution Society were indifferent to the actual organisation of human affairs, and prone to wild fluctuations in their proposals and conjectures.

But the main thrust of the *Reflections* was directed against the principles of the Revolution. Price had juxtaposed the 'rights of men' to prescriptive right, and Burke conceded that 'real rights of men' did exist, including:

> a right to justice, as between their fellows, whether their fellows are in politic function or in ordinary occupation. They have a right to the fruits of their industry, and to the means of making their industry fruitful. They have a right to the acquisitions of their parents, to the nourishment and improvement of their offspring, to instruction in life and to consolation in death. Whatever each man can separately do, without trespassing upon others, he has a right to do for himself; and he has a right to a fair portion of all which society, with all its combinations of skill and force, can do in his favor. [32]

Nonetheless, insisted Burke, these did not include, for example, a right to equal things or to judge in our own cause, man having forfeited the right to be 'his own governor' at the time of the covenant which founded civil society. Moreover, Burke denied that such rights included 'the share of power, authority, and direction which each individual ought to have in the management of the state.' These were not 'amongst the direct original rights of man in civil society', but were rather 'a thing to be settled by convention'. (But this, of course, still implied that they might be altered.) Natural liberty was thus surrendered when government was formed, and the defence of civil liberty was entrusted to it, and not retained by individuals. Thus it was entirely false to assert that government was founded upon natural rights:

Government is not made in virtue of natural rights, which may and do exist in total independence of it, – and exist in much greater clearness, and in a much greater degree of abstract perfection: but their abstract perfection is their practical defect. By having a right to everything they want everything. Government is a contrivance of human wisdom to provide for human *wants*. Men have a right that these wants should be provided for by this wisdom. Among these wants is to be reckoned the want, out of civil society, of a sufficient restraint upon their passions. Society requires not only that the passions of individuals should be subjected, but that even in the mass and body, as well as in the individuals, the inclinations of men should frequently be thwarted, their will controlled, and their passions brought into subjection. This can only be done *by a power out of themselves*, and not, in the exercise of its function, subject to that will and to those passions which it is its office to bridle and subdue. In this sense the restraints on men, as well as their liberties, are to be reckoned among their rights. But as the liberties and the restrictions vary with times and circumstances, and admit of infinite modifications, they cannot be settled upon any abstract rule; and nothing is so foolish as to discuss them upon that principle.[33]

The science of government, thus, was to be ascertained not through metaphysical postulates but prudential maxims grounded on proven success and acceptance, and a firm knowledge of the complexity of institutions and perversity of human nature. This required 'a deep knowledge of human nature and human necessities, and of the things which facilitate or obstruct the various ends which are to be pursued by the mechanism of civil institutions'. It was thus 'with infinite caution that any man ought to venture upon pulling down an edifice which has answered in any tolerable degree for ages the common purposes of society, or on building it up again without having models and patterns of approved utility before his eyes'.[34]

In the *Reflections*, then, Burke asserted that any rights possessed before civil society were greatly altered at its inception, and were now 'in a sort of middle' incapable of definition. Natural rights might have existed once, but only civil rights could be discussed and analysed in any meaningful sense.[35] Yet Burke too had used natural rights arguments on occasion in the past. A fragment from the 1760s asserted:

> Everybody is satisfied that a conservation and secure enjoyment of our natural rights is the great and ultimate purpose of civil society, and that therefore all forms whatsoever of government are only good as they are subservient to that purpose to which they are entirely subordinate.[36]

Addressing the merchants of Bristol in 1778, he had spoken of the 'natural rights' of the provinces of great empires.[37] In Parliament in 1783, he said the 'rights of men – that is to say, the natural rights of mankind' could be strengthened when they were 'further affirmed and declared by express covenants'.[38] Burke's point in 1790, therefore, was principally that no discussion of abstract right could eventuate in the conclusion, as the *Reflections* put it, that human beings possessed a right 'each to govern himself', whereby 'the whole organization of government becomes a consideration of convenience.'[39] A declaration of primitive rights now was likely to subvert any government based on preceding forms of authority, and substitute popular power in their stead, inviting not the reign of virtue but endless, shamelessly impatient anarchy, whose only resolution would be bloodshed and pillage. Burke's concern is not therefore to deny the existence of natural rights, but to emphasise their irrelevance to modern governments. Thus, as he insisted in parliament in March 1790,

> to go back abstractedly to original rights, there would be an end of all society. Abstract principles of natural right had been long since given up for the advantage of having, what was much better, society, which substituted wisdom and justice, in the room of original right. It annihilated all those natural rights, and drew to its mass all the component parts of which those rights were made up.[40]

With a self-confessed horror of 'abstract principles', thus, Burke usually maintained that 'rights' could not be discussed in theory alone:

Man he had found in society, and that man he looked at – he knew nothing of any other man – nor could he argue on any of his rights. As to abstract rights of all kinds, he thought they were incorporeal, and unfit for the body. They might be discussed in some other state; but they were totally unfit for this life, and consequently could not be fit for argument.[41]

Burke's defence of prescriptive right was interwoven with his conception of society as a closely knit organic whole where loyalties were local and limited rather than expansive, and attachments were fused organically by passion, moving from those closest to us outwards, rather than constructed artificially by reason, like mechanisms.[42] Constitutions thus emerged over lengthy periods of time; they could not be churned out to order. Consequently 'just prejudice', especially deference to rank and to the monarchy, bound the British constitution together, aided by the Church of England. The 'body' of true religion being the teaching of obedience to earthly sovereigns, religious scepticism invariably invited social disorder. Put simply, this was what 'worked' in Britain; loyalty to the constitution which was necessarily shrouded in mystery rested upon the sublime and awesome, and was inchoate and emotional rather than based on reasoned public opinion.[43] Expediency and utility were central to every political judgement and act. Political obligation, too, derived from the organic and hierarchical nature of society, and arose inescapably from each individual's social rank, not from any primordial rights given in the state of nature. The only hope for the revolution in France was to emulate Britain, and to turn away from the 'terrible revolution in property' which its confiscations of church property implied, and which left no prescriptive right secure.[44]

Crucial to the arguments of the *Reflections* is Burke's account of human nature and wants, and a notion of history and the fixity of patterns of behaviour and corresponding limits of possible change. His view of human nature was sceptical and pessimistic. The passions progressed naturally from frailty to vice, and individual moral failure largely caused social unhappiness, not political institutions or their corruption. Manners and civilisation distinguished modern from barbaric societies, and depended crucially upon the spirit of the gentleman and of nobility, owing nothing to the majority, whom Burke dismissed derisively as the 'swinish multitude' (the words would be hurled angrily back at him in nearly every radical tract of the period).[45] The lower orders, he suspected, would readily construe the appeal to an abstract 'rights of man' as a licence to plunder and pillage. Nobility was thus 'the Corinthian capital of polished society', while 'perfect democracy' could only generate the partisan tyranny of the majority over the minority. In France, however, respect for the monarchy had already markedly declined, and this for Burke symbolised the relentless assault on authority which atheism and Enlightenment principles had fomented in the previous generation. In perhaps the most famous passage of his work, Burke lamented the lack of respect paid by the revolutionaries to the French queen Marie Antoinette, whom he himself, evidently enraptured, had once glimpsed in the full bloom of her beauty:[46]

It is now sixteen or seventeen years since I saw the queen of France, then the Dauphiness, at Versailles; and surely never lighted on this orb, which she hardly seemed to touch, a more delightful vision. I saw her just above the horizon, decorating and cheering the elevated sphere she just began to move in, – glittering like the morning-star, full of life and splendor and joy. Oh! what a revolution! and what an heart must I have, to contemplate without emotion that elevation and that fall! Little did I dream, when she added titles of veneration to those of enthusiastic, distant, respectful love, that she should ever be obliged to carry the sharp antidote against disgrace concealed in that bosom! little did I dream that I should have lived to see such disasters fallen upon her in a nation of gallant men, in a nation of men of honor, and of cavaliers! I thought ten thousand swords must have leaped from their scabbards to avenge even a look that threatened her with insult. But the age of chivalry is gone. That of sophisters, economists, and calculaters has succeeded; and the glory of Europe is extinguished forever. Never, never more, shall we behold that generous loyalty to rank and sex, that proud submission, that dignified obedience, that subordination of the heart, which kept alive, even in servitude itself, the spirit of an exalted freedom! The unbought grace of life, the cheap defence of nations, the nurse of manly sentiment and heroic enterprise, is gone! It is gone, that sensibility of principle, that chastity of honor, which felt a stain like a wound, which inspired courage whilst it mitigated ferocity, which ennobled whatever it touched, and under which vice itself lost half its evil by losing all its grossness![47]

The decline of chivalry, then, had been engineered by a mechanical conception of both individual and society in which kings and women were alike reduced to mere generic human beings, their sacrosanctness and dignity dismissed as ridiculous superstition, the more easily to dangle their persons on the gallows which Burke inferred would everywhere be constructed. The natural social affections of love, veneration, admiration, and attachment, (we see here the roots of Carlyle's later theory of heroes and hero worship, as well as Coleridge's account of the organic nature of the social affections) were supplanted by mere unbridled individualism and manipulative self-interest, which in the hands of the revolutionaries became public terror. The 'old feudal and chivalrous spirit of *fealty*' was to be replaced by plots, assassination, murder and confiscation. When 'ancient opinions and rules of life', the manners and civilisation which rested upon the priesthood and nobility, were thrown to the winds, anything became permissible. A 'revolution in sentiments, manners, and moral opinions' had destroyed all respect for not only established institutions, but humanity as such. The consequence could only be bloodshed on a colossal scale. The British, by contrast, had not yet been infected with such principles:

> We have not been drawn and trussed, in order that we may be filled, like stuffed birds in a museum, with chaff and rags, and paltry, blurred shreds of paper about the rights of man. We preserve the whole of our feelings still native and entire, unsophisticated by pedantry and infidelity. We have real hearts of flesh and blood beating in our bosoms. We fear God; we look up with awe to kings, with affection to Parliaments, with duty to magistrates, with reverence to priests, and with respect to nobility. Why? Because, when such ideas are brought before our minds, it is *natural* to be so affected; because all other feelings are false and spurious, and tend to corrupt our minds, to vitiate our primary morals, to render us unfit for rational liberty, and, by teaching us a servile, licentious, and abandoned insolence, to be our low sport for a few holidays, to make us perfectly fit for and justly deserving of slavery through the whole course of our lives.[48]

Obedience to the prescribed social hierarchy of rank and station, and antipathy to unrestrained egalitarian individualism, was thus the core of what would later be called Burke's 'conservatism' and was most immediately threatened by the propagation of natural rights ideas. 'Untaught feelings' and 'old prejudices' had value in themselves and were not to be discarded because the gleaming, bauble-like novelty of illusory principles made them appear old fashioned and tarnished. We see here how far Burke perceived that the restless acquisitiveness and sense of show, and the incessant desire for novelty which characterised eighteenth-century commercial society, had penetrated into the realm of politics and abstract ideas. But governments and constitutions, he insisted, were not like 'modes of dress' to be altered as fashion and whimsy pleased, but rested on prejudice and religion, 'the basis of civil society, and the source of all good, and of all comfort'. They defined the 'great primeval contract of eternal society, linking the lower with the higher natures, connecting the visible and invisible world, according to a fixed compact sanctioned by the inviolable oath which holds all physical and all moral natures each in their appointed place'.[49] The confiscation of religious property in France thus signalled for Burke not merely a general invitation to depredation of the wealthy, but a crucial undermining of the very bases of social order itself, where what passed as democracy would increasingly resemble a tyranny in which 'oppression of the minority will extend to far greater numbers, and will be carried on with much greater fury, than can almost ever be apprehended from the dominion of a single sceptre'.[50] Absolutism, consequently, was preferable to this spectre of oppression. What began as religious intolerance would eventuate in pure and undiluted intolerance of all deviation. The 'deceitful dreams and visions of the equality and rights of men' would merely end in a 'base oligarchy'.[51] The sins of the *ancien régime*, thought Burke, were thus modest beside the frightening hubris of its opponents. The Revolution, indeed, embodied the apotheosis of evil. If its principles found favour, no crown in Europe sat securely on a regal head, and perhaps no regal head on regal shoulders. Once thrones began to topple, nothing of value was safe. For as Burke recognised, all of the awesome symbols of authority, king, priest, judge, teacher and patriarchal father, were interwoven and interdependent. The stakes being gambled for, thus, were nothing less than civilization itself. These assumptions, we will see, would become central to the ensuing debate over the next decade.

The Reception of the Reflections

Some seven thousand copies of Burke's text were sold in the first week alone, and eventually about thirty thousand circulated.[52] Though rumour had it that he had also dipped into *Rights of Man*,[53] George III commended the *Reflections* as 'a book which every gentleman ought to read, and had copies bound for his favourite courtiers'.[54] His son William, Duke of Clarence, repeated the message.[55] If, as his enemies insinuated, he had wanted to ingratiate himself with the monarch, he succeeded. In 1794 Pitt would secure him a pension of £1200 per annum from the King, the largest sum which could be granted in the circumstances, and plans were afoot to ennoble him.[56]

Burke's friends were also predictably enthusiastic. Gilbert Elliot, Earl of Minto, wrote of the book that he 'could not lay it down till I had finished the last page. I shall read it again immediately, with more deliberation and therefore, if that be possible, even with greater enjoyment; certainly with more profit ... Every Scholar, and every man who without deserving that name, has any relish for mental pleasures ... must make this book his companion and his constant resource ... Your book contains the fundamental Elements of all Political knowledge, and lays clearly open to us the just foundations of all Social wisdom'.[57] Horace Walpole was 'not more charmed with his wit and eloquence than with his enthusiasm', being particularly enamoured of Burke's description of Marie Antoinette, and 'the swords leaping out of their scabbards' – or which ought to have leapt out – in her defence.[58] Having read the text twice, he found it 'sublime, profound, and gay. The wit and satire are equally brilliant, and the whole is wise, tho' in some points he goes too far; yet in general there is far less want of judgment than could be expected from him'.[59] Burke's close ally William Windham thought that there had never been 'a work so valuable in its kind, or that displayed powers of so extraordinary a nature. It is a work that may seem capable of overturning the National Assembly, and turning the stream of opinion throughout Europe'.[60] The novelist Fanny Burney found the *Reflections* 'the noblest, deepest, most animated, and exalted work that I think I have ever read', and wrote that whatever might appear to be Burke's inconsistencies, 'When I read however, such a book as this, I am apt to imagine the whole of such a being must be right as well as the parts, and that the time may come when the mists that obscure the motives and incentives to those actions and proceedings which seem incongruous, may be chased away'.[61] Lord Auckland thought it 'a fine piece of eloquence and a splendid exercise of talents', if somewhat 'diffuse and flowery, like his speeches'.[62] Similarly Burke's friend Dr. Thomas Barnard, Bishop of Killaloe, called the *Reflections* 'indeed a capital work. The facts are undeniable, the arguments impregnable, the stile inimitable, and the whole unanswerable'.[63] The historian Edward Gibbon, setting aside his own religious scepticism, proclaimed himself 'as high an Aristocrate as Burke himself', and begged 'leave to subscribe my assent to Mr. Burke's creed on the revolution of France. I admire his eloquence, I approve his politics, I adore his chivalry, and I can almost excuse his reverence for church establishments'.[64]

Yet some who might have been expected to laud the *Reflections*, like Fox's friend the Prince of Wales, whose order had been so well served by Burke's efforts, reacted differently: 'How the Devil could your friend Burke publish such a Farrago of Nonsense?', he was reported to have said to Lord Thomond shortly after the book appeared.[65] Philip Francis, generally accepted to have been 'Junius', to whom, with Reynolds and Windham,[66] Burke had shown an early draft of the book, was equally blunt, writing that 'I find, (though with no sort of surprise, having often talked with you on the Subject) that we differ only in every thing'.[67] Francis particularly rejected Burke's description of Marie Antoinette at Versailles 'glittering like the morning star, full of life and splendour and joy', which had evoked his lament that 'the age of chivalry' was gone:[68]

In my opinion all that you say of the Queen is pure foppery. If she be a perfect female character, you ought to take your ground upon her virtues. If she be the reverse, it is ridiculous in any but a lover to place her personal charms in opposition to her crimes. ... Look back, I beseech you, and deliberate a little before you determine that this is an office which perfectly becomes you. If I stop here it is not for want of a multitude of objections. The mischief you are going to do yourself is, to my apprehension, palpable. It is visible. It is audible. I snuff it in the wind. I taste it already. I feel it in every sense, and so will you hereafter; when I vow to God (an elegant phrase) it will be a sort of consolation for me to reflect that I did everything in my power to prevent it.[69]

The Development of Burke's Thought after the Reflections

From 1790 onwards Burke's reaction to such criticisms was often focussed on the sympathetic response to the Revolution of the undisputed Whig leader, Charles James Fox. He very likely felt, as other observers did, that Fox now tended to side with another leading Whig, Richard Brinsley Sheridan, who had fallen out with Burke completely.[70] He was also deeply suspicious that Fox seemingly wished to exploit the Revolution for his own ends.[71] Similarly he warned the Society for Constitutional Information and the Revolution Society that they should 'take good care how they are involved with persons who, under the pretext of zeal towards the Revolution and Constitution, too frequently wander from their true principles, and are ready on every occasion to depart from the firm, but cautious and deliberate, spirit which produced the one and which presides in the other'.[72] Burke's motives for keeping to his course have been much debated. He risked alienating Pitt, who, bent on ignoring French developments as much as possible, wanted him to tone down his criticisms of the French constitution.[73] But he stood to gain much from the King's favour, as Fox did from that of the Prince of Wales. Burke was disaffected from a number of leading Whigs, notably Sheridan; he sought to use the Revolution as leverage in the Hastings trial, since he linked the philo-Gallicans with the East Indian 'miscreants'. He saw the Dissenters' political agitation as unfavourable to the cause of Catholic Emancipation. He was also rapidly concluding that the Revolution posed the most important crisis, both domestic and foreign, of modern times. Sympathy for the Revolution, in fact, would have served any cause near to Burke's heart, and the further it degenerated into chaos the less likely he was to shift his ground.

The break from Fox during the debate over the Quebec Bill on 21 April 1791 had been preordained for some time by this divergence of interests. Was it, however, a divergence of 'principles' which chiefly engendered the split? The answer, of course, is both yes and no. Neither Burke nor Fox had ever been committed reformers. Neither was a republican, in the sense of preferring one or two assemblies generated by popular election rather than a balanced constitution of monarch, lords and commons, which Fox commended the Americans for replicating to an impressive degree. Both had political careers of lifelong partisan Whiggism behind them. Fox was more willing to appeal to support out of doors, and to invite the Dissenters' participation in political debate, but the differences between him and Burke here were not so great. Burke, however, had rapidly come to describe the revolution as antagonistic to the principle of liberty as such, and this was crucial for their difference of opinion. Given the fact that his own influence amongst the Whigs was waning in this period, particularly after George III's madness precipitated a Regency crisis in which all the Whig leaders jockeyed for influence with the Prince of Wales,[74] Burke may have felt that such a strategy would advance his position. And there were other partisan reasons for encouraging the break: it was rumoured the King might be willing to have Fox as first minister if Pitt's government fell, as it threatened to do in the debate over Russian armaments.[75]

Yet despite this vitriolic attack on Fox we note that religion as such (as opposed to a willingness to appeal to the Dissenters) plays no role in Burke's account of Fox's motives. Despite the fact that Fox had moved for the repeal of the late seventeenth-century Test Acts (requiring conformity to Church of England dogma on the part of civil and military office holders) in March, 1790, Fox was not associated with the Dissenters by Burke; to the contrary, the latter acknowledged privately that many of the Dissenters disliked Fox, as was evidenced in the scathing comments on him in Price's sermon. It was not irreligion, in this case, which engendered disloyalty, but a misapprehension of the consequences of French developments. This was evidently linked in Burke's eyes to Fox's ambitions respecting the regency and the Prince of Wales, in which his championing of what one observer called 'higher Tory principles than could have been found anywhere' appeared no small inconsistency in principle,[76] and was thought by Pitt (according to Auckland) to be 'little short of treason'.[77]

Once the break took place the question for Burke was how to identify his opponents amongst the Whigs. In June 1791 he described these as a group who sought 'to get the Principles of Paine, Priestley, Price, Rouse, Mackintosh, Christie &ca &ca &ca magnified and extolled, and in a sort of obscure and undefined manner to be adopted as the Creed of the party'.[78] After Fox counter-attacked in May, Burke began increasingly to identify Fox with this group. This isolated Burke still further; 'the result is', he wrote in June, 'that I have the misfortune totally and fundamentally to differ with that party in constitutional and publick points of such moment, that all those, on which I have hitherto ever differ'd from other men and other Parties, are, in comparison, mere toys and Triffles'.[79] Assailed in Parliament 'with having, from corruption, or some motives not much more respectable, contradicted and disgraced the whole Tenour of my Life', Burke chose to 'draw myself within my own Circle' while preparing his *Appeal from the New to the Old Whigs* (July 1791). Yet privately, on occasion, he still voiced some support for the Revolution itself,[80] and said of Fox that their opinions were in fact quite similar,[81] despite the Foxites' industrious attempts to disseminate contrary principles.[82]

The key text for understanding Burke's views on the distance between Whiggism and 'French principles' is clearly the *Appeal*. Here Burke made four distinct points: firstly, that he did not believe that Fox himself was a 'republican', or that the parliamentary Foxites really subscribe to such views; secondly, that the 'new' or 'modern' Whigs, principally the Revolution and Constitutional Societies, both had a substantially different interpretation of the Revolution of 1688 from Burke himself, as well as of the French Revolution; thirdly, that those of the 'more sober' new Whigs, who did not belong to the 'pernicious foreign faction' dedicated to overthrowing the ancient constitution upheld in 1688, nonetheless seemed to feel that 'if antimonarchical opinions gain ground as they have done in France, they may, as in France, accomplish a revolution without a war'; and fourthly, that while mankind possessed 'obligations to mankind at large, which are not in consequence of any special voluntary pact', nonetheless this could be understood as subsumed under patriotism itself:

> If the social ties and ligaments, spun out of those physical relations which are the elements of the commonwealth, in most cases begin, and always continue, independently of our will, so, without any stipulation on our own part, are we bound by that relation called our country, which comprehends (as it has been well said) 'all the charities of all'.[83]

It was not enough, therefore, to 'assert that the destruction of an absolute monarchy is a thing good in itself, without any sort of reference to the antecedent state of things, or to the consequences which result from the change'. Such consequences might, after all, be evident at home as well as abroad; those who criticised absolutism had also formed a party which sought the 'utter overthrow' of British laws, civil and ecclesiastical, and the system of manners which underpinned them.[84] Nor was it acceptable, in Burke's eyes, to celebrate, in December 1792, the French victory at Jemappes on the grounds that, as Burke put it, those 'who were combined against France were despots, and because France itself was a republic. It was indeed a new language, to call the friends and allies of this country despots',[85] even though they sought to restore absolutism, which seemingly qualified them for the title. And on 13 December 1792, before France announced hostilities against Britain, Burke asserted that 'The French had declared war against all kings, and of consequence against this country, if it had a king'.[86] Against that 'relation called our country', Burke thus juxtaposed the ideals of these 'enemies to their country and constitution', while acknowledging that

> the leaders of party will not go the length of the doctrines taught by the seditious clubs. I am sure they do not mean to do so, moreover. God forbid! Perhaps even those who are directly carrying on the work of this pernicious foreign faction do not all of them intend to produce all the mischiefs which must inevitably follow from their having any success in their proceedings.[87]

This pointed to unintended consequences rather than conscious treachery. But Burke did clearly have a more benign view of the *ancien régime*, emphasising of French exiles who were assisting Britain that 'What were the objects of the emigrants who would enter into our service? To liberate their wives and their children, to be restored to their properties, to get possession of their vineyards, their olive-trees, and their fig-trees. This was the horrible old despotism of France. Despotism and liberty, as the honourable gentleman made use of these terms, were mere words'.[88] Stability of property, personal and ecclesiastical, in other words, rather than constitutional form or monarchical or aristocratic excess, was the key issue which legitimated the *ancien régime*.

Burke, though he privately accused Fox of being 'tainted with French politics and principles',[89] here clearly drew a line between Fox and the extra-parliamentary radicals: Fox was not among those 'men [who] publicly declare such admiration of a foreign Constitution, and such contempt of our own', for if he was guilty of the first charge, he was innocent of the second. The radicals here, however, and those new Whigs who had crossed over to join them (Grey and other members of the 'Phalanx' rather than Fox), were indeed guilty of republicanism; of believing that 1688 accorded them the right to alter the British constitution; of corresponding with the French rather than keeping their views private; of wishing the British constitution to be altered in the direction of the French; and of placing obligations to humanity, disguised as the rights of man, above those to country. These, then, were grounds for suspicions extending beyond being misguided and deluded, to treacherous impulses, perhaps even treason itself.

The *Appeal* was a considerable success.[90] Burke made it even clearer in private that the break within the Whigs had more to do with perceptions of the impact of the Revolution in Britain than its course in France itself, and that his opposition to the Revolution was motivated at least as much by its possible effects on Britain as its internal principle.[91] The most obvious worry, Burke continued to insist, lay with the Dissenters:

> But what I look to with seriousness is the Phalanx of Party which exists in the body of the dissenters, who are, at the very least, nine tenths of them entirely devoted, some with greater some with less zeal, to the principles of the French Revolution. I think, they compose a more active, a more spirited, and a more united body, than the Jacobites ever were; and as to the Republicans, (except in the time of the great troubles, near an hundred and fifty years ago) they never formed themselves into any thing like a party, until within these two years they were embodied under the French standard. Until then they were individuals who hung upon the whigg party, and by that party were look'd upon as absurd and visionary men of no sort of consequence.[92]

Those who supported the Revolution, then, were principally 'most of the dissenters of the three leading denominations', rather than the new Whigs as such.[93] The Dissenters were cunning, dissimulating, intemperate zealots, Reason-intoxicated and God-intoxicated alike, who used Priestley as a martyr to advance their wider cause. Some 700,000 strong, thought Burke, their object was 'avowedly to abolish all national distinctions and local interests and prejudices, and to merge them all in one Interest and one Cause, which they call the rights of man. They wish to break down all Barriers which tend to separate them from the Counsels, designs, and assistance, of the republican, atheistical, faction of Fanaticks in France'.[94] In late 1789 he had written to Fox that 'It would be material to you to gain entirely some of these Dissenters, who are already, I fancy, inclined to come over to you'.[95] But by January 1792 he acknowledged their great distance from Fox; the Dissenters possessed 'democratic notions', which had made them dislike Fox, and their dislike of Fox alienated them from the Whigs in general. It was vital, then, to keep the Dissenters at a distance from the French; 'the way to secure us at home is to deprive mischievous factions of their foreign alliances'.[96]

The second key problem for Burke lay with those new Whigs who had abandoned aristocratical principles, whose 'Leaders have ever since gone on, and are with all their might going on, to propagate the principles of French Levelling and confusion', and whose 'great Object is not, (as they pretend to delude worthy people to their Ruin) the destruction of all absolute Monarchies, but totally to root out that thing called an Aristocrate or Nobleman and Gentleman'. How close were they to the Dissenters? The latter had, in Burke's view, long been the Whigs' 'mortal and declared Enemies ... They had long strewn themselves wholly adverse to, and unalliable with the Party'.[97] And it is comparatively rarely that Burke does link them with 'the New French Whiggs', until late 1792. Discussing the prospect of a coalition with Loughborough on 13 June 1792, Burke speaks of 'the French and dissenting scheme of things'.[98] Yet at the same time he was willing to aver that a coalition between Fox and Pitt was still conceivable: ' "And why not!" said Mr Burke dryly [to Fanny Burney]; "why not this coalition as well as other coalitions!" '[99] In September, however, he spoke of Fox, who, Burke thought, felt George III. had 'grown quite weary of Pitt'. Fox had been engaged in various negotiations with Portland, who was keen to enlist his support, as potentially threatening thereby 'to abandon all the young and energetick part of the Party, and the whole body of the Dissenters, upon whom he has lately built his principal hopes'.[100] It now seemed clear in Burke's mind, therefore, that the new Whigs had settled upon a new constituency as the sole means of furthering their cause. And there was always, to Burke, the problem of Fox's motives. Privately Burke reported that Fox had let on that 'he is as good an aristocrate as any of us', adding that 'I really do believe him to be so; but perhaps do not the less excuse him'.[101]

Such apparent dissembling was to become even less excusable, however, as Burke's view of Fox altered. Events began to swing sharply in Burke's direction, culminating, as Pitt, swayed by Burke and the French émigrés, decided to intervene in the course of the revolution,[102] in the outbreak of war in early 1793. In *Observations on the Conduct of the Minority*, a fifty-four count indictment of the Foxites and their leader, Burke linked Fox much more closely with the dissident new Whigs, and now accused Fox of renouncing Whiggism entirely:

In all these motions and debates he wholly departed from all the political principles relative to France (considered merely as a state, and independent of its Jacobin form of government) which had hitherto been held fundamental in this country, and which he had himself held more strongly than any man in Parliament.[103]

'Under his auspices' a new society was formed, the Friends of the Liberty of the Press, which Burke described as 'was only, in reality, another modification of the society calling itself The Friends of the People'. Fox was now therefore tied more closely to the latter, Horne Tooke, and Thomas Erskine, and through Erskine to 'that Jacobin incendiary', Paine, which was clearly evidenced by Fox's opposition to war with France and his celebration of French successes.[104]

Burke naturally also rejected a petition by the Society of the Friends of the People for parliamentary reform, contending of those who wished to eliminate the power of the peerage in the Commons that 'it is natural, therefore, that they who wish the common destruction of the whole and of all its parts should contend for their total separation'.[105] All reform, therefore, now invited revolution; whether by design or consequence mattered little. No dividing line exists between the friends of Jacobinism and those of reform: 'Whether it is necessarily connected in theory with Jacobinism is not worth a dispute. The two things are connected in fact. The partisans of the one are the partisans of the other'. The Foxites now have 'sworn to live and die in their French principles'. These themes would be later developed in *Letter to a Noble Lord* (1796), which confronted two other Whig magnates, Lords Bedford and Lauderdale, and the three letters on a 'Regicide Peace' of 1796–7.

Burke's Later Reputation

The issue as to whether it was Burke or Fox who remained the more consistent Whig would overshadow Burke's reputation for about a century. Though he was often quoted subsequently as having announced himself (in 1770) 'no friend to aristocracy',[106] Burke himself regarded his efforts as protecting rather than renouncing Whiggery – a view his biographers have often taken[107] – and thought some of his leading critics were merely temporarily deluded rather than substantively at variance with his views, though this was not of course true for Paine.[108] His Whig pedigree was underscored greatly by the return to the fold of a leading reformer, James Mackintosh, of whom it was said (by Sidmouth, among others) that, a humble and penitent apostate, he 'received absolution from the Pope at Beaconsfield' at the end of 1796.[109] Disregarding the notion that Burke was an apostate Whig, Mackintosh proclaimed that 'an abhorrence for abstract politics, a predilection for aristocracy, and a dread of innovation, have ever been among the most sacred articles of his public creed'.[110] The conversion was very complete; by mid-1799 Mackintosh praised Burke 'with rapture, declaring that he was, in his estimation, without any parallel, in any age or country, except, perhaps, Lord Bacon and Cicero; that his works contained an ampler store of political and moral wisdom than could be found in any other writer whatever'.[111]

In the early nineteenth century Burke's rapid judgement about the inevitable failure of the Revolution ensured his status as 'a Political and Moral Prophet',[112] and this quality ensured the long-term reputation of the *Reflections*. The more conservative Whigs echoed George Canning's view that virtually all of the *Reflections* had 'been justified by the course of subsequent events; and almost every prophecy has been strictly fulfilled'.[113] Even liberal Whigs like Henry Brougham averred that

> For nearly the whole period during which he survived the commencement of the revolution, – for five of those seven years, – all his predictions, save one momentary expression, had been more than fulfilled: anarchy and bloodshed had borne sway in France; conquest and convulsion had desolated Europe ... The providence of mortals is not often able to penetrate so far as this into futurity.[114]

Yet Brougham also contended that Burke was inconsistent in writing that he was 'no friend to aristocracy' by contrast with 'the high monarchical tone of his latter writings'.[115] And the popular radical view was certainly, as Hazlitt put it, that Burke had by 1790 'abandoned not only all his practical conclusions, but all the principles on which they were founded. He proscribed all his former sentiments, denounced all his former friends, rejected and reviled all the maxims to which he had formerly appealed as incontestable'.[116]

Nonetheless it is not the case that Burke was simply anointed as the founding father of modern 'conservatism' (to which term Toryism was giving way by the late 1830s), and was acknowledged as such thereafter to the present. To the contrary, historians have noted, as we reach the years approaching the Great Reform Act, that Burke's star seemed to have waned. *Blackwood's Edinburgh Magazine* conceded in

1825 that 'the ashes of Edmund Burke slumber almost without notice', while John Wilson Croker lamented in the *Quarterly Review* a year later that Burke's 'mighty name was for a time obscured'.[117] The chief problem was seemingly uncertainty as to how to label Burke, and hence how to appropriate his inheritance. Some later standard accounts of Toryism, like T.E. Kebbel's *History of Toryism* (1886), though acknowledging the impact of the *Reflections*,[118] pay scant attention to Burke, and it is tempting to conclude, as James Sack has done, that 'Burke had no paradigmatic influence on most leading Conservative politicians of the Victorian age', this 'widespread neglect' by Tories being derived in part because 'Burke may never have appeared completely convincing as at Tory'.[119] Burke was thus not a 'Tory' as such for many nineteenth-century commentators, but rather what Keith Feiling would later term a 'converted Whig'.[120] Whilst Burke was cited constantly throughout the nineteenth century on the Irish question, his *Reflections* were often condemned as (to take an account from 1854) 'most inadequate. He could neither see the necessity of the consequence upon the hopeless corruptions of the old system, nor yet the promise which it held out for the future.'[121] As Britain began to embrace democracy, then, the *Reflections* seemed increasingly outmoded. Yet this perception, too, would alter in the later nineteenth century, when, in light of the International Working Men's Association and the Paris Commune, the threat of socialism loomed, Burke became increasingly seen as having anticipated a new form of tyranny still greater than that of Jacobinism. Now the consistency of his 'instinctive and undying repugnance to the critical or revolutionary spirit'[122] (in John Morley's words) was increasingly stressed, in face of the threat of a European-wide revolutionary conflagration. Bolshevism emphatically recast the *Reflections* in a contemporary light, and the text was often reprinted in the twentieth century as exemplifying the dangers of revolutionary principles and communistical egalitarianism. Today, thus, Burke's reputation rests chiefly upon his prophetic denunciation of what is usually termed totalitarianism, and the substantial revival of interest in his principles is chiefly indebted to the ideological conflicts of the Cold War era.

Chapter Three: Thomas Paine
Rights of Man *(1791–2) and*
the Origins of Radicalism

Background

Thomas Paine was born in Thetford, Norfolk, 29 January 1737, the son of a Quaker stay-(corset)maker. He assumed the family trade, then briefly became an exciseman (tax-collector), and emigrated to America in 1774. Here he quickly joined the colonists' cause and befriended Jefferson, Franklin, and Washington. His famous pamphlet, *Common Sense* (1776), was crucial in persuading the Americans to part from England. After serving in the revolutionary war, Paine worked as a farmer and inventor. In England in 1790, he wrote the main response to Burke's *Reflections, Rights of Man* (2 parts, 1791–2), for which he was prosecuted and the book proscribed. Forced to flee to France, Paine was first welcomed as hero, and elected as one of only two foreign members of the National Convention, but was then imprisoned during Robespierre's Terror (1793–4) and nearly guillotined for supporting exile rather than execution for Louis XVI. He was later greatly disappointed with the course of revolution. His *The Age of Reason* (1794) was written against 'priestcraft', though his religious views were deist rather than atheist. But the tract did much to make him widely unpopular in the United States, where he died in 1809.

Rights of Man *(1791–2)*

Rights of Man can be described as a classic exercise in political demystification, and a vigorous defence of the first principles of modern democratic political thought in an accessible and persuasive fashion. Britons, Paine thought, had been essentially well disposed towards French developments until Burke's attack upon the Revolution. Yet the *Reflections* had so far erred in its interpretation of events that to Paine it was a mere 'dramatic performance', full of wild assertions and driven by an obsession with outmoded precedents.[1] But it was an interpretation, nonetheless, which required refutation. In both parts of *Rights of Man* Paine commended against Burke's gothic ideal, or idealised British constitution, the European imitation of the American model, with the provision of a written constitution approved by the voting public, an elected executive, representative institutions based upon a wide franchise, the abolition of aristocratic monopolies and the Established Church, and a general reduction of the expenses of government. Through the extension of universally recognised rights and of the system of commerce Paine hoped not only for the greater enrichment of the labouring classes, but a closer unity of the international system through the recognition of the advantages of mutual trade. Government thus founded on 'a *moral theory, on a system of universal peace, on the indefeasible hereditary Rights of Man*' would prove vastly more just and efficient than existing European systems.[2]

Paine's starting point in Part One concerns the authority of past legislation over existing generations, for Burke had contended against Price that the settlement of 1688 bound all posterity. Burke thus denied the people's right to choose their own governors, to cashier them for misconduct, and to frame their own government. But the Parliament of 1688 had done just this, Paine thought, and then restricted its own successors from performing any similar act. This was inconsistent and unjust:

> Man has no property in man; neither has any generation a property in the generations which are to follow. The Parliament or the people of 1688, or of any other period, had no more right to dispose of the people of the present day, or to bind or to control them *in any shape whatever*, than the parliament or the people of the present day have to dispose of, bind or control those who are to live a hundred or a thousand years hence. Every generation is, and must be, competent to all the purposes which its occasions require.[3]

'Governing beyond the grave', or forcing the living to be compelled by the actions of the dead, was tyranny: what we might term the 'wisdom of ancestors'[4] was now accordingly always in question. Consequently rebellion against French despotism had been justified. Louis XVI might have been a moderate king, but despotic principles had infiltrated into every corner of France, assuming variously the guises of feudal, ministerial, monarchical, parliamentary or ecclesiastical tyranny. Burke, concentrating on the personality of the king, lamented the loss of what was for Paine a merely Quixotic 'age of chivalry'. But Burke did not sympathise with the victims of the Bastille and other prisons, only the few killed liberating them. In one of Paine's most memorable phrases, Burke was ridiculed because he 'pities the plumage, but forgets the dying bird'.[5] In his sycophantic applause for aristocracy and monarchy he simply passed over the human tragedy of despotic rule.

Paine then turned to rights. Burke appeared to deny that men possessed any natural rights at all. But this could not be his meaning, Paine assumed. Rights of one kind or another existed, everyone agreed. The chief problem was their origins, and to discover these it was essential to go back 'the whole way', not merely a hundred or a thousand years. The origin of the rights of man was the origin of man himself, at the Creation. All histories thereof, and particularly the Mosaic account, 'whether taken as divine authority or merely historical', agreed 'in establishing one point, the unity of man; by which I mean that men are all of one degree, and consequently that all men are born equal, and with equal natural rights'. Consequently each generation possessed identical natural rights 'in the same manner as if posterity had been continued by creation'.[6] On these rights were founded civil rights, including, crucially (as the American Declaration of Independence had recognised),[7] the right of resistance. Such rights included 'all the rights of the mind' as well as 'all those rights of acting as an individual for his own comfort and happiness, which are not injurious to the natural rights of others'. Civil rights existed for the same reason civil society did, because not all natural rights, especially self-protection, could be guaranteed by the individual. Those natural rights 'in which the power to execute is as perfect in the individual as the right itself', such as freedom of religion, remained intact in civil society. Others, such as the right to judge in one's own case, were surrendered in exchange for the guarantee of just redress in society, which secured the right more fully, civil power having no mandate to invade any natural right.[8]

But the only government which could secure such rights had to be based upon equal and full representation, which entailed recognising the principle of popular sovereignty, freedom of commerce, and the abolition of primogeniture, aristocratic monopoly and established religion. Governments based solely on power or superstition would not maintain rights properly. Paine at first denied that he recommended any particular form of government, arguing that 'That which a whole nation chooses to do, it has a right to do', and promoting 'the common interest of society and the common rights of man'. Nonetheless he then sided clearly with anti-monarchical republicanism, as he would do when he reached France, hoping that with a true 'renovation of the natural order of things ... combining moral with political happiness and national prosperity ... the cause of wars would be taken away'.[9] Nor would Paine contemplate government by an aristocracy, who possessed no hereditary claims to wisdom, and were a debased, corrupted, and tyrannical order.

'The most impressive of all his writings', as a distinguished philosopher has termed it, Part Two of the *Rights of Man* again took as its point of departure the American Revolution, and indeed the text has been described as considerably more American than French in outlook. America had been 'the only spot in the political world, where the principles of universal reformation could begin'. The diversity of its immigrants and their different religious backgrounds had enforced a spirit of compromise. Conquering the wilderness demanded great co-operation, by which the colonists came to see one another 'not with the inhuman idea of a natural enemy, but as kindred'. Moreover, America's increasing opulence proved that its government assisted prosperity. By contrast, Europe abounded with 'hordes of miserable poor', and 'the greedy hand of government' could be found 'thrusting itself into every corner and crevice of industry, and grasping the spoil of the multitude', making 'universal civilization and commerce' impossible.[10]

The connection of democratic republicanism and prosperity led Paine to elaborate upon the distinction between 'society' and 'government' first tentatively explored in *Common Sense*. Society was a 'great chain of connection' based upon 'mutual dependence and reciprocal interest' between landholders, merchants, tradesmen, manufacturers and other occupations whose strong common interest regulated their affairs almost entirely. Thus society performed 'for itself almost every thing which is ascribed to government', while 'a great part' of 'government' was 'mere imposition'. Compelled to co-operate because their wants were greater and more diverse than their individual capacities, people were ultimately drawn together by 'a system of social affections' which produced a 'love for society'.[11] There is no worry here about the corrosive effects of luxury and avarice on either individual morals or public virtue. The more perfect civilization was, rather, 'the less occasion has it for government, because the more does it regulate its own affairs, and govern itself'. Uncivilised governments upset rather than reinforced the natural harmony of society. But America, where 'the poor are not oppressed, the rich are not privileged', taught the world that 'government is nothing more than a national association acting on the principles of society', and that representative, not hereditary, government, was the only polity based on reason:

> All hereditary government is in its nature tyranny. An heritable crown, or an heritable throne, or by what other fanciful name such things may be called, have no other significant explanation than that mankind are heritable property. To inherit a government, is to inherit the people, as if they were flocks and herds.[12]

America also proved that while simple democracies were incapable of governing great populations, 'ingrafting' representation upon democracy permitted both a diversity of interests and an extensive territory and population. What Athens had thus been to the ancient world, America would be to the modern.[13]

The conception of a system of interdependent needs which Paine usually termed 'society' was drawn largely from natural law writings, and their adaptation by the early political economists, though this is a tradition usually associated with Burke rather than Paine.[14] Paine, who referred to Adam Smith approvingly, was manifestly a modern, commercial republican, and no friend to primitive or Spartan equality of the type associated with Rousseau.[15] Commerce, he thought, was 'a pacific system, operating to unite mankind by rendering nations, as well as individuals, useful to each other'. Since each individual was improvable principally 'by means of his interest', if 'commerce were permitted to act to the universal extent it is capable of', it would 'extirpate the system of war, and produce a revolution in the uncivilized state of governments'. Commerce was 'the greatest approach towards universal civilization, that has yet been made by any means not immediately flowing from moral principles'. Its essence was merely 'the traffic of two individuals, multiplied on a scale of numbers; and by the same rule that nature intended the intercourse of two, she intended that of all'. Consequently nature (meaning God) had 'distributed the materials of manufactures and commerce in various and distant parts of a nation and of the world; and as they cannot be procured by war so cheaply or so commodiously as by commerce, she has rendered the latter the means of extirpating the former'. By war and taxation uncivilised monarchical governments merely inhibited commercial growth at home as well as abroad. But when nations trading with Britain were harmed, their capacity to buy her goods also lessened. Thus 'the prosperity of any commercial nation is regulated by the prosperity of the rest. If they are poor, she cannot be rich'.[16]

The most novel and controversial proposals in Part Two – and those which most clearly provoked the accusation of 'levelling' – were contained in the final segment of Chapter Five.[17] Here Paine detailed his schemes for the redistribution of wealth, proclaiming that the aim of government was to provide 'for the instruction of youth, and the support of age, so as to exclude, as much as possible, profligacy from the one, and despair from the other'. This proposal has consequently often been seen as helping to originate the welfare state.[18] These partly republican-inspired goals thus allowed for a more virtuous electorate and greater social equality. Though Paine saw some sense in a national debt, since it served 'to keep alive a capital, useful to commerce', vast increases in current expenses were unnecessary to pay for this programme. Instead all unnecessary costs could be reduced, and the remaining legitimate existing revenues would be used to provide for the necessitous poor. Poor children would receive a minimal education. Of the aged, those over fifty and unable to support themselves would be granted a pension of £6 per annum until the age of 60, or about a ninth of a skilled labourer's average wage, and £10 thereafter. Assistance would be given to women on the birth of each child, and £20,000 made available to defray the funeral costs of all who died away from home. Two workhouses would be funded in London to provide temporary employment, meals and lodging to some 24,000 people annually. Money would also be set aside for the maintenance of disbanded soldiers and sailors. Finally, and most dramatically, Paine proposed a system of progressive taxation on inheritances. On estates annually worth from £50 to £500, the tax would be only some 3d per pound ($1\frac{1}{2}$ per cent) of value, but at £23,000 (equivalent to several million pounds today) it would reach 100 per cent. Estates so large were simply a 'prohibitable luxury', though property acquired by honest industry would not be affected, only that received by bequest. By this means the aristocracy would carry its burden of just taxes. But it is important to point out, given the subsequent debate about the *Rights of Man*, that these proposals would hardly have destroyed the existing property system. Estates of up to some £13–14,000 a year – a very considerable sum earned by probably only 200 families in Britain – would still produce a profit to their holder, Paine estimated. In addition, that old republican bugbear, primogeniture or the inheritance of landed estates solely by the eldest son, would be abolished, and greater social equality promoted.[19] Yet given the subsequent debate it is worth underscoring the fact that Paine was a moderate rather than an extreme egalitarian, and in modern European terms, a social democrat rather than a socialist.

Paine's Religious Thought: The Age of Reason (1794)

It is now generally conceded that Paine is better classified as a Deist, or one who generally believes in God but not revealed religion, than a Quaker, despite his upbringing among and many affinities with the latter sect.[20] But even within Deism there was a fairly wide spectrum of belief, and the implications of apparently minor shifts of theological doctrine for the social, political and economic theory of particular thinkers remains a contentious topic. And theology and social theory, and in particular, theories of property, remained intimately intertwined in this period in a manner which has become unfamiliar to us today. It is worthwhile, therefore, assessing the major elements of Paine's controversial religious beliefs.

The Age of Reason was published in 1794 not to advertise Paine's atheistic views, but rather to defend the cause of Deism against what Paine himself saw as the harmful trend towards atheism in France, where 'in the general wreck of superstition, of false systems of government and false theology', the danger emerged that 'we lose sight of morality, of humanity and of the theology that is true'. The principles of Paine's Deism included the belief in one God, and the hope 'for happiness beyond this life'. Beyond this, however, the Christian religion was too far subverted by 'priestcraft' and superstition to suit the true Deist. This was particularly true of its claim to revelation, and thus the pretence that the Bible was the work of God. Most of the Bible, as far as Paine was concerned, was only hearsay and mythology. The account of creation in 'Genesis', therefore, was probably 'a tradition which the Israelites had among them before they came into

Egypt; and after their departure from that country they put it at the head of their history'. Elsewhere, too, Paine wrote of the 'whimsical account of the Creation', the spuriousness of the Book of Genesis and related works, concluding that it was nothing but 'an anonymous book of stories, fables and traditionary or invented absurdities, or of downright lies'.[21] It is scarcely surprising that many a believer, like the young tailor Francis Place, arose from the text a freethinker.[22]

Revelation was to be discovered not in the Bible, therefore, but in nature itself. Only here was the universal message of God apparent:

> The Creation speaks a universal language, independently of human speech or human language, multiplied and as various as they be. It is an ever-lasting original, which every man can read. It cannot be forged; it cannot be counterfeited; it cannot be lost; it cannot be altered; it cannot be suppressed. It does not depend on the will of man whether it shall be published or not; it publishes itself from one end of the earth to the other. It preaches to all nations and to all worlds; and this Word of God reveals to man all that is necessary for man to known of God.

All of the attributes of the Deity were thus evident in the natural world. The power of God was demonstrated in 'the immensity of the Creation'. His wisdom was discernable in 'the unchangeable order by which the incomprehensible whole is governed'. His munificence was revealed 'in the abundance with which he fills the earth', and his mercy, 'in His not withholding that abundance even from the unthankful'. God, then, was the 'first cause' of the Creation, but could otherwise be known only through the scientific exploration of the natural world, though Paine conceded at one point, somewhat inconsistently, that 'the power and wisdom He has manifested in the structure of the Creation that I behold is to me incomprehensible'.[23]

The revelation of nature was thus hardly devoid of moral meaning to mankind. Divine intention in fact suffused nature in the form of Providence. Though he derided 'the God Providence' as one of the five Gods of Christian mythology, Paine was deeply convinced that the Creator had 'organised the structure of the universe in the most advantageous manner for the benefit of man', and that there existed 'an Almighty Power that governs and regulates the whole'. The religion of Deism thus consisted in 'contemplating the power, wisdom and benignity of the Deity in his works, and in endeavouring to imitate

Him in everything moral, scientifical and mechanical'. Were the benevolent designs of the Deity not a part of Paine's religion he would merely have become a worshipper of nature. As it was, his views clearly relied very strongly upon a belief in Providence, which underpinned the optimistic theory of commerce outlined above. Elsewhere we find him praising 'the hand of Providence', describing God as 'an infinite protecting power', and implying that Providence had intended America to become an asylum for the persecuted virtuous of Europe (and had even played a role in saving Paine himself from the guillotine). He also paid homage to the 'unerring order and universal harmony reigning throughout the whole' of the works of creation, particularly as evidenced by the operations of the planetary system (and he remained a devotee of Newton's, in 1797 using the rotation of the planets as a key argument to prove the existence of an external Cause of the world).[24]

What implications might this theology have for a theory of property? In *Agrarian Justice* (1796), we will see, Paine would introduce divine authority in the gift of all land to the human species. Yet if *The Age of Reason* discounted the Biblical account of Creation, how was such a supposition possible? It is unlikely that he altered his views on the Bible during this period. During his defence of *The Age of Reason* in 1797, in fact, Paine specifically mocked the apparently confused account of Creation in Genesis, arguing that it inconsistently asserted that the first man and woman were given dominion over the whole earth and then over only a single garden.[25] How could land then be 'the free gift of the Creator in common to the human race'? Upon what basis could the will of the Creator be known in such circumstances if the authority of the Bible was questionable or even unusable? In following natural law discussions of the problem of original communal property, Paine accepted an account of its dissolution which was broadly historical (in a conjectural sense). He emphasised that landed property arose with cultivation, and did not exist in the first state of man, that of hunters, nor in the second state, that of shepherds, where property existed only in flocks and herds. So far he only adopted the four stages theory of the progression of modes of subsistence which many of the Scottish writers, following the natural law tradition, had popularised.[26] But this did not necessarily entail the notion that any common property rights were given to all in the state of nature which could be drawn upon in later stages of society. The claim to common property rights was thus suspect unless such rights inhered in individuals as individuals, and not as the result of Divine behest. This might have corresponded to Paine's notion of natural rights, each of which he saw as 'an animal right; and the power to act it, is supposed, either fully or in part, to be contained within ourselves as individuals'.[27] But it is also inconsistent to deduce from the mere fact that rights inhere in individuals any right to an original portion of communal property. Such a right could not possibly be intrinsic to existence outside of the state of nature, without the assumption that all mankind were God's children and as such vested with this right, which Paine's sceptical Deism did not indicate as such. Nor could it be deduced from the motion of the planets. It had to be, therefore, either historically grounded, or divinely granted.

Reinforcing Property Rights: Agrarian Justice (1796)

As we have seen, the conclusion to *Rights of Man*, Part Two, indicates that Paine had moved some distance from a Smithian conception of the *laissez-faire* state as outlined in the *Wealth of Nations* (1776), and towards a justification of greater intervention to assist the poor. By 1796 Paine came to believe that in 'old countries' like Britain and France poverty might indeed be endemic, even under a republican constitution, and had to be countered by a still greater redistribution of existing tax revenues and of income from the largest landed estates. In the *Rights of Man*, Part One, he acknowledged only that rights 'which appertain to man in right of his existence', or which thus 'inhered' in individuals, not those present in any conjectural state of nature. No mention was made here of property rights, either individual or collective, positive or negative, in relation to the state of nature or divine intent.[28] Compared to the *Rights of Man*, *Agrarian Justice Opposed to Agrarian Law and to Agrarian Monopoly* made far more sweeping claims for the poor's right to what Paine now argued was common wealth, especially agricultural improvements, doubtless partly inspired by the French egalitarian communist Gracchus Babeuf's views, which became widely known after his abortive conspiracy in 1795–6, and by French discussions of the *Loi Agraire*.[29] Crucially, Paine now saw poverty as originating partly in inadequate wages and an economic oppression in which all employers, not merely corrupt aristocrats, participated, and less in the heavy taxation imposed by government which he had chiefly stressed earlier. This shift advertised a growing concern with the labouring classes generally, and not only the poor.

Central to *Agrarian Justice*'s new claims was Paine's discussion of the original community of property ordained by God. Here he distinguished for the first time between 'natural property' bequeathed by the maker of the universe, 'such as the earth, air, water', and 'artificial property' created by mankind. Equality in the latter was 'impossible; for to distribute it equally it would be necessary that all should have contributed in the same proportion, which can never be the case; and this being the case, every individual would hold on to his own property, as his right share'. But of 'equality of natural property … the subject of this little essay', Paine insisted that 'every individual in the world is born therein with legitimate claims on a certain kind of property, or its equivalent'.[30] This 'natural birthright' Paine thought was still recognised among primitive societies like the North American Indians. But while early societies were blissfully unaware of 'those spectacles of human misery which poverty and want present to our eyes in all the towns and streets of Europe', they had also lacked 'those advantages which flow from agriculture, arts, science and manufactures'. To retain these benefits while avoiding the evils of progress, it was necessary to acknowledge 'the first principle of civilization … that the condition of every person born into the world, after a state of civilization commences, ought not to be worse than if he had been born before that period'.[31] Thus Paine proposed that landowners pay a lump sum as well as an annuity to all deprived of their birthright. Much of his new plan to tax landed property seemingly hinged upon conceding this right of restitution.

Paine's second main proposition was the claim that 'the earth, in its natural, uncultivated state was, and ever would have continued to be, the common property of the human race', with every man being 'born to property' in the land. If this was true, only 'the value of the improvement', not the earth itself, was 'individual property', even though it was admittedly 'impossible to separate the improvement made by cultivation' from what the earth itself provided. Paine could have argued that at some point not industry but inheritance generated unacceptable inequalities in wealth. That was where *Rights of Man* had left the matter. Or he could have simply defined 'a limit to property, or the accumulation of it by bequest'. Instead he now justified a tax upon all landed wealth without having to measure 'improvement', by arguing that every landed proprietor owed the community a 'ground-rent'. Upon this, rather than the mere condemnation of the excessive 'luxury' of great estates, Paine's new taxation plan was to be based.[32]

It was not merely the claim that land historically had once been held in common, but the original intentional bequest of the whole earth to all by God at the Creation which was vital here. This supported rights claims which merely acknowledging an historical state of nature with common use rights did not necessarily uphold (and of course there were disagreements about what rights had existed then). Moreover, it lent Paine's case an important pedigree. For this argument was central to natural jurisprudence accounts of property, which developed the Biblical assertion that at the Creation, dominion over the earth was vested in the first man and woman and all their descendants. By the 1790s most Christians, however, and the chief natural jurists Paine probably read, Grotius and Pufendorf, believed that God gave the earth to all in common only 'negatively', that is, to develop individually as the need arose (principally from the pressure of population). God had not intended a 'positive' community of property where goods remained in common in perpetuity, and which could be used as a justification for communistical proposals in the modern world.[33]

Yet if *Agrarian Justice* did not entertain such proposals, Paine nonetheless contended that some communal property rights were still retained in the civilised state. He thus promoted a contemporary right to property which a strictly stadial theory (emphasising the progression of all societies through major phases of development, notably the four stages of hunting and gathering, pastoral, agricultural and commercial) – insofar as it historicised rights claims, acknowledging only those original rights which had been unsecured by subsequent contracts – necessarily rejected, at least in this form. Natural law texts usually conceded the recurrent validity of original common property rights in one crucial respect. For some, at least, argued that the needy, if facing starvation, could invoke the right of charity from the rich, and could demand that grain be sold to them at the normal market price, and even (a few added) rightfully steal in cases of dire necessity. But Paine's conception of the application of original rights to the modern world was wider than this, and only succeeded because of a theologically based workmanship model. Man had not made the earth, and 'though he had a natural right to occupy it, he had no right to locate as his property in perpetuity any part of it; neither did the Creator of the earth open a land-office, from whence the first title-deeds should issue'.[34] Since cultivation began, however, landed monopolies had dispossessed at least half the population of their portion of the soil. If they were compensated by receiving £15 at age 21 (or about half a year's wage for an agricultural labourer) and £10 annually from age 50 onwards, a 'revolution in the state of civilization' analogous to a republican revolution in government would result.[35]

It can certainly be contended, then, that *Agrarian Justice* uses an argument for an original community of goods in order to favour a limited redistribution of property. Paine did not, however, believe that a positive community of goods was possible or accept the communistic implications of Babeuf's theories. In fact there is no reason to suppose that he retreated far, if at all, from the view he expressed in mid-1795, or some six months before *Agrarian Justice* was composed, in which he firmly asserted:

That property will ever be unequal is certain. Industry, superiority of talents, dexterity of management, extreme frugality, fortunate opportunities, or the opposite, or the means of all those things, will ever produce that effect, without having recourse to the harsh, ill-sounding names of avarice and oppression ... All that is required with respect to property is to obtain it honestly, and not employ it criminally.[36]

The Reception and later Reputation of Paine's Ideas

Rights of Man was astonishingly successful, selling some 300–500,000 copies in the next decade, probably more than any work in a similar period of time. Paine could have been rich; instead he gave the copyright and £1000 worth of royalties to the Society for Constitutional Information. Much of the debate the book spawned during the 1790s will be considered in chapter five. Paine's reputation as a radical critic of the British constitution extended well into the next century. The events of the 1790s probably set back the cause of parliamentary reform for more than a generation, and did much to forge a new Toryish nationalist identity in which that belligerent symbol of British national character, John Bull, reigned undisputed.[37] But Paine was far from forgotten. The London Corresponding Society leader Thomas Hardy wrote him in 1807 that 'there are many who are silently reading and reflecting on what you have written'.[38] In 1817 we find Paine being termed 'the greatest political reasoner that ever existed'.[39] A pamphlet attacking *Rights of Man* was published as late as 1831,[40] while plebeian reformers celebrated his birthday regularly, and his works circulated widely in the Chartist period and beyond, becoming classics of republican argument. But for the time being many reformers avoided the taint of Jacobinism, disdaining, as the popular leader Sir Francis Burdett did in 1808, any interest in 'speculative plans ... new systems, or novelties of any kind'.[41] Reasoning in politics according to first principles or abstract speculation was indeed to be difficult in Britain for many decades, in part owing to the reaction to Paine. Paine also became widely associated with the Victorian secularist tradition.[42] But his theologically based rights arguments, particularly respecting land, would also remain influential until the twentieth century and were still prominently used by the land nationalisation advocate Alfred Russel Wallace.[43]

Chapter Four: Mary Wollstonecraft
Vindication of the Rights of Woman
(1792) and the Origins of Feminism

Wollstonecraft's Life

Mary Wollstonecraft was born on 27 April 1759 in Spitalfields, London, the daughter of reasonably affluent weaver whose fortunes declined in her youth. For a time in the 1780s she taught school at Newington Green, where she befriended the philosopher and pro-American Richard Price, agreeing with his Rationalist Dissenting optimism respecting social and individual change, though remaining an Anglican. She also worked as a governess in Ireland before becoming a journalist and a woman of letters. Wollstonecraft's career as a writer began with *Thoughts on the Education of Daughters* (1786). Thereafter she assisted the leading publisher Joseph Johnson, notably with the *Analytical Review*, wrote a children's book (*Original Stories*, 1788), and soon entered into the inner circles of London radical society, meeting Thomas Holcroft, William Godwin, Thomas Christie, and others. She may have heard of the French writer Condorcet's plea for equal rights for women, written in 1790.[1] When Burke's *Reflections* appeared in November 1790, Wollstonecraft was its first respondent, producing her *Vindication of the Rights of Men* (1790) within a matter of weeks. The famous *Vindication of the Rights of Woman* followed in 1792. Wollstonecraft lived in France between 1792 and 1795 with an American sea-captain, Gilbert Imlay. She later wrote an important historical account of the French Revolution, and began a novel, later published as *Maria, or the Wrongs of Woman*. She married William Godwin, and died in childbirth in 1797.

From the Vindication of the Rights of Men *to the*
Vindication of the Rights of Woman

Mary Wollstonecraft's *Vindication of the Rights of Woman* (1792) first centrally established the claim that 'feminist' argument (the term being here applied anachronistically) had to be included in the canon of political texts which define the modern tradition. The text forces upon us, similarly, the realisation that the pre-existing canon of political thought had omitted any discussion of women on many occasions, or had seemingly subsumed their role under the generic label of 'man' while in fact supporting the patriarchal domination of men over women.

Any account of Mary Wollstonecraft's most famous work must necessarily commence with an assessment of the so-called first *Vindication*, the *Vindication of the Rights of Men*, which offers important clues as to the central themes of the second *Vindication*, and particularly the issue as to why, despite its title, most of the second *Vindication* seems to have far more to do with 'manners' than with 'rights' *per se*.[2]

Until fairly recently Wollstonecraft was rarely located within histories of the critique of manners in this period.[3] But the 'main argument' of the second *Vindication*, as Wollstonecraft herself expresses it, is that those who support the 'cause of virtue' must permit women to become educated to be the companion of man. Failure to do so will result in women halting 'the progress of knowledge and virtue'.[4] This was a striking argument in itself for its time. What is most radical in the second *Vindication*, however, particularly in light of the development of later feminist thought, is the assertion that private morality is the chief 'source' of public virtue, and that male tyranny in the domestic sphere thus inhibits public morality, notably by imposing an education in tyrannical principles upon children who are destined to become citizens under what was widely trumpeted as the freest constitution in the world. Rather than the domestic sphere of the family and household being thus 'separate' from and contradistinguished to the 'male' public and political sphere, Wollstonecraft demands their reintegration, and the assessment of the influence of each on similar criteria. Mandeville, emphatically, had been wrong: private vices begat public vices.

It is, however, paradoxical that it is precisely where Wollstonecraft seems to be at her most 'radical', in eroding a crucial distinction between public and private forms of virtue, that she also appears in some respects most 'traditional', in supporting the view that marriage and motherhood remain the chief occupation and fulfilment for most women. Moreover, it was Wollstonecraft's 'second' argument about rights, derived from a notion of divine intention, which seems to be most traditional and alien to more secular modern readers, yet which was in fact far more radical in its implications. This concept of equality, which was, we will see, not gendered, pointed towards a much more all-encompassing egalitarianism by arguing that the Creator did not intend any difference in character to exist between men and women. Seen from this perspective, Wollstonecraft's much-neglected religious views – whose sources and development cannot be explored here – were not tangential to, but central to the main arguments of the *Vindication of the Rights of Woman*.[5] For these reasons in particular it is worth examining the arguments of the first *Vindication*.

Wollstonecraft's starting point in the *Vindication of the Rights of Men* (1790) is the 'rights of humanity', or 'the rights of men and the liberty of reason'.[6] But while she early on introduces the theme of rights, Wollstonecraft in fact is more concerned to juxtapose two notions of manners, one, challenging the status quo, based on reason; the other, already widely accepted as the dominant role model for female behaviour, unduly fixated on sensibility. Burke's reaction to the French revolution, and his effusive affection for the *ancien régime* and the trappings of aristocratic and courtly life, Wollstonecraft claims, succumbs to the sensibility and chivalry which are the grand mania of the day. Burke's 'pampered sensibility', the fumes of his emotionalism rising to 'dispel the sober suggestions of reason', prevents him from recognizing the cause of justice as embodied in the French revolution.[7] But justice, Wollstonecraft says, now entails the defense of 'such a degree of liberty, civil and religious, as is compatible with the liberty of every other individual with whom he is united in a social compact, and the continued existence of that compact'. This liberty, everywhere fenced in by 'the demon of property', must be recognised by all those who build their morality and religion on 'the attributes of God'.[8] Burke, by contrast, reverences not reason, but only 'the rust of antiquity ... the unnatural customs, which ignorance and mistaken self-interest have consolidated'. Those who uphold similar principles, the few who tyrannise over the many, are not cultivated as a result of their education, but warped by its tendency, according to the dictates of European civilization, to refine 'the manners at the expence of morals, by making sentiments and opinions current in conversation that have no root in the heart, or weight in the cooler resolves of the mind'.[9] We see quite early on, thus, that Wollstonecraft's main strategy concerns a juxtaposition of one form of manners, or more properly morals, based on sincerity, to the 'courtly insincerity' and 'politeness' which, by merely making 'sport with truth', demand disguising our sentiments and perpetrating an ethos of falsehood throughout social relations.[10]

It is usually recognised that this is a common radical and Dissenting claim against the ruling classes and courtly culture; a plea for sincerity would also play a crucial role, with a similar aim, in Godwin's *Enquiry Concerning Political Justice* (1793). The ideal of politeness under attack was a fairly recent invention. Since the end of the seventeenth century, writers like Shaftesbury, Addison, Steele, and Hume had attempted to construct a new model of commercial, and increasingly urban manners which could dispel the myth of the supposed, much vaunted, superiority of ancient patriotism, especially of the Greek and Roman republicans, by comparison with the more refined, self-indulgent, private but sociable manners of the moderns. In the second half of the eighteenth century David Hume, most notably, had attempted to defend as intrinsic to the achievements of commercial society a notion of politeness which was partly modelled on courtly culture, while avoiding the extremes of 'affectation and foppery, disguise and insincerity'. Hume asserted that modern politeness, whose essence was a 'mutual deference or civility, which leads us to resign our own inclinations to those of our companion, and to curb and conceal that presumption and arrogance so natural to the human mind', owed its origins to gallantry. This form of civility arose in particular where a chain of dependency from prince to peasant existed, which provoked 'in every one an inclination to please his superiors, and to form himself upon those models which are most acceptable to people of condition and education'. Its great social advantage lay in the suppression of natural feelings, and affectation of polite deference and respect 'which civility obliges us to express or counterfeit towards the persons with whom we converse'. Gallantry, Hume assumed, tended to correct the gross vices between the sexes, and by comparison with the ancients, who left their women at home, and the barbarians, who simply enslaved them, men now compensated for their physical superiority over women by deference and generosity. Indeed Hume conceded that men would themselves find their manners softened, polished and refined by the company of virtuous women. It was for these reasons, among others, that Hume proclaimed the age of refinement to be both the happiest and most virtuous in history, with the increasing sociability and, even more, humanity, incident to urban life compensating sufficiently for the growing individualism of commercial societies. In Hume's account of manners, politeness in an urban context thus bears much of the weight which would otherwise fall on a theory of justice, morality and civic duty. For Hume is persuaded that greater humanity results from the social intercourse of commercial society than from that of any preceding social stage.[11]

Yet this account of the improved treatment of women by men, and the consequent superiority of modern civilization, was still reliant upon an ideal of gallantry to regulate men's behaviour towards women. This aroused Wollstonecraft's ire. Her own views echoed similar claims by John Brown, James Burgh (whose widow Wollstonecraft had befriended) and other republican writers who sought a more austere, stoic and puritanical reformation of manners against the general trend towards libertinism which is now usually regarded as characterising relations between the sexes from the Restoration until about 1800.[12] From the start of her career as a writer, Wollstonecraft had developed the theme of moral reform through piety. It was central to her first published work, *Thoughts on the Education of Daughters* (1787), which warns of the refinement of female manners unchecked by religious sentiment.[13] It reappears in some of the works she translated for Joseph Johnson, such as *Young Grandison. A Series of Letters from Young Persons to Their Friends* (2 vols, 1790). It looms large in her first novel, *Mary: A Fiction* (1788), with its injunctions to Christian virtue to 'govern the wayward feelings and impulses of the heart'.[14] It also plays a role in her occasional essays for Johnson's *Analytical Review*. One such piece reminded readers that God was 'the source of all perfection';[15] while another condemned that 'sickly feminine sensibility' which was too often the product of female education in the period, and derided female novelists for poisoning 'the minds of their sex, by strengthening a male prejudice that makes women systematically weak'.[16] A third insisted that education need treat men and women similarly, there being no 'characteristic difference' between them.[17]

Such demands were also echoed in more conservative, and especially evangelical quarters, by a major campaign against aristocratic profligacy led by Hannah More, whose *Thoughts on the Importance of the Manners of the Great to General Society* appeared in 1788. This attacked, amongst other things, 'The substitution of the word "gallantry" for that crime which stabs domestic happiness and conjugal virtue' [adultery], terming this 'one of the most dangerous of all the modern abuses of language'.[18] The efforts of William Wilberforce, too, were crucial in encouraging the restraint of excessive drinking, gambling and philandering amongst the upper classes early in the new century. Wilberforce's *A Practical View of the Prevailing Religious System of Professed Christians in the Higher and Middle Classes in This Country Contrasted With Real Christianity* (1797) appeared at the same time as the furore over Godwin's ruthlessly honest *Memoir* of Wollstonecraft, ensuring that her early ideals were forgotten amidst the censorious abuse heaped upon her conduct in the late 1790s.[19] And even at the level of high theory, Archdeacon William Paley's *Moral and Political Philosophy* (1790), a standard text for educated discussion of ethical issues over the next several generations, reminded readers of the perils of fornication, seduction, and adultery, and condemned 'All behaviour which is designed, or which knowingly tends to captivate the affection of a married woman' as 'a barbarous intrusion upon the peace and virtue of a family'.[20]

There was thus some common ground between Wollstonecraft and the evangelicals early in the decade. For Wollstonecraft, who quotes Hume in this context and clearly frames him as a target, gallantry was merely a 'cold unmeaning intercourse ... this vestige of gothic manners'.[21] Polite culture masks an inequality of ranks which inhibits 'true happiness', which derives solely 'from the friendship and intimacy which can only be enjoyed by equals'.[22] It emanates from that arrogance of the propertied which prevents them from looking for natural rights 'which men inherit at their birth, as rational creatures'. Inequality leads them to concede, with Burke, the value only of precedent, of the rights of the Englishman instead of those of the human being, of the virtues of the citizen rather than those inspired by the image of God.[23] Such prejudices are typical of 'the vulgar', by whom Wollstonecraft means both the rich and the poor, all of whom are mostly 'the creatures of habit and impulse', the rich from laziness and lack of mental exercise, the poor from necessity and inadequate education. Incapable of higher thought, the rich in particular achieve at the most Burke's 'Gothic affability', a form of politeness which is a mere substitute for true humanity and which is, other radical Whigs like James Mackintosh agreed, a reversion on Burke's part to an earlier, pre-commercial moral ideal.[24] Those beneath them, particularly the middle classes, in turn multiply their vices by 'apeing the manners of the great'.[25] Such arrogance, Wollstonecraft charges, prevents Burke from recognising the inhumanity of the game laws and impressment, and leads him to turn a blind eye to the corruption of Crown and government. Reverence for property, in particular, limits benevolence within the family, and encourages the brutal treatment of children. Daughters suffer 'legal prostitution' in arranged marriages, after flirtatious coquetishness, thus exchanging their bodies for wealth, while younger sons are sacrificed to the elder heir. Most, prevented from early marriages by parental will, descend into immorality and weaken both mind and body thereby. Here is the well of morality first poisoned, though 'natural parental affection' was meant to be 'the first source of civilisation'.[26]

Inequality of property thus undermines family morality as well as producing 'an unmanly servility, most inimical to true dignity of character'.[27] Luxury, 'effeminacy' (which like most republican writers, Wollstonecraft equates with personal weakness and civic inadequacy), vice and idleness pervade the world of wealth. The ethos of romance and chivalry, the spiritual by-product of aristocracy, are now however on the wane, for the passions underlying them are slowly being dispelled by the advance of reason. Burke claimed that Britain could make little progress in morals, politics and the idea of liberty, and contended that morality originated in 'untaught feelings'. Wollstonecraft instead forces the point that virtue derives from the understanding, is based in justice, and is 'concentrated by universal love'. This is in turn underpinned by a fear of as well as a reverence of God which aids self-reverence, and which indeed can alone promote it.[28] Wollstonecraft follows with what most modern readers may treat as a digression on the dangers of religious establishments, the immorality of tithes and of the corruption of the clergy by their association with the nobility. These religious themes, however, would remain vital to her perspective in the second *Vindication*. Indeed, they would provide Wollstonecraft with her most powerful argument in favour of sexual equality.

So far we have seen that most of Wollstonecraft's concentration in the first half of the *Vindication of the Rights of Men* is upon the roots of morality rather than upon rights *per se*. Moral behaviour, in turn, rests upon the capacity for reason. Wollstonecraft's central contention in this respect is that since 'those men who are obliged to exercise their reason have the most reason', these are 'the persons pointed out by Nature to direct the society of which they make a part'. Talents are not hereditary, and this disqualifies from rule 'the profligates of rank, emasculated by hereditary effeminacy'. This is by no means an unqualified republican idea. Wollstonecraft concedes the point (in reference to the members of the French National Assembly) that the founders of the Roman state, for example, had only been partially civilised, and had sometimes refined the manners, but rarely the morals, of their people. (She otherwise commends 'that enthusiastic flame which in Greece and Rome consumed every sordid passion'). What Wollstonecraft instead seeks is a moral meritocracy, 'everything respectable in talents', which is clearly not represented in the British House of Commons. Nor could it be, for few there have laboured for their knowledge, much less their bread, and hence they know not that 'every thing valuable must be the fruit of laborious exertions'.[29]

The improvement in morality Wollstonecraft seeks will, she claims, result only from an increase in liberty, 'the mother of all virtue', by which she means in part greater social equality of the type associated with the United States. This helps her to justify the seizure of church lands in France. But it must also result from increased humanity, though less from benevolence than from the recognition of just rights, particularly the right of the poor to 'more comfort than they at present enjoy', which she proposes might be aided by, for example, dividing great estates.[30] Yet by and large the practical politics of the first *Vindication* are extraordinarily moderate. Despite her own friendship with Richard Price, the leading British target of the *Reflections*, Wollstonecraft surprisingly even concedes to Burke, 'for a moment ... that Dr Price's political opinions are Utopian reveries'. Her sympathies here, despite the invocation of the rights of man, do not in all matters lie with the 'democratists'.[31] For it is here, not among the majority, that morality and the sources of enlightenment should be sought. For while the rich have 'polished vices', insincerity, the debauchery of luxurious ease, the poor are 'scarcely above the brutes', debauched not by riches and power but the crushing burden of life at the subsistence level.[32] Wollstonecraft is not here, thus, a social and political egalitarian; her radicalism, rather, is of a very different, if distinctive, type.

Let us now turn to the arguments of that 'very bold and original production', as Godwin termed it,[33] the much better known second *Vindication*. Completed in a mere six weeks it is, like the first *Vindication*, more concerned with manners than rights, proclaiming, famously, that 'it is time to effect a revolution in female manners'.[34] Its chief target is those, like Rousseau, who have sought to foist what Wollstonecraft regards as an inferior character upon the female sex, in order the bolster the rule of a 'male aristocracy'. The barrier to the progress of morality which Wollstonecraft is concerned to assail now, however, is less the overly deferential respect paid to rank and custom which Burke had commended, than tyranny within the family. This inhibits, by coercion, the freedom of women, and consequently the wisdom and virtue of both sexes. This is particularly the case because women who are insufficiently educated cannot foster that love of mankind in their families which needs to be passed on to their children, both because they are not active citizens, and because of the overbearing authority of the husband and father. Wollstonecraft's crucial assumption here is that 'every family might ... be called a state', whose morality, when 'polluted in the national reservoir, sends of streams of vice to corrupt the constituent parts of the body politic'. The principles of rule within the family are thus exactly analogous to those in society at large, and there is an interesting parallel here, as we will see below, with Godwin's assessment of all individual relations as involving the propensity of the strong to dominate the weak. But we also see here how crucial Wollstonecraft's account is for our sense of what the canon of modern political thought consists in. For rather than, as is usually assumed, having been seemingly vanquished by the events of 1688, the pestiferous principles of divine right and patriarchalism have in fact found their last great refuge hidden in the bastion of the family, where children are normally raised in despotic principles of unconditional obedience and blind respect whose suitability to 'public' life was now widely dismissed. This theme had been hinted at in the *Vindication of the Rights of Men*, where Wollstonecraft had suggested that 'the character of a master of a family, a husband, and a father, forms the citizen imperceptibly, by producing a sober manliness of thought, and orderly behaviour'.[35] But this notion is now expanded into a full-scale theory of the relations between public and private morality. Wollstonecraft's starting point is well known, but nonetheless worth quoting once again:

> Contending for the rights of woman, my main argument is built on this simple principle, that if she be not prepared by education to become the companion of man, she will stop the progress of knowledge and virtue; for truth must be common to all, or it will be inefficacious with respect to its influence on general practice. And how can woman be expected to co-operate unless she know why she ought to be virtuous? unless freedom strengthen her reason until she comprehend her duty, and see in what manner it is connected with her real good? If children are to be educated to understand the true principle of patriotism, their mother must be a patriot; and the

love of mankind, from which an orderly train of virtues spring, can only be produced by considering the moral and civil interest of mankind, but the education and situation of woman, at present, shuts her out from such investigations.[36]

Private morality thus subverts the public, for children can themselves scarcely become good citizens in these circumstances. Moreover, the reverse was also true, for as Wollstonecraft would emphasise elsewhere, 'the private duty of any member of society must be very imperfectly performed when not connected with the general good'.[37]

Important as this conception is in foreshadowing later feminist discussions of the public/private dichotomy, the rights claimed for women here are nonetheless contingent and limited in two crucial ways. Firstly, they depend on a wider theory of the progress of reason and virtue and the repression of passion. That is, Wollstonecraft assumes that public virtue, and a claim for the extension of citizenship and greater social equality, are crucial elements in a necessary reform of public life and politics in order to halt the slide towards oligarchy and despotism, themes in this period which are now widely associated with a broadly 'republican' world view. But it is also quintessentially Christian, since here, for Wollstonecraft, as in the first *Vindication*, the character of God provides 'the only solid foundation for morality'.[38]

Indeed, we can now appreciate that the importance of her religious mission to Wollstonecraft in the second *Vindication* has been much underestimated. For Wollstonecraft even demands of her female readers that they recite a sort of (admittedly latitudinarian, or theologically broad-minded) catechism of belief in one God, powerful and wise, who has ordered all harmoniously.[39] Moreover, women's claims to equal rights are also contingent on the social role of education and the rearing of children, which Wollstonecraft concedes is 'the peculiar destiny of woman', and which gives them special claims *vis à vis* the advancement of citizenship. This view leads Wollstonecraft to give stress to the improved performance of women's traditional roles which would result if they were freed from male tyranny. 'The conclusion I wish to draw, is obvious', writes Wollstonecraft: 'make women rational creatures, and free citizens, and they will quickly become good wives, and mothers'. Now, therefore, women languished as merely inferior mothers and housekeepers. 'Women cannot be confined to merely domestic pursuits', Wollstonecraft elsewhere notes, because 'they will not fulfill family duties, unless their minds take a wider range'.[40]

Wollstonecraft here thus claims that women themselves have a right to be educated based on the wider social good which would result from their improved role as family members, rather than a right based in their inherent status as rational creatures. Though she argues that the aim of all education is 'to enable the individual to attain such habits of virtue as will render it independent', the basis for proclaiming this right is one of utility and function, namely women's contribution to education and to public virtue, rather than a claim based on the innate capabilities of women.[41] And this right in turn presumes that they can renounce the prevailing notion of the ideal character of womanhood, forced upon them by the lack of recognition of their rights, in order to practise greater modesty, chastity, virtue and rationality. In this sense, despite the later assertion that the *Vindication* gave 'utterance to startling and extreme opinions respecting marriage',[42] marriage remains 'the foundation of almost every social virtue'. Earning one's own subsistence might still be 'the true definition of independence'. But it is not an ideal to which most women would be able to aspire.[43] Instead, women's domestic roles are reinforced, though these functions themselves, for Wollstonecraft, will clearly be considerably more pleasurable, fulfilling, and meaningful to exercise.

The theme of female virtue and character thereafter becomes central to the second *Vindication*, which considers women in the middle and upper social ranks in particular (though sometimes Wollstonecraft's generalisations appear to apply to all women). The general question of woman's character had been touched on, though tangentially, in the first *Vindication*. Here Wollstonecraft had challenged Burke's view of women, which seemingly insisted 'that littleness and weakness are the very essence of beauty; and that the Supreme Being, in giving women beauty in the most supereminent degree, seemed to command them, by the powerful voice of Nature, not to cultivate the moral virtues that might chance to excite respect'. Here, too, Wollstonecraft had condemned the resulting 'laxity of morals in the female world', which occurred when women were forced to coquet themselves in order to counterbalance male hostility to their just claims, and insisted that true virtue could flourish 'only among equals'.[44]

But among the shifts in approach we witness in the *Vindication of the Rights of Woman*, a religious argument now emerges as central to a new rights claim offered by Wollstonecraft. Whatever biological differences there are between men and women, both are 'human creatures' whose capacities are regulated by 'the governing passion implanted in us by the Author of all good, to call forth and strengthen the faculties of each individual'. For 'the grand end of existence' is 'the attainment of virtue', and 'the nature of reason must be the same in all, if it be an emanation of divinity'. If women lack souls, or are otherwise designated as inferior to men on theological grounds, this argument will be difficult to make, for Wollstonecraft's second rights claim is based not on function, but on nature. Wollstonecraft's God, the grand creator of nature, the instiller of the 'sublime and the amiable' (in Godwin's description), was 'not less amiable, generous, and kind, than great, wise and exalted',[45] far too wise, indeed, to have ever intended excluding half the human race from his bountiful legacy.

By contrast to this divinely guided natural ideal, however, women's character now derives from circumstances, not innate propensity. Women are now educated to be sweet, docile, delicate, dependent, and full of sensibility, their whole beings straining to be fulfilled in marriage. But for Wollstonecraft, 'elegance is inferior to virtue ... the first object of laudable ambition is to obtain a character as a human being'.[46] Clearly the idea of virtue, and the antitheses of 'manners' and 'morality', centrally juxtaposed in the first *Vindication*, are also crucial here.[47]

Much of the second *Vindication* in fact covers similar ground as the first. We find here the same general critique of Britain's 'preposterous distinctions of rank, which render civilization a curse, by dividing the world between voluptuous tyrants and cunning envious dependents'. Derided, again, is an overly respectful attitude towards property: riches and honours prevent men from cultivating their understanding. Virtue, defined in terms of independence, 'the grand blessing of life, the basis of every virtue', is now extended to encompass women's virtue in turn, in an comprehensive widening of oppositional, and particularly republican, ideology.[48] Condemned, too, is the system of British political patronage, prone to multiplying 'dependents and contriving taxes which grind the poor to pamper the rich'.[49] Some other standard radical themes of the era also crop up, such as an opposition to a standing army and the vices of an established clergy. An overly affected sensibility which excites the emotions and subverts reason, virtue and 'austerity of behaviour' is again the target, and one solution again preferred is that liberty generally diffused produces virtue and wisdom, and that the cause of progress requires greater social equality. Indeed any improvement in women's position is contingent upon increasing equality, which implies that women must become more independent of men just as the poor must of their masters.[50] As in the first *Vindication*, Wollstonecraft here also contrasts the character of the rich to that of the middling ranks, who are paid homage as possessing the 'most virtue and abilities', often because they place education ahead of marriage for money. Nonetheless Wollstonecraft also concedes, rather unusually, given her readership, that most female virtue is to be found in 'low life', where greater heroism emerges in the face of true adversity. For the maxim she elsewhere invokes, that 'pleasure is the business of woman's life, according to the present modification of society', hardly applies.[51]

Wollstonecraft's main assault here is clearly on the distinction between 'a supposed sexual character' and a 'human character', her chief emphasis being that women are educated to be weak and submissive, and have foisted upon them these manners, the insincere semblance of authentic being, a mere role, which is to be contrasted to true morality.[52] Crucial here is the parallel Wollstonecraft establishes between the character of women and that of the wealthy, who, like women, says Wollstonecraft, quoting Adam Smith, do little labour, engage in little abstract thought, and are overly sentimental: 'women in general, as well as the rich of both sexes, have acquired all the follies and vices of civilization, and missed all the useful fruits'. Clearly this parallel, the most important analogy in the second *Vindication*, is not meant to apply to all women, but to Wollstonecraft's chief audience, the middle and upper classes, where 'morality is very insidiously undermined, in the female world, by the attention being turned to the shew instead of the substance'. Nonetheless it is here, and in the character of the courtier, whose 'artificial mode of behaviour' is equally condemned by Wollstonecraft, that we see most clearly the extension of a wider eighteenth-century radical critique of corruption in the *Vindication* to the treatment of women in British society.[53] In this regard, the analogy Wollstonecraft draws between the character of a standing army and that of women is also important, however: in both, manners are learned before morals, and largely from the same source: the puffed-up ideal of gallantry. Instead, Wollstonecraft argues, both men and women should base their behaviour upon 'the character of the Supreme Being', the wise, the good and potentially perfect.[54] Both sexes should eschew the effects of luxury, which leads men to indulge their appetites more than women, and which engenders, through the debauched inclinations of men, the chief cause of both female depravity and the subversion of public morals. Both should recognise that one set of virtues, 'chastity, modesty, public spirit, and all the noble train of virtues, on which social virtue and happiness are built, should be understood and cultivated by all mankind'.[55]

Thus, Wollstonecraft insists, in a profound critique of radical as well as more traditional forms of political thought, there is no point in searching, with philosophers, for public virtue in the (male) citizen's willingness to place public duty before private interest, and to sacrifice the particular to the general will. No isolated public sphere, excluding the relations of fathers, husbands, wives and mothers, exists, for the distinction between a female domestic sphere and a male political sphere has been burst asunder: 'public spirit must be nurtured by private virtue, or it will resemble the factitious sentiment which makes women careful to preserve their reputation, and men their honour'. This, then, must be the task of the legislator, who should endeavour 'to make it the interest of each individual to be virtuous; and thus private virtue becoming the cement of public happiness, an orderly whole is consolidated by the tendency of all parts towards a common centre'. But this in turn requires, if women's private virtue is to become a 'public benefit', that they 'have a civil existence in the state, married or single'. There is thus a reciprocal relationship between public and private virtue. The second *Vindication* concludes, with explosive implications for traditional concepts of political virtue and the public sphere, that:

> To render women truly useful members of society, I argue that they should be led, by having their understandings cultivated on a large scale, to acquire a rational affection for their country, founded on knowledge, because it is obvious that we are little interested about what we do not understand. And to render this general knowledge of due importance, I have endeavoured to shew that private duties are never properly fulfilled unless the understanding enlarges the heart; and that public virtue is only an aggregate of private.[56]

Much of the plea of the second *Vindication* is thus cast in the shape of a paean to the advantages of a 'revolution in female manners'. Better educated women would make better friends and wives, as well as lending dignity to single life. Men would be released from slavery to their appetites, and marriages would flow from affection alone. Children would be better educated, and less blindly obedient once an overly selfish respect for property had been removed. The effects of circumstances on character are thus the same for women as for men; in both, fashion, delicacy and sensibility corrupt, debase and foster dependence. But given equal opportunity, women can avoid false notions of beauty and delicacy, and instead, giving less stress to politeness, cultivate sincerity and humanity.

Yet feminists have often been exasperated by the limits of this vision. To Wollstonecraft, marriage would become 'the foundation of almost every social virtue', with passion subsiding into friendship and greater modesty prevailing with both sexes.[57] But we must recall that Wollstonecraft regarded as her 'main argument' the value of domestic but truly virtuous and more independent women to the general cause of social virtue. As Ursula Vogel has stressed, Wollstonecraft's idea of domestic virtue thus forms an integral part of her moral critique of a civilised society corrupted by wealth and privilege'.[58] Family and public life are seamlessly integrated rather than parallel or mutually exclusive spheres. This is a substantial departure from the republican and dissenting tradition out of which Wollstonecraft largely emerges, which while it clearly also supported the cause of private morality, did so on a broadly patriarchalist foundation. Yet, while women are to become citizens, to emerge into the harsh light of the public from the shadows of the private sphere, they remain for Wollstonecraft within a more or less traditional conception of the sexual division of labour, and are still assigned a specialised, distinctive sphere of competence, which some have associated with a romantic notion of a distinctive female nature, based primarily upon Wollstonecraft's idea of God's design in creating the human species.[59]

Clearly there is thus some conflict between the two types of rights claims Wollstonecraft puts forward. Where the rights of women are subordinated to the cause of the progress of virtue, and it is the reformation of women's manners which is of crucial importance, women's demands are set within a traditional context of the nuclear family, where their role as agents of education is paramount; and in a largely republican image of society, where the aim of creating virtuous citizens is fundamental. Women are here far from equal with men; for they are still separated by function, if at least eventually considerably more equal than they had been in the past. In Wollstonecraft's second rights claim, however, based on theological premises, the intent of the Deity in creating humanity implies that women become as independent as possible, 'the grand end of their exertions' being to unfold their own faculties and acquire the dignity of conscious virtue'.[60] Here no such subordination to male-dominated systems of power (or theories of politics) is evident.

Like Paine, thus, – a man of 'strong sense' in Wollstonecraft's view[61] – who derived subsequent rights claims from the notion that God had created human beings in his image,[62] Wollstonecraft also rests her most radical argument on divine intention, indeed upon the same supposition about the Creation. As mere citizens, women remained tied to a specialised function dictated by the nature of citizenship, for their special contribution to the public good was the education of virtuous youth. Only as divine creatures, destined to reason exactly like men, are they truly equal and free, and no longer shackled by function. Wollstonecraft's conception of rights remains much the same in both 'Vindications', being based on the notion that all have a right to independence granted by God. In this sense the second *Vindication* does not extend the theory of rights of the first *Vindication*, as is often assumed, though Wollstonecraft's emphasis on the right of women to independence is clearly stronger, and comprises also a right to education based on the social and political consequences, especially increased patriotism, which would ensue. Instead, it is the critique of manners which is extended, and the analogy between public and private morality, which in this form goes well beyond republican writers, most of whom (even including the feminist historian Catherine Macaulay, a role model for Wollstonecraft) had not stressed women's rights in this way.

But Paine, and the overwhelming majority of radical and republican writers in this period, had not extended such arguments to women as such, but, while condemning unchastity as a vicious aspect of aristocratic culture, often lent their weight to ideas of dual, unequal natures. Thus Thomas Christie, in his *Letters on the Revolution of France* (1791), commended the new French government for 'not raising [women] out of their natural sphere; in not involving them in the cares and anxieties of State affairs, to which neither their frame nor their minds are adapted' by allowing women to succeed to the throne.[63] And Capel Lofft, too, while dismissing a 'frivolous and insulting Gallantry', even upheld an idealised notion of chivalry, indeed insisting that a republican form of government would be most likely to restore 'not its Pomp indeed, but its true Value: its Simplicity, its Purity, and Elevation'.[64]

The Development of Wollstonecraft's Thought

Following the second *Vindication* Wollstonecraft's main work of non-fiction was her *Historical and Moral View of the Origin and Progress of the French Revolution* (1794). The work as a whole is essentially a narrative history of the progress of events during the preceding five years. It also contains, however, reflections on the causes of these events, and upon the deflection of the Revolution from its original course. While acknowledging that the anarchy and bloodshed which had occurred could not 'fail to chill the sympathizing bosom, and palsy intellectual vigour', Wollstonecraft nonetheless insisted that the Revolution was the

> natural consequence of intellectual improvement, gradually proceeding to perfection in the advancement of communities, from a state of barbarism to that of polished society, till now arrived at the point when sincerity of principles seems to be hastening the overthrow of the tremendous empire of superstition and hypocrisy, erected upon the ruins of gothic brutality and ignorance.[65]

Having said this, however, she conceded that the French had not in fact been 'properly qualified' to make revolution at the time events forced one upon them. A spirit of inquiry, fuelled by philosophic investigation and wedded to an insatiable attachment to 'novelty and ingenious speculations', was undermined by the luxury of the *ancien régime*. This degeneracy of morals, coupled with a desire for vengeance on the part of the poor, facilitated the excesses of the Revolution. These had been exacerbated, moreover, by the progress of modern commerce, and the propensity of manufactures to concentrate artificers in workshops, where the mind tended to become 'entirely inactive'. The strength of character present in the rural artisan, indeed, was eroded so far by the division of labour that the town-dweller was debased to the level of 'machines'.[66] Clearly drawing upon Adam Smith's account of the division of labour in the *Wealth of Nations*, and probably Adam Ferguson's considerably more critical assessment of the effects of specialisation, Wollstonecraft thus offered a sophisticated interpretation of the dual causes of moral debasement not only of the *ancien régime* but also the progress of commercial society in France, thus explaining both the sources and development of the revolution in France. Nor did she retreat from the conclusion that 'a barbarian, considered as a moral being, is an angel, compared with the refined villain of artificial life', even if at bottom it was 'unjust plans of government' which finally accounted for the progress of modern degeneracy.[67]

Wollstonecraft's Reputation

Most assessments of the origins of feminism commence with Mary Wollstonecraft, though the term itself had not yet been coined, nor did a 'movement' as such exist until the late nineteenth century. There is nonetheless some evidence of support for Wollstonecraft's ideas in the early 1790s; at least one radical toast, for instance, is recorded as having been to 'THE RIGHTS OF WOMEN'.[68] Reaction against the cause of reform, however, dampened any nascent feminist inclinations. The few reformers we know of this period who apparently adopted feminist ideas, such as the physician William Hodgson, active in the London Corresponding Society, who planned to publish a work entitled Proposals for Publishing by Subscription, A Treatise Called the Female Citizen, or, A Historical, Political, and Philosophical Enquiry into the Rights of Women (c. 1796), did not advance far in such endeavours. And the reaction against the cause of the rights of 'women', in the wake of that against the rights of 'men', was even more pronounced, vicious and long lasting. Horace Walpole famously derisively dismissed Wollstonecraft as a 'hyaena in petticoats' because of the persistence of her attack on Marie Antoinette, even after her execution, and it would be several generations before a more balanced assessment of her merits became possible.

Much of the early nineteenth-century assessment of Wollstonecraft hinged on the frank assessment of her practice of 'free love', first with Gilbert Imlay, then William Godwin, which offered a marked contrast to the conservative approach to sexuality of the second *Vindication*, and which was detailed, without, as Godwin himself confessed, 'any motives of prudence or delicacy', in his memoir of his wife, which the philosopher Samuel Parr told him 'shocked ... all wise and good men'.[69] Thus, although a number of important theoretical works advocating feminist arguments appear in the first half of the nineteenth century, most notably William Thompson's *Appeal of One-Half the Human Race, Women* (1824)[70] and John Stuart Mill's *The Subjection of Women* (1869), Wollstonecraft was not infrequently condemned – even by such an 'advanced' liberal as Harriet Martineau, as but 'a poor victim of passion' who was neither a 'safe example, nor as a successful champion of Woman and her Rights'.[71] It was not until the late 1860s that a substantial movement seeking female enfranchisement and other reforms commenced, and an historiography tracing its genesis and pedigree emerged. Early studies of Wollstonecraft include Elizabeth Robins Pennell's *Mary Wollstonecraft Godwin* (1885), which lamented the fact that few people 'have been the objects of such censure' on account of their 'immorality' and 'unwomanliness';[72] and Emma Rauschenbusch-Clough's *A Study of Mary Wollstonecraft and the Rights of Woman* (1898), which drew on the sympathetic account of Godwin and Wollstonecraft in C. Kegan Paul's *William Godwin: His Friends and Contemporaries* (2 vols, 1876). From the late 1870s it was commonly asserted that Wollstonecraft had sown the seeds from which the nascent feminist movement was rapidly growing.[73] By the turn of the century most accounts of feminism included an introductory chapter on Wollstonecraft summarising the arguments of the second *Vindication*, which was reprinted in 1891.[74] Some indeed thought the work 'might well be used, possibly is widely used, as a text-book by the woman suffrage movement, so well does the argument used more than a century ago fit the present situation'.[75] Yet it is also the case that much of the late nineteenth-century feminist movement was extremely cautious respecting – if not downright hostile to – anything smacking of 'libertine' 'free love'.

Chapter Five:
The Spectre of 'Levelling':
Loyalists and Paineites, c. 1791–5

Introduction

The coming of revolution in France provoked what has been termed 'perhaps the most crucial ideological debate ever carried on in English'.[1] Raging most fiercely between 1791 and 1793, this pamphlet war has often been described as a 'Burke-Paine' controversy. Both at the time, and subsequently, it has too often been caricatured as the uneven contest of an ill-educated, angry, conceited and ignorant Paine against an *eminence grise*, the greatest statesman of his generation, Burke.[2] But this is somewhat misleading.[3] Burke responded in the first instance to the Richard Price's sermon lauding the revolution in the context of a complex pre-existing set of issues, while much of *Rights of Man* was not a direct reply to Burke at all, but an independently grounded exposition of Paine's own political principles. Moreover, many issues marginal to Burke and/or Paine, such as the plea for women's rights we have just examined, were nonetheless taken up by other participants in the controversy. Furthermore, if we can generalise respecting the perhaps six hundred contributions to the debate,[4] much of both the loyalist assault and the Paineite defence of revolutionary principles came to centre upon the question of the degree to which these principles promoted 'levelling', or social equality, and what the consequences thereof would entail. Prominently and lengthily detailed, the accusation of 'levelling' was in some respects merely a tactical ploy to frighten off Paine's middle class supporters. Nonetheless it was also a consequentialist account of the implications of popularising radical and republican ideas among the lower orders, and pushed to the fore a language which by 1793 came virtually to dominate the entire revolutionary controversy. Interpreters of later eighteenth-century radicalism have suggested that we should see either a Lockean 'liberal' view centring on the protection of rights and expansion of commerce, or a 'neo-Harringtonian' republican inheritance more concerned with civic virtue as the principal component of pre-revolutionary Whiggism.[5] Various shifts in Whiggism in this period can certainly be understood in light of a conflict between these ideals, and particularly in terms of a supposed opposition of republicanism to commercial modernity. But given the fact that most of the literature about the revolution controversy consisted of 'anti-Jacobin' loyalist tracts, the central issue in the political writing of the 1790s was neither the nature of the Lockean contract nor the limits of republican virtue, but the relationship between economic inequality and social progress, defined in terms of both commerce and manners. Rights theories were central to the revolution debate, but were refracted through the prism of a new set of historical and economic assumptions which for loyalists dictated the rejection of Locke's appeal to the state of nature as too close philosophically to radical republican or 'Jacobin' ideals.

As J.G.A. Pocock has proposed, this suggests that a third language anchored in the new, essentially Scottish science of political economy was already central to political debate by 1790 which attempted to avoid appeals to both Lockean rights concepts and republican civic virtue while remaining essentially Whiggish and progressive.[6] The crucial argument levelled against the Paineites, we will see, was not merely that natural rights were non-existent, but that appeals to such rights masked an economic and social agenda which threatened the progress of that very commerce, and its accompanying polished manners, which had made Britain the wealthiest if not quite the politest nation in Europe by the end of the century. Although Paine himself was as we have seen a 'modern' republican sympathetic to commerce, both he and his followers were accused of seeking to reinstate primitive equality and even community of goods through their emphasis on natural rights. They never succeeded, as we will see, in persuading their opponents to the contrary. The intellectual centre of gravity of this dispute, then, was the accusation that republicanism was incompatible with the inequality which underlay the achievements of commercial society, and that the language of natural rights and appeal to norms established in the state of nature was at least tacitly primitivist, because of the implications of its egalitarianism. This argument helped loyalism to bridge Whiggism and Toryism, and thus to achieve much of its popular success. It also exposed what would become the single greatest theme of subsequent modern political thought: the relationship between liberty and equality, and the explosive incompatibility of these principles in certain combinations.

This defence of British opulence and the mixed constitution in these terms was not, however, widely associated with Burke's *Reflections*, but was instead closer to the moderate Whiggism of some of Burke's middle class opponents like James Mackintosh. These accused Burke of appealing to a pre-commercial 'Gothic' system of aristocratic *mores* instead of defending modern Britain. Such moderation, then, rather than Toryism, was triumphant in the reaction to the revolution. Seen in these terms, too, the revolution debate in Britain had far more to do with the application of the American republican model to Britain and France than it did with the imposition of French republican principles on Britain, for the principal issue was the compatibility of republicanism with societies far more advanced than the United States. Moreover, this reading also challenges the common assumption that natural rights language had been substantially eroded by the sceptical and utilitarian attacks mounted by David Hume, Jeremy Bentham, William Paley and others before 1790. This was, rather, principally a result of the debates of the 1790s. Radical Whigs like Richard Price and Granville Sharp continued to use natural rights arguments up to the first years of the revolutionary debate.[7] But when Paine and his followers appropriated this inheritance, and appealed to the lower orders to act on its implications, moderate Whigs came to see the language of commerce, manners and civilization as a surer means of vindicating the British constitution. Thereafter Whiggism came quickly to be defined by its adherence to Benthamite utilitarianism and classical political economy, while the language of natural rights, dismissed by Bentham as a mere 'anarchical fallacy', 'nonsense upon stilts',[8] was appropriated by nineteenth-century working class radicals in particular.

We will examine the unfolding of these issues by considering firstly, the chief responses to Burke's *Reflections*; then the emergence of both popular radicalism and loyalism; the main responses to Paine's *Rights of Man*, and more briefly, alterations in the debate in the later 1790s.

Responses to Burke

Opposition to Burke's provocative assault on the Revolution, which one account said 'astonished wise and shocked consistent men',[9] was not long in forthcoming. Within weeks, responses against Burke's 'libel on human nature' began to appear.[10] By the spring of 1791, about fifty replies had been published, and the tide began to run in the opposite direction.[11]

The first printed response to the *Reflections,* as we have seen, was Mary Wollstonecraft's *Vindication of the Rights of Man* (1790).[12] Following Wollstonecraft several other brief responses to Burke merit mention. The historian Catherine Macaulay's *Observations on the Reflections of the Right Hon. Edmund Burke* (1790)[13] focussed on Richard Price's and the radical Whigs' interpretation of the 'Glorious' Revolution of 1688, which they believed France had emulated, Louis XVI having been 'cashiered' for misconduct by an assembly acting wholly within its rights, which included the formation of a new constitution, and a more popular form of government and ecclesiastical arrangements. George Rous's *Thoughts on Government: Occasioned by Mr. Burke's Reflections* (1791)[14] charged the *Reflections* with retailing 'neither more nor less than the exploded doctrine of the old school revived in a new dress', that is, the Toryism of 1688 which supported any form of despotism, rather than any Whiggish liberty. Rous took the view that despotic principles had so far penetrated the political and ecclesiastical system of France that their overthrow was inevitable, and that kingly power must rest upon popular approbation, as established in 1688 and reiterated in Price's 1789 sermon. 'The whole fallacy of Mr. Burke's reasoning consists in confounding the right of the people with its abuse', Rous insisted, public happiness being the test of monarchical as well as any other form of government. Similarly Brooke Boothby's *A Letter to the Right Hon. Edmund Burke* (1791) defended Price's leading principles, justified the causes of inevitable revolution in France against 'an unqualified monarchy, a feudal nobility, a domineering hierarchy,' and praised 'the most magnificent spectacle that has ever presented itself to the human eye. A great and generous nation animated with one soul, rising up as one man to demand the restitution of their natural rights.' Burke seemed 'to have been so awe-struck with the magnificence of the court and so enamoured of the rising beauties of the Dauphiness' that he 'had no attention left to bestow on the people.' Nor was Burke consistent in his opposition to monarchical encroachments on popular power in the 1770s and 1780s, in his prosecution of the arbitrary rule in India of Warren Hastings (a theme addressed in John Scott's *A Letter to the Right Hon. Edmund Burke,* 1791),[15] by contrast to the views outlined in the *Reflections.* A defence of ideas of popular right and the choice of governors against 'indefeasible hereditary right' or 'divine right' was also at the centre of Benjamin Bousfield's *Observations on the Right Honourable Edmund Burke's Pamphlet* (1791), Charles Pigott's *Strictures on the New Political Tenets of the Right Hon. Edmund Burke* (1791) and other responses. Few critiques of the *Reflections* fail to comment on Burke's paean to Marie Antoinette, his apparent inconsistency in supporting the despotic rule of the *ancien régime*, his failure to appreciate the power of ecclesiastical 'superstition' in upholding the *ancien régime*, and his apparent opposition to the principles of 1688.

Besides *Rights of Man*, three other leading responses to Burke merit special attention: Thomas Christie's *Letters on the Revolution in France* (1791), James Mackintosh's *Vindiciae Gallicae* (1791) and Joseph Priestley's *Letters to the Right Hon. Edmund Burke, Occasioned by His Reflections on the Revolution in France* (1791).

Thomas Christie, who had witnessed the Revolution at first hand,[16] focussed on six themes in his *Letters*: the general principles of the *Reflections*, especially in contrast to those of 1688; the necessity of a revolution in France; the evils attending that revolution; the judicial and territorial changes made since; and the monarchical system. Taking as his starting point Price's defence of natural rights, including a people's right to choose their own governors and frame their own government, Christie denied that the British constitution was unalterable, or based solely on prescriptive right. The *ancien régime*, rotted throughout by corruption, was 'an arbitrary and wretched system of Government', and merited a 'radical reform' as Britain had done a century earlier. Christie was similarly surprised that a 'liberal scholar' like Burke who knew 'the patriots of Greece and Rome' should immerse himself in 'gothic feudality' and spurned Burke's 'miserable deformed gothic idol'. Once this principle was acknowledged, the violent episodes of the revolution, the occasional fury of the mob, paled into insignificance, and the right of the people to devise a constitution and assembly to their liking could be conceded.[17]

Better known than Christie's *Letters* was James Mackintosh's *Vindiciae Gallicae* (1791).[18] Complimented by Fox in the Commons,[19] it became the one response for which Burke, while first dismissing it as 'Paine at bottom',[20] eventually acknowledged a grudging admiration, after Mackintosh had recanted his revolutionary enthusiasm in 1796, and writing that 'it is on all hands allowed that you were the most able advocate for the cause which you supported'.[21] The structure of the *Vindiciae* is fairly similar to Christie's *Letters*, being divided into a justification for the necessity of the revolution; an analysis of the composition and character of the National Assembly; a defence of popular 'excesses' as fuelled by the cruelties of the *ancien régime*; an account of the new French constitution; and a vindication of the British supporters of the cause and their fundamental allegiance to the principles of 1688, admiring but not wishing to imitate the French revolution.

Like most of Burke's antagonists, the *Vindiciae* asserted centrally that the *ancien régime* had been an 'incorrigible' outmoded feudal despotism incapable of gradual and moderate reform by that enlightened commercial 'monied interest' or 'middle rank among who almost all the sense and virtue of society reside',[22] which was the harbinger of modern civilisation and basis of modern Whiggism. As such it was antithetical both to the British constitution and its Whiggish underpinning, and to the doctrine of natural rights (to which Mackintosh, while hostile to a titled aristocracy, pays less heed than, for instance, Paine or Wollstonecraft, by contrast to rights based on utilitarian expediency).[23] On the issue of the confiscation of Church lands and elimination of the 'sacerdotal aristocracy', of great interest and importance to the *Reflections*, Mackintosh was insistent that 'The lands of the Church possess not the most simple and indispensable requisites of property. They are not even pretended to be held for the benefit of those who enjoy them'. As such they were not inalienable, but could be disposed of for the public good without subverting the laws of property as such or eradicating the spirit of true Christianity. Against Burke's Gothic support for the ancient aristocracy and its ethos, then, Mackintosh gave stress to the progressive aims of an enlightened commercial society:

> commerce has overthrown that 'feudal and chivalrous system' under whose shade it first grew. In religion, learning has subverted the superstition whose opulent endowments had first fostered it. Peculiar circumstances softened the barbarism of the middle ages to a degree which favored the admission of commerce and the growth of knowledge.[24]

Mackintosh thus describes the natural development of society as entailing the overthrow of a feudal and chivalric system of manners by commerce, while Burke seemed to identify both. This 'Gothic' reading of Burke's text has been challenged by some modern historians, notably J.G.A. Pocock, who argues that the *Reflections* also defended modern politeness and commerce, which Burke saw as rooted in 'ancient manners'. But Pocock also argues that Burke in many ways now feared the growing influence of the middle classes, and in some respects tried to displace the Scottish vindication of their social, economic and cultural position by arguing that both 'modern manners' and commerce owed much to feudal *mores*, and might indeed decay if the latter, their 'natural protecting principles', disappeared. Burke did not explain why commerce still depended upon chivalry.[25] But this interpretation seems to imply that the *Reflections* was less 'modern' than others of Burke's works. Certainly it concedes the point that Burke was less 'liberal' than many loyalists in his emphasis upon the virtues of monarchy and aristocracy rather than the balance of the constitution, and upon Gothic *mores* rather than commercial manners, though he was not more conservative than Tory loyalists like Reeves, Hannah More or many High Churchmen.[26]

As might be expected from a leading Dissenter, Joseph Priestley's *Letters to the Right Hon. Edmund Burke* pays greater heed to the religious issues raised by the Revolution than most responses to the *Reflections*, and indeed described the reception of the latter in terms of religious divisions.[27] Much of Priestley's work does cover similar ground to that of other respondents, examining the general causes of the revolution; the emergence of the new constitution and popular character of the new form of government, whose preponderance of lawyers paralleled that in America, and held out no dangers for Priestley; and doctrines of natural rights, whose utilitarian justifications are strenuously supported against the ideals of 'passive obedience and non-resistance', peculiar to the Tories and the friends of arbitrary power. Proportionately more effort, however, is devoted to condemning the corruptions of an established clergy maintained by public property. This 'naturally tends to debase the minds of those who officiate in it', and demonstrated the dangers of governmental interference by contrast to individual effort. Instead an elective clergy, parallel in its virtues to elected representatives compared to hereditary legislators, is praised as supporting a 'general enlargement of liberty', when civil wars, colonies, grievous inequalities and intolerance would be abolished.[28]

The leading responses to the *Reflections* thus reveal both a consistency of argument, a concentration on half a dozen main themes in the text and the general consensus that Burke had 'unwhigg'd' himself in departing so far from the established interpretation of the principles of 1688 with respect to natural rights and the popular nature of the British constitution. Burke was commonly criticised for apparently leaving 'not a shadow of distinction between possession and right' where the legitimacy of any government was at issue.[29] Burke's critics declaimed against his 'raptures with the French *noblesse* as "imperfect", "deceived" and "unpardonably credulous"'.[30] They generally assumed that once the old French despotism had been destroyed, 'the higher order, and the most enlightened class, will feel, and really possess, all the natural advantages of their fair superiority; while the lower orders of the people will fall into the rank of useful industry'.[31] Burke was not universally understood as defending the British constitution as such, but was often accused of bolstering both monarchical absolutism and an odious Catholic hierarchy. The effect of such criticisms between 1790–2, and especially Paine's, was considerable. As a young Whig lawyer, Samuel Romilly, commented in May 1791, 'it is astonishing how Burke's book is fallen; though the tenth edition is now publishing, its warmest admirers at its first appearance begin to be ashamed of their admiration. Paine's book, on the other hand, has made converts of a great many persons; which, I confess, appears to me as wonderful as the success of Burke's'.[32] From 1792, however, a new phenomenon emerged: a popular radical movement, whose character would render the debate vastly more complex.

West of Hounslow: The Growth of Popular Radicalism

Far more than the 'Glorious Revolution' of 1688, those of 1776 and 1789 implied not only an appeal to the legitimacy of popular sovereignty as expressed through a 'natural' governing class, but an invitation for actual popular involvement in the political process, and for the assumption for the first time by hundreds of thousands of a civic identity based on this participation. If, to return to the quote from Lord Acton with which we began this investigation, the French Revolution was widely perceived as a 'middle class' or 'bourgeois' revolt, this was the moment, in Britain, when it began to assume a more popular character. Among the new constituency of reformers, the overwhelming majority were tradesmen.[33] Most were probably not republicans, in the sense of wishing the abolition of the monarchy,[34] but certainly were democrats. They were often inspired by Paine, though Burke's role in encouraging this popular movement, notably through his arrogant dismissal of the populace as a 'swinish multitude', is undisputed.[35] Virtually all were deeply struck by Paine's doctrine of rights, which was widely perceived as having an empowering, liberating effect when viewed as the antidote to prevailing emphases on the social duties of the lower orders to their superiors. For this, for the average observer, was probably what the Revolution in France embodied, more than anything else.

In this sense, the turning point in the early years of the debate was the formation in January 1792 of the London Corresponding Society, the first large-scale plebeian democratic organisation in Britain.[36] Earlier reformist associations, such as the Society for Constitutional Information and the Revolution Society,[37] (derided by Burke as the 'society for Revolutions') or the soon to be formed (26 April 1792) 'association of gentlemen', the Society of the Friends of the People, (see below, Ch. 6) had generally disdained popular political activity. By contrast the LCS and organisations like the Sheffield Constitutional Society, formed in December 1791, openly solicited mass political participation, notably through meetings with tens of thousands of participants. Fond of deploying powerful symbols like the 'liberty tree',[38] they offered an entirely new style of reform politics, modelled in part on popular debating societies,[39] and partly on the ideals of direct democracy popularised by Rousseau. LCS members addressed one another as 'citizen', and were hostile to manipulation by Whigs, aristocratic reformers, and even the former popular hero, Fox, now sometimes denounced as a 'sham patriot'.[40] Some indeed rejected leadership of every type. Most would have accepted the loyalist judgement that they aimed at 'such a government as should acknowledge no other source of authority and no other rule of conduct, than the will of the majority'.[41] In conjunction with developments in France in 1792, particularly those of 10 August and following, which impelled the revolution onto a new democratic course, then, the events of this year, 'one of the turning-points in English history',[42] thus ensured as fundamental a transformation in political thought and action as those of 1789.[43] This process culminated in the organisation of 'conventions', firstly by the Scottish Society of the Friends of the People at Edinburgh in December 1792 and May 1793, then as the 'British Convention', held from 19 November–6 December 1793.[44]

What else, besides greater democracy, did this new group of reformers want? Their chief goals were to extend the franchise, shorten parliaments and eliminate ministerial corruption in order to lighten taxes and purify the process of representation. They also wished to reduce the national debt, the frequency of wars and the expense of the monarchy, and to address the game laws, impressment, primo-geniture, tithes and a host of other issues.[45] Rather than supplanting the Hanoverian monarchy with a republic, most radicals sought instead to restore the constitution to its 'original purity'.[46] This might lie in the Saxon mode of government,[47] or in shoring up the princi-ples of Magna Charta and the Bill of Rights of 1689.[48] At some earlier period, most agreed, much greater political liberty had existed; the epoch following the Bill of Rights was the favourite choice. But it was also usually lamented that 'From that time, we have been gradually losing what it was the declared object of that declaration to establish'. 'Corruption' was the agreed cause of this decline.[49] There were also clearly economic issues underlying this constitutionalist emphasis. Rejecting the loyalist interpretation of Providence, that Britons lived in the best of all worlds, radicals often asserted that the existing social system secured 'to the rich and powerful their luxuries, extorted from the toil and miseries of the poor', and warned that its continuance might introduce 'the most abject slavery'.[50]

Travelling west of Hounslow, so to speak, where the radical John Horne Tooke described himself as prudently alighting from an imag-inary coachload of still more extreme reformers,[51] we see what a vast distance separates even the Society of the Friends of the People from firstly, the Society for Constitutional Information, which the SFP declined to co-operate with because its 'views and objects appeared to them irreconcilable with the real interests of the People, and the gen-uine principles of the Constitution',[52] and even more importantly the London Corresponding Society. The LCS plumped explicitly, as Thomas Hardy later recalled, for 'restoring' universal manhood suffrage as 'the only reform that can be effectual and permanent', while denying the charge that it opposed the existence of either the monarchy or parliament.[53] Its addresses of the period invoke 'only the Restoration of the lost Liberties of our Country', and reiterate that 'To obtain a compleat representation is our only aim'.[54] 'If we once regain an Annually elected Parliament, and that Parliament to be fairly chosen by all, the people will again share in the Government of their Country', was a common formulation.[55] Yet in its more dramatic proposals, for payment of MPs and equal electoral districts, linked to annual elections and universal male suffrage, no historical precedent was cited, and the LCS could be accused of designing a new constitu-tion.[56] It deflected this charge principally by reprinting William Pitt's reform proposals from April 1780, which included the proviso 'That all members serving in Parliament be entitled to reasonable wages, according to the wholesome practice of ancient times'.[57]

This appeal to precedent was thus widespread among the more plebeian reformers. Even the Edinburgh convention invoked the practice of Alfred and 'the established usages of our ancestors', which had been crushed by the Norman imposition of feudalism, and insisted that it sought only the 'restoration' of annual parliaments and universal suffrage.[58] The Edinburgh convention in particular, however, was accused of aiming to 'subvert our limited monarchy, and to substitute in its place ... a *republic* or *democracy*'.[59] This of course was also the thrust of the accusation against Thomas Paine, particularly through the charge that Paine had described even limited monarchy as 'an oppressive and an abominable tyranny'.[60] Much of this aspect of the debate thus hinges on whether the reformers sought political novelty and innovation or the restoration of past custom. Though some of the language of fraternity and citizenship was new to Britain, much was not. As John Horne Tooke made clear at his 1794 trial, Pitt himself had been a 'delegate' at a 'convention' a decade earlier; the difference was that in 1794 many delegates were working class. But the LCS did offer many hostages to fortune; when it sent delegates to the French National Convention in November 1792, one remarked, leaving too little to the imagination, that 'it would not be extraordinary if in a much less space of time than can be imagined the French should send addresses of congratulation to a National Convention of England'.[61]

By the spring of 1792, support for Paine's 'infamous libel upon the constitution', as Burke dubbed it, mounted steadily.[62] Yet this might have been channelled towards a more moderate and traditional rather than a more explicitly innovative and plebeian ideal. With the founding of the Society of the Friends of the People there emerged the prospect of just such a moderate reform movement which might unite the entire middle ground between Burke and Paine behind powerful and respectable leaders who supported a property qualification for the franchise rather than universal suffrage.[63] Much depended here upon what happened in Parliament. At the end of April the government pronounced that 'This is not a time to make hazardous experiments',[64] and defeated by a vote of 282 to 41 Charles Grey's reform proposals (which were supported by twenty-three petitions, some with 15,000 signatures). It then persuaded the King to issue a Proclamation against Treason and Sedition[65] on 21 May, aimed directly at Paine. This was read in public in many towns and villages and was hotly debated in the

Commons in particular.[66] Such publicity merely provoked greater interest in the doctrines the government aimed to suppress.[67] But it also invited a public, if government-sponsored, counter-offensive from loyalist opponents of the Revolution.

The Emergence of Loyalism

The enormous popularity of *Rights of Man* prompted many Whigs to lament Paine's style and appeal to the lower orders, while coupling this with a grudging degree of admiration.[68] More conservative loyalists reacted chiefly by forming numerous local associations (eventually some two thousand), which were soon busily suppressing the radical contagion.[69] Chief amongst these was John Reeves's Association for Preserving Liberty and Property against Republicans and Levellers, based in London.[70] A former Newfoundland magistrate and placeman *extraordinaire*,[71] Reeves was so zealous in the 'anti-Jacobin' cause that he was eventually (though unsuccessfully) prosecuted for the absolutist assertion that the King could rule without parliament.[72] In the early 1790s, however, his propaganda efforts were crucial in coordinating the loyalist offensive. The Prime Minister, Pitt, who feared a French republic would be far stronger than the old monarchy, was anxious to assist.[73] The counter-revolutionary blasts of disillusioned reformers like Calonne,[74] helped him to prepare the public for the prospect of war with France, and to secure the widespread condemnation of 'French principles'[75] of every cast. Government pamphleteers were enlisted by the droves.[76] Postmasters were ordered to report the circulation of seditious material. Reformers were hounded from their meeting places.[77] *Rights of Man* was proscribed, and Paine was torched in effigy throughout the country. Loose words with vaguely disloyal implications were prosecuted ruthlessly, and employers were encouraged to sack radical workmen. Dissenters in particular were targeted as having caused the American Revolution and leaning notably to the French; Priestley indeed was assailed as 'even more infamous than Paine'.[78] In July 1791, his house was destroyed by frenzied 'Church and King' rioters, though bystanders later recalled them as having 'better understood thirty-nine bottles of wine than Thirty-Nine Articles'.[79] (But the rioters were also motivated by a variety of factors, including a fear of a monopoly in the corn trade.) To counter the spirit of democracy there was whipped up what one reformer described as 'a spirit of Toryism more indiscriminate, more abject, and more rancorous than has existed in England since the accession of the House of Hanover'.[80]

Panic and hysteria soon proved more effective in mobilising and manipulating opinion than polite debate about political principles. This was the point at which, over the course of about a year, the French revolutionary 'debate' became an actual 'war of opinion', (the phrase was later popularised by the leading anti-Jacobin George Canning) in which no holds were to be barred on the government side to ensure victory. By the end of the year, the tone set for much of the subsequent debate – epitomised in Justice Ashurst's widely distributed *Charge to the Grand Jury of the County of Middlesex*,[81] issued on 19 November – was no longer polite, genteel and parliamentary. Instead, as force supplanted reason, it was more akin to the rough-and-tumble brawl of a sailor's tavern or the hustings at a British election. And yet this was not deemed inappropriate.[82] For the image of reform Reeves succeeded in impressing on public opinion was more like Hogarth's 'Gin Lane' than a portrait of the gentlemanly Revolution Society at dinner. The effect of the activities of the LCS and various 'conventions' was clearly to persuade many that 'they who are most clamorous for a reform, only wish for it as a step towards the total overthrow of our constitution, and the reducing to practice the whole system disseminated by Thomas Paine and his followers'.[83] Many now concluded that such assemblies aimed 'to procure a general commotion of the people' rather than parliamentary reform.[84] Arrests, show trials, and sentences of lengthy transportation (permissible for sedition in Scotland though not England) to Botany Bay followed swiftly.[85] Finally, in late 1795, legislation drastically curtailed the reformers' freedom of correspondence, assembly and speech.

Responses to Paine

In the two years or so before dialogue gave way to intimidation, the loyalists wrote an immense number of pamphlets, broadsides, sermons and books to refute the 'Jacobinical' cause, indeed to fuse in the public mind the identification of 'radical' with 'Jacobin'. Some eighty works, approximately, responded directly to *Rights of Man*. These ranged over many themes: the reassertion of the glory of the British system of checks and balances, the wisdom of virtual representation, the right of substantial property owners to a preponderant power over legislation, the benefits of limited, historically grounded rights and liberties, and the location of sovereignty in the legislature rather than the whole people.[86] Also important was the defence of a natural social hierarchy bound together by 'duty, affection, and respect', contrasted to Paine's principles, which in their French practice meant that 'All the ties which formerly bound the individual to the community have been destroyed, and every man has been left free to act from the unrestrained impulse of his own free will'.[87] The core loyalist contention against the reformers, however, was the argument that the form of society and government invoked by Paine's account of natural rights was incompatible with the opulence and inequality of modern Britain. This charge was not offered as a prelude to a sophisticated analysis of Paine's economic thought.[88] Instead, it was asserted that Paine sought to destroy the British system of property as such: his abstract, egalitarian system of rights thus also only suited a primitive, poor country. Republican egalitarianism could not therefore be combined with modern commercial prosperity.

There were two components to this defence of British opulence, the first concentrating upon Paine's theory of rights and its appeal to an original state of nature, the second on the implications of Paineite republicanism for an unequal society. Loyalists of course defended modern property rights, and, following Burke, played down or rejected entirely the language of natural rights generally. In dismissing Paine's account of rights, discussions of the state of nature and the rights possessed in it were prominent, for the debate about both equality and rights rested largely upon notions of the origins of society, and the implications of an appeal to restore or reintroduce natural rights which invited, necessitated, or might result in a return to 'natural society', or a condition of primitive equality.

Loyalists thus commonly asserted that Paine had misunderstood the relationship between natural and civil society (Richard Price and Joseph Priestley had been similarly accused in 1789–90). His attempt to replicate natural rights in civil society underlay his misconceptions about rights, 'natural equality' being 'incompatible with the advantages of social life'. On this question, as elsewhere in this debate, extreme views emerged; one cleric, for example, seemed to admit only a natural right to celebrate the blessings of the English constitution. More serious critics usually rejected Paine's distinction between society and government as implying that mankind had once been so good as not to have needed government, or that America had ever lacked such an authority, or that any security of property could exist without one. Many similarly accused Paine of forgetting 'a very essential and operative part of human nature, the passions', and assuming that 'the people will all be regenerated with the government'. The *Rights of Man* thus ascribed 'more virtue and knowledge to mankind than they are really possessed of'. To Paine's claim that the system of trade mitigated the need for extensive governments, too, one retort was that commerce was only pacific because governments protected its promoters.[89]

Many of Paine's opponents also denied that rights existed in the state of nature, at least in any positive or beneficial sense. Everyone was admittedly independent in the state of nature, one wrote, but everyone was also miserable, and the strong preyed continuously on the weak. Yet this 'was a state which modern philosophers have commended'. Nonetheless it was also surely a condition in which no rights existed. Power alone had regulated human relations then, with rights emerging only with society proper, support for this view being elicited from Grotius, Pufendorf, Burlamaqui and others. 'Natural rights' did not exist for practical men and women: 'all rights ... are properly civil' (as Edward Tatham put it) or were only 'real' because they were 'secured ... by that form of government under which we live' (wrote the Duke of York's chaplain).[90] A similar argument, close to Burke's, was that some rights preceded society, but 'no natural rights are retained after entering into society'. Another variation on this theme was to define these original rights as merely 'the rights of a savage, to prey upon the weak and helpless', which had been surrendered for civil rights, 'the rights of society, uniting us for our general happiness, and mutual assistance, and protection'. But this also virtually implied that 'in a natural state, men were possessed of no rights at all', since 'none can be called natural rights which were not possessed in a state of nature; and where the rules of justice are not established, where the strong can enforce obedience, and the weak must yield to oppression, what becomes of the Rights of Man?' Or correspondingly, if such rights were 'natural', they included only the right to eat, drink, sleep, hunt, fish and the like. Some critics further contended that even if an original contract had marked the passage from the state of nature it would not have obliged future generations, who would not have been the real descendants of those who signed such a contract, and who, even if they were, would now be landed proprietors rather than 'the people at large'. If only historical rights were meaningful, too, it was thus legitimate to confine the definition of terms like 'rights' and 'liberty'. In a typical caricature of plebeian political discourse, the evangelical pamphleteer Hannah More's widely circulated *Village Politics*, for example, began with workman Tom demanding 'I want liberty', and workman Jack responding 'Liberty! what, has any one fetched up a warrant for thee?' 'Liberty' was not admissible as a general concept, thus, but only as a specific grant, in the sense of the 'liberty of the city', embedded in British law.[91] A nostalgic image of a quintessentially rural Britain was now conjured up, where patriotic, hard-working peasants, a generous and patronising aristocracy and benevolent curates coexisted in a symbiotic relationship of timeless harmony until threatened by an invasion of Gallic cannibal-atheists.

Some quite extensive and sophisticated arguments were employed against Paine's supposed appeal to the state of nature. In the 620 page jurisprudential account by a conveyancer of the Middle Temple, Francis Plowden, 'state of nature' meant a 'mere theoretical and metaphysical state, pre-existing only in the mind, before the physical existence of any human entity whatever'. Writers like Locke, Plowden asserted, never implied that any historical transition from a state of nature to civil society took place, and used the concept only as 'a method of philosophers to discuss the nature of man, before they enter upon peculiar attributes of existing beings'. This meant that rights were primarily psychological qualities. A similar argument was that if 'state of nature' meant 'what is independent of society and exists at all times, without any consideration of any thing but itself', as the Edinburgh Professor of Civil Law argued, natural rights were neither created nor abrogated by society but only fully enjoyed there, since they had no security prior to the institution of government. Natural rights could thus signify *jus gentium*, or rights 'co-extensive and coeval with social man', or the 'simple, pure, perpetual, universal dictates of our feelings and our understanding', which increased or diminished anyone's happiness. This could be understood as part of the instinctual law of nature, but also implied an appeal to 'general convenience and utility through experience and history', which was exactly what in 'the modern rights of men is not appealed to'. The principle of utility, thus, which had been slowly growing in popularity before the 1790s through the writings of Bentham, Priestley and Paley among others, was now to become the new basis of Whig political thought, and, in Plowden's words, 'the great principle on which Government is to be established and maintained'.[92]

The gist of this line of attack was that Paine's appeal to natural rights either theoretically implied reinstating something like natural society, or, consequentially, that the egalitarian scramble which would result from popularising such ideas would induce a reversion to an anarchic, pre-social state. And the portrayal of this state, of course, was Hobbist rather than Rousseauist: a condition of cruel anarchy, as described by Thomas Hobbes in his famous *Leviathan* (1651), rather than that of sociable harmony as portrayed in Jean-Jacques Rousseau's *Discourse on the Origins of Inequality* (1755). The fact that Paine thought rights preceded society implied that men could exist individually, outside of society, and that all possessed 'individual sovereignty to govern' themselves. Paine was thus the 'reducer of civilized society into individual independence'. The counter-argument, of course, was that rights were only secured by laws where sovereignty normally resided with government, and where individuals were far from wholly independent. Some of Paine's opponents also stressed that children were born dependent upon their parents, and in addition possessed different abilities. Many more asserted that if the Garden of Eden had been idyllic, the Fall had provoked continuous violence as well as the threat of overpopulation, which necessitated the formation of civil society. Pufendorf and Burlamaqui, among others, were enlisted to support the view that while the laws of nature regulating self-preservation and the pursuit of happiness might have governed during natural society, appetites and passions soon led to their relaxation, and to each judging the value of his or her own actions. Consequently all were soon reduced to avarice, envy and mutual oppression. Finally independence was renounced and all lodged their rights in the supreme power of the state, which at last permitted 'true liberty' and 'intire independence'. Returning to natural society would thus be reinstating anarchy.[93]

One of the more substantial responses to Paine which concentrated on defining the state of nature was written by one Robert Thomas, minister of Abdie in Scotland, printed at Dundee in 1797, and supported by subscriptions from, among others, Adam Smith's successor at Edinburgh, Dugald Stewart, and a leading clerical luminary, the Rev. Hugh Blair. This 430 page book assumed that the state of nature was a fiction insofar as any arrangements made within it could be binding thereafter, and that any early stage of society should be reconstructed through conjectural history rather than philosophical speculation. Here a Christian conception of the state of nature was again important, with the earliest stages of mankind being characterised by sin as well as

misery. But Thomas also presumed that society was the natural condition of mankind. All were born within it with 'natural rights', but the
state of nature did not define these. Instead natural rights, as part of
human nature, were summarised in 'the right which every man has to
himself', especially the right to life, and included the rights to liberty
and property. Within society, however, men were naturally unequal.
Thus, asserted Thomas, 'Mr. Paine's error lies in misrepresenting the
original state of man, and in overlooking those variations in the character and situation of men, produced by an original inequality in the
formation of their minds and bodies, and by numberless adventitious
causes'. A similar view was taken in another lengthy account by a
Professor of Moral Philosophy and Natural Law at the University of
Utrecht, William Brown. His *An Essay on the Natural Equality of Man* levelled an entire classical armoury against Paine, citing extensively from
Cicero, Seneca, Pliny, Epictetus and Marcus Antonius as well as Bacon,
Grotius, Cumberland, Pufendorf, Hutcheson and many others. Brown
also conceded that natural rights existed, being equal rights to life,
the fruits of labour, the preservation of a fair and honest character,
and to liberty and private judgement. Nonetheless society rested
upon the necessity of subordination and the just demands of authority.
Inequalities arose through different talents and dispositions, and
though a 'natural equality of man' existed, this meant an equality of
obligation and mutual dependence, or the equal duty of all to ensure
the preservation and well being of society.[94]

The clergy thus clearly played an important role in loyalism. Pulpits
reverberated throughout the land in 1792–3 with exhortations to
obey the divinely sanctioned civil authority,[95] with clerics insisting that
the new spirit of equality was 'highly criminal in the sight of God'.[96]
Instead 'Equality', as one of their dialogues bluntly put it, was 'only
another name for Atheism', as liberty was for licentiousness.[97] There
were of course exceptions, notably amongst the Dissenters. But when
the Baptist minister William Winterbotham was tried in 1793 for
preaching a seditious sermon, his accusers contended that no 'rights
of man' existed 'in opposition to the supreme being, while in a state
of civil society, man has no rights but what that society which he lives
in allows him', any defence of 'absolute' rights thus being 'blasphemy
to their Creator, and treason to the constitution'. Other authors
agreed that while all rights were derived from God, none existed
where no title could be shown. The Rev. John Riland thus entitled his
response to Paine *The Rights of God, Occasioned by Mr. Paine's Rights of*

Man. Some clerical critics moreover thought Paine's proposals for relief of the poor, ill and aged would undermine existing rights to charity and eventually degrade the poor further. (This accorded with the clerical explanation that God permitted the existence of rich and poor to ensure the exercise of those virtues necessary to salvation, a theodicy common to natural law texts as well). Clerical critics also objected to any use of the Mosaic account of the Creation to justify modern rights. Some protested that Genesis was Paine's only cited authority for the doctrine of equality, but that since only one man was first created, his sons could not have been his equals. No original equality thus existed, and monarchy was a more likely form of original government, a familiar argument to students of seventeenth-century patriarchalism. Paine's inference that if Genesis was not a divine account it was at least historically accurate was also contested.[98]

Paine's treatment of natural rights and the state of nature was thus widely understood as diverging from the mainstream eighteenth century position on such questions. Paine, some felt, was 'very anxious ... to disclaim the authority of those who have gone before us'. On doctrines like the right of resistance, his views were seen as quite dissimilar from those of natural law writers like Pufendorf, whose definition of a right was also contrasted to Paine's supposed notion of a 'simple power', which might include a right to do wrong (which in fact was not Paine's view at all). Jurists like Burlamaqui were also frequently quoted on the disadvantages of popular government, with evidence cited from Greece, Rome, Carthage, Sparta and elsewhere, and in fact such writers were more commonly deployed against Paine than was Burke's *Reflections*. Many writers also attempted to show that Paine had departed from the Whig canon on these matters. One tract for example asserted that 'Those natural rights, whatever they may be, are placed by their new champion above the law; so that he directly contradicts Mr. Locke (whom we are not yet prepared to exchange for him) who says, where there is no law, there is no freedom'. Another thought that for Locke and Sidney natural rights meant that man was 'born with a capacity to acquire that freedom, and all those rights which any other man is capable of enjoying or acquiring' rather than being born with this freedom and these rights himself. Because of Paine, clearly, natural rights doctrines became increasingly dangerous to retain in any Whiggish account of the origins and nature of the British constitution, and with them the associated ideas of the original contract and state of nature.[99]

Interlocking with the loyalist treatment of natural rights and the state of nature was the defence of inequality of property. For Hume, Smith and the other Scottish theorists of commercial society whose accounts underlay much loyalist argument, the attainment of opulence entailed accepting greater inequality than had existed in earlier historical stages. But in absolute terms the poor were now better off than they had been under feudalism, much less earlier agricultural or hunting and gathering societies, and could even boast, in Adam Smith's image, of surpassing the standard of living of 'many an African king, the absolute master of the lives and liberties of ten thousand naked savages'.[100] In a masterfully ironical, sweeping accusation, thus, republicans were described as demanding a primitivist equality from which not even the poor would benefit, and France was to be condemned, as a London doctor put it, for reviving 'these exploded dreams of the golden age, the terrestrial paradise, the millennium'. The image of Britain's permeable, flexible aristocracy, by contrast with the closed castes of the European nobility, was here often adverted to. British inequality was based on merit, not on birth as such. In Britain even the poor could be ennobled, like the obscure barber and inventor, Richard Arkwright, who 'by his superior merit and ingenuity' gained a Baronetcy.[101] And the professions, too, relied upon the existing distribution of wealth. Inequality of property permitted doctors, lawyers, and other trades and professions to thrive and in turn to distribute their largesse to meet the real wants of the poor, the only equality possible between the two being, as one loyalist put it, in the act of charity. Division of labour secured opulence; doctor, weaver and farmer alike would be 'gone a digging', as Hannah More put it, if the reformers had their way.[102] Paine's tract was thus to More only a way of 'making ourselves poor when we are getting rich'. Inequality was not unfair since the rich employed the rest, insisted a Buckinghamshire farmer. One 'Plain Man', probably a shopkeeper, similarly noted that 'I have a set of wealthy customers who put a great deal of money into my pocket in the year, whose expenses, suitable to their rank and situation in life, enable me to enjoy all the solid comforts suitable to mine'. High taxes, too, could be understood as benefiting the working classes because labourers' wages had to be greater to pay them.[103]

Politically, then, the public were doubtless swayed by what the *Analytical Review* termed 'the fascinating power of the belief of the excellency of the English constitution', a form of government which, as Pitt put it, 'we do not flatter from prejudice or habit, but which we

cherish and value, because we know that it practically secures the tran-
quillity and welfare both of individuals and the public ... beyond any
other frame of government which has ever existed'.[104] Ultimately the
loyalists were largely successful in portraying every effort at reform as
'an intention, design, and effort to subvert and annihilate' the constitution,[105] and those whom Burke termed the 'new Whigs'[106] as little
better than the most feckless Parisian Jacobins. Yet what was much
more important to the success of the loyalist cause than the defence
of the British constitution as such was the fact that by 1793 the debate
about the revolution in France became, as Arthur Young put it, not a
contrast of liberty to tyranny, but 'alone a question of property. It is a
trial at arms, whether those who have nothing shall not seize and possess the property of those who have something'. Property-owners were
thus warned that they would soon face beggars with 'the sword in one
hand, and Rights of Man in the other', demanding 'that which good
government tells me is my own'.[107]

Satirical treatments of the theme of 'levelling' were common. *A Trip
to the Island of Equality* described Paine's principles as operating successfully on an island off Alaska, where all were reduced to wearing
fox-skins (there was a small pun here at radical Whig expense) and
living in caves. Parodies of the *Rights of Man*, such as *Buff; or,
A Dissertation on Nakedness*, accused Paine of relinquishing religion, literature, the arts, sciences, manufactures and the polite professions.[108]
'Levellers', it was asserted, would 'draw the people in to overturn
the government, and put all property under confiscation, as they have
done in France, hoping to get pretty good shares for themselves in the
scramble'.[109] What most people understood by 'equality', then, was
'an equal right at this moment to equal property – this after all the dis-
putes on the matter, is the only sense the common people could
understand it in, and was in fact the sense which Tom P—— meant
them to understand, and the sense in which they really did understand it in'.[110]

Paine, then, had 'disclaimed all ideas of subordination' and had
'more than insinuated, that men ought to be equal'. He had thus
'endeavoured to excite, in the people's mind, a desire of establishing
equality'.[111] Indeed some insinuated that he even wished children to
become equal to parents, apprentices to masters, women to men,
blacks to whites.[112] But republicanism, it was frequently reiterated,
suited only poor, pre-commercial societies which were incapable of

being 'congenial to science, or friendly to commerce' (as a Canterbury printer wrote) and implied a return to 'ancient rusticity'. Paine sought 'to mow down all distinctions of rank and titles, and thereby reduce civilised society to the primitive level of hunters and shepherds' (which explained why the French Jacobins were, logically, as ferocious as Indians). Moreover, as one Royal Navy Captain put it, not merely opulence but manners and refinement depended on inequality of property. Other critics similarly insisted that 'Arcadian schemes of polity are only fit for Arcadian manners', that only Spartan simplicity could maintain a government like Paine's, or that the latter was 'calculated for infant society, for shepherds, fishermen, and huntsmen, where the riches of the state is scarce become an object of temptation, or an excitement to plunder'.[113] Such comments could be greatly multiplied, for it is clear that the most successful loyalist argument deployed against Paine did not concern the danger of extending political participation, but the problem of reconciling republican ideals with unequal, and especially modern commercial societies, without destroying their opulence. Put slightly differently, the issue was not whether all men possessed a natural right to the franchise, but what sort of society would result if they did. In essence Paine's critics simply rejected the idea that a commercial republic much more egalitarian than Holland or Venice was even possible, often by pretending that 'republic' could be understood only in classical, pre-commercial terms. By greatly idealising the social and legal system, loyalist authors could insist that:

the only equality that man can know upon the earth, is that political equality which forms the leading feature in our own glorious constitution; where the laws are equally binding on all; whether exerted for the purpose of protection or punishment they extend alike to the rich and the poor; in England, thank Heaven, the power to oppress is unknown; the sovereign himself has no right to enter the cottage of the peasant, without the permission of its owner. Under the influence of such laws, freedom is secure, and property safe; no invidious exclusions, no monopoly of wealth or power is authorized; the road to wealth and honours is open to every man; the means of elevation are infinite: industry, application, genius, either separate or combined, can raise men from the lowest to the highest stations of life.[114]

In the eyes of loyalists Paine's principal aim was thus to establish
social equality. In loyalist 'dialogues' reformers were caricatured as
asserting that 'We have nothing to do but to plant the Tree of Liberty,
I think they call it, which will make us all equal, and then I shall be as
great as a lord'.[115] But these assertions of rights were in reality 'not a
jot better than those of highwaymen and housebreakers; for the
object of both is EQUALIZING PROPERTY'.[116] The taxation scheme in
the *Rights of Man Part Two* was typically condemned as 'so unprincipled, as to surpass anything that is to be found in the history of the
Buccaniers of America. It is an advertisement for general pillage.'
Sometimes Paine was assumed to want to divide all property equally,
which, one loyalist calculated, would leave three acres for each to cultivate, and since no one would be left for specialised labour, all would
quickly sink into barbarism.[117] A leading anti-Jacobin, John Gifford,
thought Paine wanted every man 'to resign all he possesses, and put
all his property into one common stock-purse, whence it might be distributed in equal parts to all the different members of the community:
the indolent and the industrious, the lazy and the laborious; the
extravagant and the frugal'. Other loyalists asserted that the Paineites
promised labourers three guineas a week without working by dividing
property. And if such promises were not explicit, many feared they
were understood as tacit; who knows how many labourers harboured
the fantasy of Robinson Crusoe, so immensely popular in the period,
to be 'monarch of all I survey' – for was this not also the magnetic
source of attraction for many to the new world? A Durham letter of
late 1792 reporting local opinion said that local workers 'talk of equality and expect, that all property will be divided in case of a Republic'.
An Edinburgh pamphlet insinuated the same, while another report
said that the poor had been told each would get ten acres, and that
'French equality meant an equal distribution of land, which Paine
had told them was their natural and original right'. During a distur-
bance amongst the keelmen at Shields and Sunderland, it was
reported, 'General Lambton was asked: "Have you read this little work
of Tom Paine's." "No." "Then read it – we like it much. You have a
great estate, General; we shall soon divide it amongst us." "You will
presently spend it in liquor, and what will you do then?" "Why then,
General, we will divide again." ' Often the accusation was that whatever Paine's followers protested and Paine had written, his system
implied equality, though every sane person knew that inequality
based upon differential productivity had been necessary since the

state of nature to support an increasing population.[118] If Paine had not urged equality of property in so many words, thus, he had 'insinuated it', and intended others to seek it, or, at least minimally, was read by others as having done so. For many loyalists the issue was thus not what the radicals meant 'or what they now say they mean, but what ... men of plain understandings and common sense would naturally understand them to mean'. Political opinions thus had economic consequences. Claiming an equal right to vote might be also understood as tending 'to subvert the natural order of things'. In France, after all, a wide suffrage had resulted in 'no laws, no government, no order or rule'.[119]

Loyalist argument thus hinged upon the assertion that any appeal to natural rights would necessitate a return to the conditions of the state of nature, where man's 'rights were many, but his power feeble, and his enjoyments few'. There, possessing 'perfect independence of all control', mankind had also been 'by far the most wretched ... the most brutal, selfish, and unfeeling towards each other'.[120] Invoking 'natural rights' thus meant seeking 'natural liberty', 'the power of acting as one thinks fit, without restraint or control'.[121] By contrast the Bill of Rights, for example, had defined 'not the rights of man as a solitary independent savage; but the rights of Englishmen, in the social compact, and civilized life; who knew that subordination was essential to freedom'.[122] It was 'the wildest and most fantastic of all chimeras' to dream of replicating natural conditions in a civilized society, or indeed anywhere except Atlantis, Utopia or the City of the Sun.[123]

As to the assertion that such rights had already been replicated in America, loyalists disclaimed the applicability of any such parallel. America had no indigent poor to support and thus lacked the chief burden of other governments, said the agricultural writer Arthur Young, emphasising that its population had 'scarcely become a settled and mercantile people'. Luxury, another observer added, was 'but beginning to be known there', though eventually 'wealth and ease' would 'produce ambition'. Ambition in turn would engender faction, and soon an American commercial and manufacturing aristocracy would overturn the relative equality of the colonial era. Some who rejected Paine's conception of the American model were not ill disposed towards the United States, or at least hastened to insist that its powerful President and Senatorial check on popular government did not imply 'like the French, a wild species of republicanism'. John Adams' hostile response to the *Rights of Man* was thus welcomed as proving 'that the American Government is not founded upon the absurd doctrine of the pretended rights of man, and that, if it had been, it could not have stood for a week'. Some also argued that Paine had used the American model dishonestly, since universal suffrage did not prevail there. Most agreed, however, that if Paine's views applied anywhere, it was only to countries like the United States, where commerce and manufacturing had made no extensive inroads and much free land existed. Such ideas were 'totally inapplicable to Britain' because it was corrupted by the luxuries and vices of refinement.[124] The principles of 1776, in other words, could never be those of 1789, and any attempt to make them such was bound to terminate in disaster.

The Popular Debate in Decline c.1793–1800

The publication of radical tracts became more difficult after the *Rights of Man* was proscribed in December 1792, and several printers and booksellers were prosecuted for disseminating it and similar works. (Bowdlerised editions which omitted the offensive sections continued to be sold.)[125] And, as the Sheffield reformer Henry Redhead Yorke lamented, the 'wicked manoeuvres' of Reeves' Association were very damaging to the radical cause.[126] While repeatedly denying 'the Agrarian position of equalizing property', insisting only on 'equal protection of the law, whereby ... the poorest man [has] an equal chance of obtaining the impartial administration of justice', London Corresponding Society leaders acknowledged in 1797 that loyalist propaganda had been 'unfortunately too successful'. 'The word equality became the constant theme of abuse, and was construed to mean, not equality of rights, but an equality of property also, in which perverted sense the French had never used it', lamented one Paineite, while conceding that once 'we became familiarized with the name, and ... some of those who do not take the trouble of thinking for themselves, may possibly not detect that absurdity of the doctrine'. Paineite pamphlets like *An Explanation of the Word Equality* and *Political Dialogues upon the Subject of Equality* (both *c.*1792) railed against the 'perverse sense imposed on the word', and denied that the 'ridiculous idea' of equality of property had been proposed either by Paine or 'the most violent reformers in France'. In Ireland, the United Irishmen insisted that 'By liberty we never understood unlimited freedom, nor by equality the levelling of property or the destruction of subordination'.[127] But to little avail: Yorke even felt that 'the general terror occasioned by such an insinuation' had brought about war with France.[128]

The atmosphere which prevailed from 1793, and even more from 1795, was extraordinarily repressive. Allowing free political debate, Pitt maintained, 'amounted to a toleration of the worst species of anarchy, sedition, and treason'.[129] Consequently, the casual mention in the street that a reform of Parliament might be desirable could result in being hauled up before a magistrate.[130] To mimic the same words favouring reform as ministers like Pitt and the Duke of Richmond had themselves used nine years earlier was to court arrest.[131] Tension reached a peak during the great treason trials of 1794, when, after many months' imprisonment, and the failure of facile government efforts to manufacture evidence using spies and informers, the chief working-class leaders, Thomas Hardy and John Thelwall, together with John Horne Tooke and others, were acquitted.[132] The Attorney General, with two hundred similar indictments awaiting signature upon their expected conviction, was grievously disappointed.

Yet much of public opinion had clearly begun to swing behind loyalism before this. The Jacobin coup of 10 August 1792 and the increasingly popular character of what was sometimes called the 'second revolution', alarmed many,[133] as did reports of massacres of aristocrats and, in September 1792, of imprisoned nobles and others in Paris.[134] Louis XVI's execution in January 1793 convinced many that France was 'not capable of receiving liberty, and of preserving it for any time'.[135] Crucially, the outbreak of war with France in February 1793, and the steady stream of Gallic successes, made France seem 'at least as much inclined to universal monarchy as the greatest of her despots ever were',[136] if not aiming at 'the extermination of the human race'.[137] The government was now enabled to identify the reformers' principles with those of Britain's 'hereditary enemy' even more completely.[138] Many moderates now abandoned the cause, even insisting, with Burke, that the war be pursued until 'French principles' had been eradicated. When the Jacobin dictatorship under Robespierre (1793–4) liquidated the Girondin opposition such sentiments intensified still further.[139] By 1794, many middle class moderates, in particular, were prone to concede that even partial parliamentary reform might invite revolution, republicanism, civil war and national bankruptcy.[140]

Nonetheless the unpopularity of the war, higher taxation, political repression and growing social problems helped to swell plebeian radical ranks in 1793–4.[141] Some claimed that Britain had provoked France by assisting counter-revolutionaries like the Duke of Brunswick, and by conspiring with the continental great powers from the convention of Pilnitz in 1790 onwards.[142] The principles of the Revolution could still be defended, even if their application had been less than successful. Even after the execution of Louis some insisted that 'we ought not to feel lukewarm in the cause of Liberty, because some of its assertors have done wrong; nor disclaim a grand, general principle, because it may have been partially disgraced'.[143] Probably about three thousand strong in early 1794, the London Corresponding Society staged a number of hugely successful mass meetings in 1795, and attracted large numbers of new members. But following a supposed assault on the life of the king when a window of his carriage was broken, and against the threat 'that a great part of the nation was now strongly in a state of rebellion',[144] Pitt moved decisively.[145] A further proclamation against seditious activities was issued on 4 November, and the notorious 'Two Acts' were passed at Christmas time.[146] Anything likely to incite hatred or contempt of the King, government or constitution could now be prosecuted. Meetings of more than fifty persons required governmental supervision, and were hampered by other restrictions. Rejecting such 'ACTS FOR THE EXTINCTION OF BRITISH LIBERTY', reformers denounced Pitt for dragging the nation 'into the most abject slavery'.[147]

These measures were successful. The LCS declined dramatically. The Society of the Friends of the People closed its doors in 1795, and other provincial political societies the following year. The official parliamentary opposition, led by Fox, was cowed into silence. Thousands of reformers emigrated to the United States, where they made a considerable political impact.[148] Some who remained recanted their radicalism loudly enough to rescue their reputations.[149] From the end of 1795 until early 1797 there were thus few attempts either hostile or friendly to analyse the principles of the revolution.[150] In the late 1790s and early years of the nineteenth century, however, a vigorous campaign emerged to stamp out what were regarded as the 'philosophic', that is, atheist, 'causes' of democratic sentiment. Here the assumption that religious belief was the key to all other forms of subordination was central, as was the belief that no government could 'long subsist, if the bulk of the people have no reverence for a supreme being, no fear of perjury, no apprehension of futurity, no check from conscience'.[151] Here, while Paine's *The Age of Reason* was proscribed in

1797, William Godwin, whom we treat at length below (Ch. 7) was a particular target in the creation of a counter-Enlightenment ideology. Burke had already pinned the label of atheist on the English revolutionaries,[152] though opposed by Mackintosh and others,[153] and the anti-Priestley riots proved that the cry, 'The Church in Danger' could be used to rally the mob.[154] Now a philosophical conspiracy by freethinking literati was mooted as a principal cause of the Revolution, with Godwin, the English apostle of Reason, its great local votary. Spearheaded by well-attended lectures by the now anti-Jacobin James Mackintosh in 1799, and a well-publicised *Spital Sermon* by a leading Whig intellectual, Samuel Parr, in 1801, a literary sub-genre, the anti-Godwinian novel, now emerged, in which the 'new philosophy', exposed to the dazzling light of criticism, was condemned as anti-authoritarian infantilism.[155] United to an emerging and increasingly powerful evangelical agenda led by Bishop William Wilberforce, these efforts belittled the powers of Reason by contrast with the awesome inevitability of Original Sin. A well-orchestrated campaign for the reform alike of public and private morals was commenced which was to prove profoundly influential for virtually a century.[156] And, ironically, this campaign would proclaim its fervent opposition to the corrosive effects of luxury upon morals both public and private in much the same way as the radicals had in the early 1790s.

Most reformers vainly protested that their principles and motives had been misconstrued and caricatured.[157] When the Society of the Friends of the People was founded it disavowed 'THE EXISTENCE OF ANY RESEMBLANCE WHATEVER BETWEEN THE CASES OF THE TWO KINGDOMS', adding that 'WE UTTERLY DISCLAIM THE NECESSITY OF RESORTING TO SIMILAR REMEDIES'.[158] But other reformers did propose turning waste and common lands over for cultivation, complaining that the poor in Britain were oppressed 'to enrich our nobles',[159] and justified the expropriation or redistribution of clerical revenues, *à la mode française*. A few even denounced all aristocrats as monsters 'of rapacity, and an enemy to mankind'.[160] And some radicals did carry such principles well beyond Paine's. While Godwin's primitivism spawned romantic plans by the young poets Coleridge and Southey for a 'Pantisocracy' on the Susquehannah, his ideas on property are rarely encountered among the lower orders. The utopian strand in republicanism, derived from Plato, Thomas More, Gerrard Winstanley, and others, if theoretically significant, was never widely popularised during the 1790s.[161] But the writings of a London bookseller, Thomas Spence, do merit greater

attention in this context.[162] The father of the modern land nationalisation movement, which through A.R. Wallace and others was to have
considerable appeal in the late nineteenth century, Spence like Paine
commenced from the premise that property had originally been held
in common (his sources included the Bible, Locke and Pufendorf),
and was then slowly monopolised by 'a few usurpers and tyrants'.[163]
But Spence protested that no other reformer was willing to acknowledge the full implications of this fact. Paine and his ilk had mistakenly
levelled 'all their artillery at kings, without striking like Spence at
the root of every abuse and of every grievance', he complained,
denying in 1796 that Thelwall, too, had gone far enough in reasserting
the rights of man.[164] Once all realized that their common rights
were still retained, however, these could be reclaimed, and the
land wholly nationalised, with each parish being reorganised as a corporation to own and manage the land. Farms would be rented out to
individuals, and the proceeds used to pay expenses, including the
national parliament.[165] The parish was to be the basic unit of social
organisation because, among other reasons, it was too small a community to wage war on others, and because Spence insisted on local,
rather than provincial or national, control over both estates and taxes.
(This included public control over education, medical care and poor
relief).

The monopoly of land Spence thus regarded as 'the mother of all
other monopolies', since once land had been redistributed equally,
'farms would be so small, that the farmers would hardly be rich enough
to hoard much, neither would they be so few in number as easily to
combine to raise the price of their produce'. Public granaries would
make corn hoarding unprofitable, while scarcities of other goods could
be similarly prevented. This concentration on the results of inequality
of land ownership left Spence little disposed to scrutinise the workings
of trade more carefully. Although he envisioned a decrease in both
manufacturers and tradesmen, Spence nonetheless thought that considerable trade would still exist, and even suggested, somewhat inconsistently given his expectation that the number of manufacturers might
well decline, that good taste would be extended throughout the population, leading to an increased demand for a wide range of goods.[166]
The abolition of taxes and of land monopolies, indeed, he considered
would be such a spur to mercantile activity that merchants and manufacturers could sell their produce so cheaply as to ensure 'a very extensive foreign and domestic trade'. While all other forms of property

except land were to be permitted in his future system, Spence was in fact little concerned with commerce or wage-relations, and happily acknowledged that anyone would be free to 'engage his services and his time', short of slavery.[167] Spence and his followers thus remained at the extreme, agrarian radical wing of the Harringtonian tradition of British republicanism, and are of considerable theoretical significance even if Spence's 'Plan for Parochial Partnership' does not appear to have circulated widely outside of London in this period.[168]

Conclusion

The anti-Paineite case was constructed out of old materials, but these were not essentially 'Tory', though Toryism was now more respectable than at any previous point in the eighteenth century. For the French revolution debate took place in terms of, while also reshaping, Whig discourse, killing off the now dangerously radical myths of an older Whiggism. It was the need to disavow Paineite claims to the right of mass political participation which finally put paid to strictly Lockean arguments for many reformers unwilling to risk revolution for the cause of a fairer representation. Many loyalists, however, remained loosely Whiggish. If they admired what they took to be Burke's energetic avowal of the British constitution, they abjured the extreme of 'reviving doctrines superannuated and obsolete even in Spain and Portugal', which some claimed had actually 'brought Paine's Rights of Man upon our backs'. Some loyalists indeed objected in particular to the 'erroneous political inference' that the nation had relinquished 'the right of electing their Kings, or any other political right' in 1688. Their concern was not to defend the divine right theory of monarchy, or to increase the king's powers, but to shore up the constitution as a whole. In this sense, because it defended the status quo, and not some British version of the French *ancien régime*, loyalism was more Whig than Tory, and less 'a conservative reaction' than 'an attempt to maintain the most liberal constitution in Europe', as an important account has argued. The extreme Toryism of John Reeves, defined by the belief that the King could govern without the Lords or Commons, was thus of less account than the Whiggism of William Paley, who argued that the king was no master of the common man, and could not interfere with the liberty of any of his subjects. It is for this reason, in particular, that the 'Burke-Paine debate' is something of a misnomer when applied to the wider French revolution controversy in Britain. For unlike Burke, most loyalists were not only defending Britain, but believed her achievements rested on distinctly modern, indeed what a later generation would call specifically 'bourgeois' achievements, rather than 'Gothic' ideals. Thus they sought to defend not only an inequality of ranks generally, but British inequality and commercial wealth in particular.[169] The Paineite appropriation of rights language in order to further claims for popular political participation in fact drove most Whigs to abjure older rights arguments in favour of claims based upon utilitarianism and political economy as well as historical precedent. This 'liberal' condemnation of natural rights was as we will see crowned by Malthus' merciless assault on the notion of a natural right to subsistence in his *Essay on Population* (1798). Thereafter, natural rights arguments remained popular in working class radicalism through the Chartist period and beyond.[170] But mainstream Whig radicalism reacted strongly to the threat of popular participation during the 1790s, and it is thus clear that the transformation of Whiggism into liberalism, already well under way, increased rapidly as a consequence of loyalist intellectual strategy during the revolutionary period.

Chapter Six: Varieties of Whiggism: Fox, Sheridan and the Whig Party, 1791–3

'I'll unwhig the gentleman for the rest of his life.'
(Pitt on Fox's role in the Regency debate, 10 December 1788)[1]

Introduction: Whigs Unwhigged?: Fragmented Loyalties

The unhappy history of the Whig party in this period is well known and can be restated briefly.[2] Most Whigs were neither anti-monarchist republicans nor revolutionaries, and while many had considerable sympathy for France in 1789–90, this had begun to cool by late 1790 and was transformed widely into antipathy by the publication of Burke's *Reflections*. A few, however, led by Charles Grey, formed the Society of the Friends of the People (SFP) in order to link outdoor agitation to the parliamentary party.[3] The Whig grandee, Charles James Fox, was also wooed by the government, and sought to defend a middle ground between these competing pressures, but failed to accommodate any group. Eventually a large group of Whigs led by the Duke of Portland agreed to support the government, in early 1793, and then joined Pitt in a coalition government in mid-1794. This left the Foxites isolated in opposition, and powerless to halt the crushing of the extra-parliamentary plebeian reformers by the suspension of habeas corpus and the passage of the treason and sedition laws of 1795. From about the spring of 1792, then, the Government had one main strategy, and the reformist Whigs two. Pitt, under considerable pressure from Tories and conservative Whigs, aimed to portray all reforming activity as unpatriotic and un-English if not downright seditious and treasonable. Amongst the reformers, some sought to argue that their applause for French developments was commensurate with a tradition of British liberty stretching far into the past. Others, however, insisted that their ideals innovated upon and/or broke from such a tradition.

This Chapter aims to explore the evidence for seeing the split amongst the Whigs as a matter of principle, or as a function of party and, beyond this, personality. Characteristically, of course, any such party fissure is a function of all three: the devil lies in the details. That the French Revolution revealed a substantial underlying disagreement about the nature of Whiggism is evident; the break among the Whigs was clearly a matter of principle, and had been forecast by some very early in the debate.[4] This principle, stated most simply, was whether any stable monarchical government was legitimate as such, including that of Louis XVI; or whether even a republic, if freely chosen by the French nation, was preferable to monarchical absolutism. What rendered these principles far more complex was that support of the first – legitimacy – could be construed as support for despotism, if the *ancien régime* was 'despotic', while applause for the second – popular choice of government – could be viewed as republicanism, even verging on, indeed to the doorstep of, particularly in humbler abodes, treason. It is these issues, firstly, of hidden motives, and secondly, of unintended consequences, we will see, which most bedevilled the debate during the years 1790–3.

Whigs and Newer Whigs:
Charles James Fox and Richard Brinsley Sheridan

Charles James Fox

Central to any such examination are the views of Charles James Fox (1749–1806), third son of the first Lord Holland, a leading Whig MP, and an ally of Burke's respecting both the American colonies and East Indian corruption. Long suspicious of French national and imperial ambitions, Fox welcomed the Revolution warmly as much 'the greatest event … that ever happened in the world! and how much the best', and writing in late July 1789 that 'all my prepossessions against French connections for this country will be at an end … if this Revolution has the consequences that I expect'.[5] Fox had a possible motive for developing, and a much stronger motive for 'appearing' to develop, a republican sympathy (but republicanism, of course, did not need to be either anti-monarchical or anti-aristocratic as such): he was greatly disliked by George III, who resented his scheming with the Prince of Wales, whom his father detested, (notably respecting the Prince's right to become regent, which in view of the King's illness was a very serious matter).[6] At the time of the break from Burke in February 1790, Fox was, however, insistent as to his attachment to the British constitution. He was not an enemy to 'every species of innovation', but:

> He begged, however, not to be misunderstood in his ideas of liberty. True liberty could only exist amidst the union and co-operation of the different powers which composed the legislative and the executive government. Never should he lend himself to support any cabal or scheme, formed in order to introduce any dangerous innovation into our excellent Constitution.[7]

He was not, therefore, Fox insisted, a friend of democracy as such:

> He declared himself equally the enemy of all absolute forms of government, whether an absolute monarchy, an absolute aristocracy, or an absolute democracy. He was adverse to all extremes, and a friend only to a mixed government, like our own, in which, if the aristocracy, or indeed either of the three branches of the constitution, were destroyed, the good effect of the whole, and the happiness derived under it, would, in his mind, be at an end.[8]

To Burke Fox thus insisted that 'His right honourable friend might rest assured, that they could never differ in principles, however they might differ in their application,' and that 'ultimately, it would be for the advantage of this country that France had regained her freedom'.[9] But this was the point Richard Brinsley Sheridan (1751–1816), a dramatist and leading Whig orator, and another confidant of the Prince of Wales, chose to accuse Burke of 'being an advocate for despotism'.[10]

Fox clearly spoke the language of patriotic reform, echoing the principles of Locke and Somers and of 1688. He was not here far distant from Burke. Nor did he wish to link the cause of Dissent to that of the Revolution. He did propose in March 1790 the repeal – not supported by Burke – of the Test and Corporation Acts, pointedly proclaiming that 'he did not hesitate to stand forward the advocate of civil and religious liberty, even in favour of men, who had, on different occasions, acted hostilely towards him'.[11] He also spoke favourably of Price and

Priestley. But he cautioned that 'To make of the pulpit, the altar, or sacramental table, political engines, he must ever condemn, whether in a dissenter or a churchman. The clergy, in their sermons, ought no more to handle political topics, than the House to discuss subjects of morality and religion'.[12]

Events might have kept the two great Whigs, Fox and Burke, together across the course of the next few years. But when the *Reflections* appeared, Fox called the book 'Cursed Stuff.' In Parliament, debating the Quebec bill, he said that, 'as soon as his book on the subject was published, he condemned that book both in public and private, and every one of the doctrines it contained'. He felt that 'his right honourable friend's conduct appeared as if it sprung from an intention to injure him, at least it produced the same effect, because the right honourable gentleman opposite to him had chosen to talk of republican principles as principles which he wished to be introduced into the new constitution of Canada, whereas his principles were very far from republican in any degree'.[13]

Fox's main charge against Burke thereafter was that of political inconsistency.[14] But this was capable, of course, of being turned back on Fox: how far, indeed, did his support for France weaken his claim to uphold the British constitution as the best model? His remark on 15 April 1791, following the break from Burke on 4 March, that 'he for one admired the new constitution of France, considered altogether, as the most stupendous and glorious edifice of liberty, which had been erected on the foundation of human integrity in any time or country',[15] has often been thought to indicate a lapse of principle. On its face it seems to declare the French to be freer than they would have been under a constitution modelled on Britain's.[16] Even if, as his kinsman Lord John Russell later concluded, Fox did not intend to use the Quebec bill debate on 21 April 1791 'to make his difference of opinion on the French Revolution a subject of personal quarrel'.[17] When the bill was recommitted on May 6, Burke insisted on discussing the subject. Fox could only retort that

[o]n the French Revolution he did indeed differ from his right honourable friend: their opinions, he had no scruple to say, were wide as the poles asunder ... On that revolution he adhered to his opinion, and never would retract one syllable of what he had said. He repeated that he thought it on the whole one of the most glorious events in the history of mankind.[18]

On this occasion Fox could not resist taunting Burke with ignorance of current affairs in France. Burke responded angrily, insisting in turn that 'what principally weighed with him' was the potential consequence for Britain of a rising domestic radical movement. Fox, however, denied that

> the way to do justice to the excellence of the British Constitution was never to mention it without at the same time abusing every other constitution in the world ... he had ever thought that the British Constitution in theory was imperfect and defective, but that in practice it was excellently adapted to this country ... because he admired the British Constitution, was it to be concluded that there was no part of the constitution of other countries worth praising, or that the British Constitution was not still capable of improvement?[19]

In the debate on May 6, Fox declared explicitly that admiration of France did not entail imitation:

> Let those who said, that to admire was to wish to imitate, shew that there was some similarity of circumstances. It lay on his right honourable friend to shew that this country was in the precise situation of France at the time of the French revolution, before he had a right to meet his argument; and then, with all the obloquy that might be heaped on the declaration, he should be ready to say, that the French revolution was an object of imitation for this country.[20]

His principles, he insisted, 'were very far from republican in any degree'.[21] Indeed Fox went so far as to concede that 'he would not say that the government of France was good. It was undoubtedly capable of improvement, and would be amended by degrees'.[22] He repeated his view that no government could 'be a fit one for British subjects to live under, which did not contain its due weight of aristocracy, because that he considered to be the proper poise of the constitution, the balance that equalized and meliorated the powers of the two other extreme branches, and gave stability and firmness to the whole'.[23] Such comments did not prevent Fox from being caricatured as a Jacobin in a contemporary Gillray engraving, for the Tory hounds were clearly baying for Fox's blood. But we see here the space created for a liberal, even a radical, Whiggism, in which praise for the French Revolution could be accommodated to loyalty to the British constitution, and innovation within it of the sort – economic retrenchment in particular – that Burke had also previously championed. When the Canada bill was debated again, and the issue was whether Canada should have an hereditary peerage, Fox, while opposing the imposition of a landed aristocracy on Canada (which brought the charge from both Pitt and Burke that this was republican), reiterated his view that 'prejudice for ancient families, and that sort of pride which belonged to nobility, was right to be encouraged in a country like this, otherwise one great incentive to virtue would be abolished'. Those who said he favoured democracy, Fox said, failed to see that when he praised the American government he meant 'that form of government which was best for themselves; most of which consisted of the powers of monarchy, aristocracy, and democracy blended, though under a different name'.[24] He was only a republican, he added, insofar as 'he approved all governments where the *respublica* was the universal principle, and the people, as under our Constitution, had considerable weight in the Government'.[25] His own views, then, permitted praise for both America and France to be combined with loyalty to Britain.

It was Fox's support for Charles Grey which seemingly led this formula to come unstuck. For Fox, while acknowledging his unwillingness to join the SFP,[26] supported Grey in Parliament, avowing that 'while he was strongly attached to our form of government, he thought the power of the Crown too great, and he wished to diminish it'. Despite his avowed neutrality respecting the SFP, thus, everyone knew that 'it was plain where his heart was'.[27] This provoked a predictable reaction from Burke and Pitt. Yet to support reform as such was not, Fox insisted, to go the length of, in particular, Thomas Paine: 'the truth was, that the book, called 'Rights of Man,' was a performance totally different from all ideas of reform in our government. It went the length of changing the form of it'.[28] Fox was well aware of the delicate line he was treading. The Royal Proclamation against sedition of May 1792, he claimed, had no other intent than 'to strive to make a division between that great body of united patriots, known by the name of the Whig interest'.[29] In this debate the crucial question again arose of how far sympathy for France entailed a wish to alter the British constitution. Again Fox was resolute that there was no connection as such between the two.[30] The result of current prosecutions, he insisted, was merely that 'Those who dread republicanism, fly for shelter to the crown. Those who desire reform and are calumniated, are driven by despair to republicanism. ... These are the extremes into which these violent agitations hurry the people, to the gradual decrease of that middle order of men who shudder as much at republicanism on the one hand, as they do at despotism on the other'.[31] Private reports reinforce the view that Fox thus continued to feel that 'the danger to this country chiefly consisted in the growth of Tory principles, and what happened in France was likely to be useful to us in keeping alive and invigorating the spirit of liberty'.[32]

These principles were to be sorely tested when the campaign against France began in earnest. In mid-December 1792 Fox insisted that a sympathy for French resistance to invasion from without could not 'be considered as a sign of discontent and of a preference to republican doctrines'. Why, he said, should men

> droop and be dejected in their spirits, when they heard that the armies of despotism had triumphed over an army fighting for liberty? If such dejection be a proof that men are discontented with the Constitution of England, and leagued with foreigners in an attempt to destroy it, I give myself up to my country as a guilty man, for I freely confess that when I heard of the surrender or retreat of Dumouriez, and that there was a probability of the triumph of the armies of Austria and Prussia over the liberties of France, my spirits drooped, and I was dejected. What, sir, could any man who loves the Constitution of England, who feels its principles in his heart, wish success to the Duke of Brunswick, after reading a manifesto which violated every doctrine that Englishmen hold sacred, which trampled under foot every principle of justice and humanity and freedom and true government; and upon which the combined armies entered the kingdom of France, with which they had nothing to do; and when he heard or thought that he saw a probability of their success, could any man possessing true British feelings be other than dejected? I honestly confess, sir, that I never felt more sincere gloom and dejection in my life, for I saw in the triumph of that conspiracy not merely the ruin of liberty in France, but the ruin of liberty in England, the ruin of the liberty of man.[33]

Again, therefore, support for French military success did not entail either republicanism or treachery (from the 'left') at the end of 1792, but failure to support France might well, by the same principle, imply both support for despotism as well as treachery (from the 'right').

The question was how long this principle could merit public support; the answer: not long. By the autumn of 1792, Fox was willing to acknowledge that treaty obligations – to the Dutch respecting the French interference in navigation on the river Scheldt, for instance – could provoke a just war in response, and that 'the same national spirit' which had animated France under Louis XIV might be 'more likely to collect and act now than at the former time'. In November the trial of Louis was resolved upon; on 21 January 1793 Louis was executed. Fox, even now, resisted war, insisting that the true reason motivating the war party was the wish to restore the *ancien régime*, a wish which conflicted with 'principle inviolable, that the government of every independent State was to be settled by those who were to live under it, and not by foreign force'. A 'war of opinion' of the type sought by Burke and Pitt, could not be justified by such a principle. But if the Whig party might have held together over the issue of parliamentary reform alone, the war with France permitted no such papering over of differences.[34]

As 1793 dawned, then, Fox continued to insist that 'whatever progress the doctrines of France might make in other countries, they would make but little here, where rational liberty was enjoyed and understood'.[35] He had, he said,

> signed a declaration of attachment to the constitution, because he thought it of importance at the present moment to let foreigners, and especially the French, see that men of all descriptions were firmly attached to it; that they had been grossly deceived by the addresses from this country, which told them that their doctrines were very generally adopted here; that they had been deceived by the minister's proclamations, stating that there was great danger from their doctrines.[36]

The outbreak of war did not curtail this debate entirely within the walls of St. Stephens', but it made Fox's position virtually indefensible, though he continued to assail both the causes and conduct of the war. France had declared war first against Britain, and though Fox could query the government's motives for war, and Pitt's aims in conducting it, and urge negotiation, he could not effect more. Sabotage was out of the question, and in any case he was himself appalled by the execution of Marie Antoinette in particular, calling it 'more disgusting and detestable than any other murder recorded in history'.[37] His position, however, was becoming increasingly untenable. 'Though', Fox insisted in March 1793, 'he had objected to the war in the strongest terms, he wished, as he believed every gentleman did, that it should now be carried on with vigour'.[38] In May, 1793, however, Fox supported Grey's parliamentary reform proposals, though reiterating that 'He had always disliked universal representation'.[39] It seems more than likely, thus, that Fox was courting the left wing of the Whig party rather than altering his own views on parliamentary reform.[40]

After the Parisian massacres of August 1792, and the extension of French citizenship to Priestley, Paine, and others, such assurances were clearly necessary on Fox's part, for the course of the Revolution was not one which he could be seen to approve. The delicate line he had adopted throughout 1792 was now closed. Any expression of sympathy for France now verged on sedition; all that remained was to minimise the damage to the constitution itself which the war and domestic scaremongering threatened, especially by containing the ever-widening accusations of treason, and the creeping insinuation that all opposition was disloyal, that every hint of reform whispered revolution. Fox affirmed his confidence that 'the king and the House of Lords were felt and believed by the people ... to be not only useful but essential parts of the constitution', but was also 'ready to say with Locke, that government originated not only for, but from the people, and that the people were the legitimate sovereign in every community' (but Rousseau's *Social Contract* was 'extravagant').[41] It was, he averred, consistent to remind the Whigs that in 1780 they had rallied round the slogan 'that the influence of the crown had increased, was increasing, and ought to be diminished'.[42] If the principles of the French Revolution had now undergone a 'scandalous perversion', moreover, Fox still affirmed that 'The extreme ... of their principles in favour of democracy was not worse than the species of principles which he had heard urged in favour of royalty'.[43] Moreover, in early 1794 he 'reprobated the conduct of Austria and Prussia, in attacking the French, for no reason but because they were attempting to regulate their internal government – a conduct which has, I fear, been more fatal to the political morality of Europe than any thing the French have yet done'. He therefore condemned the Duke of Brunswick's manifesto urging a Europe-wide counter-revolution against France as the cause of much of the ensuing carnage which the Revolution's opponents blamed on the French government.[44]

Yet to dismiss the motives and aims of the war was not to assail its successes on the British side. As far as the conduct of the war was concerned, Fox also stressed his loyalty from time to time. On the occasion of Howe's naval victory of 1 June 1794, for example, he exclaimed that 'he rejoiced in it as much as any man in England could rejoice in it'. But even here he still hoped, since the threat of French invasion was now removed, 'that Lord Howe had not only conquered the French fleet, but reconquered the habeas corpus act'.[45] Throughout the treason trials Fox contended against Pitt that the Edinburgh convention had aimed 'not to oppose the power of government, but to seek redress of grievances'.[46] Reforming parliament was not the same as overthrowing parliament, as Pitt seemed to insist.[47] Moreover, Fox, as we have seen, wholly accepted the legitimacy of the Hanoverian monarchy, if not the encroachments of the monarchy in the Commons. To avoid these was, for Fox, the meaning of Whiggism; the meaning, indeed, of 'Briton', in his eyes. Such opposition was not 'un-English', but what one could be proud of, in maintaining the inheritance of 1688, as part of the definition of 'English', seeing the threat to the constitution as far more likely to come from the monarchy than the populace. To support the reactionary cause, 'this abominable confederacy of kings',[48] in restoring the most powerful of absolutist monarchies on the Continent was not in keeping with this heritage. Fox felt secure in his Whiggism, even as most of his party had begun to abandon him.

Richard Brinsley Sheridan

The second leading Whig to break publicly from Burke over the Revolution was Sheridan, who confronted Burke formally over the French Revolution during the Army Estimate debates of 9 February 1790. He commenced by arguing that

> he could not conceive how it was possible for a person of such principles, or for any man who valued our own constitution, and revered the Revolution that obtained it for us, to unite with such feelings an indignant and unqualified abhorrence of all the proceedings of the patriotic party in France. He conceived their's to be as just a Revolution as ours, proceeding upon as sound a principle and a greater provocation. He vehemently defended the general views and conduct of the National Assembly.[49]

Asserting that the cruelties evidenced so far in the Revolution resulted from its form of government, he denied that the French could have received a constitution from Louis, and hoped that it could be introduced without any 'wanton persecution of the nobility, or any insult to royalty'. He concluding by contending that the Revolution of 1688 had 'established, on a permanent basis, those sacred principles of government, and reverence for the rights of men'.[50] Sheridan did not return to the theme at length until April 1792, when, in the context of Scotch burgh reform, he expressed 'exultation and joy at the downfal of the despotism of France, the greatest enemy England ever had.' He stressed 'that the destruction of a despotic government is an act of the highest wisdom in a people': and recommended that Britain aim at nothing other than 'a rational and sober reformation of abuses, at a time when there was nothing to interrupt us. This was the only way by which we should be sure of avoiding the evil that might attend a reformation by violence'.[51] Sheridan became a leading figure in the Society of the Friends of the People, but he did not construe its goals in terms of innovation, proposing in December 1792 that

> if a convention were nominated by the free vote of every man in the country, for the purpose of framing a government, he firmly believed they would express no other wish than for the constitution which had been transmitted to us by the virtue of our ancestors, and would retain the form, the substance, and principles of that constitution.[52]

As the government began its prosecutions for sedition, Sheridan insisted that 'if there were really any seditious persons in this country, who wished to overturn the constitution, their numbers were as small as their designs were detestable'. He 'hoped it was not understood that those who rejoiced in the revolution in France likewise approved of all the subsequent excesses'. 'Bad dispositions' might be evident, but there 'was no proof of treacherous designs':

> Such was his idea of the character of Englishmen, that he should take upon him to assert, that were but one French soldier to land upon our coast, the idea of effecting any change in our government, every hand and heart in the country would be roused by the indignity, and unite to oppose so insulting an attempt.

In December 1792, Sheridan also met privately with the French envoy, Chauvelin, and argued that the French had been mistaken in issuing a decree 'offering French assistance to all revolted subjects'. This, he thought, might imply support for rebellion in Ireland. But he made it clear that the opposition would resist any French attempt to meddle with internal British affairs.[53]

On 15 December Sheridan spoke again in support of Fox's motion to send a minister to France to treat with the provisional government, rather than preparing for war. He lamented 'that one English guinea should be spent, or one drop of British blood be shed, to restore the antient despotism of France'. He returned to the theme on 30 December, and joined Fox on 12 February 1793 in deploring the outbreak of war with France. On 4 March he again spoke on sedition, now, however, more cautiously querying whether it 'was not at least premature at the time it was uttered, and consequently that nothing had happened in this country that could justify government in the steps they had taken, and the proceedings they instituted'. He added that

> we were at war with a great, a powerful, and hitherto victorious republic – it was idle to conceal the truth – and he added, that there was not in that house, of in this country, any man who wished more sincerely than he did that we might be able to check them in their career.[54]

In the absence of any proof of conspiracy, he contended, the government's plan was firstly that 'the public were to be alarmed at the apprehension of the progress of French principles, in order that they might the more readily be induced to go to war with the French'; and, moreover, 'secondly, an inclination to divert the public mind from the question of parliamentary reform, for the purpose of concealing the apostacy of certain individuals, who do not chuse to be put to the test, and tried by the public upon the standard of their own professions'. This was the line he continued to pursue in 1793 as bills against traitorous correspondence were introduced by the government, still opposing the restoration of 'the ancient tyranny and despotism' of France, and resisting Pitt's contention that this was no time to introduce measures of parliamentary reform:

> He wished the Chancellor of the Exchequer would either tell the friends of parliamentary reform when he thought he should lend them his assistance, or declare that he never would. He had proved he was of opinion that a season of permanent prosperity was not the time. He had proved too that a time of war was not the time – Should they have the assistance of the right honorable gentleman

after the war with France was over; or should we then be told, that the French being subdued, we should not suffer any alteration in our own constitution?[55]

Sheridan's strategy, thus, was not only to deny that there was nothing seditious in Whig proposals of parliamentary reform, in keeping with the principles of Pitt and Richmond in 1784, but that there was precious little sedition out of doors either, a view he maintained through the 1795 debates on the treason and sedition bills.[56] By 1794, however, while blaming the war on Britain as much as France, he was willing 'for the present', to 'grant that it was a war of sound sense, policy, and justice ... commenced in self-defence and necessity on our part'.[57] Sheridan certainly accused Burke of political inconsistency.[58] But though Fox's partisans have usually seen him as wishing to widen the breach between Burke and Fox,[59] this, too, is indisputably the language of loyal opposition.

Whig Radicalism: The Society of the Friends of the People and the Revolution Society

To appreciate the spectrum of positions definitive of Whiggism we need also briefly to define what lay further to its 'left', beyond 'Hounslow', for this period of course witnessed an expansion of the political spectrum to encompass, for the first time, working class participation in a systematic and partisan manner, as we have seen, with the founding of the London Corresponding Society. On the Whig side we need to consider briefly two organisations: the Society of the Friends of the People, and the Revolution Society.

The key question here is how far more 'radical' Whigs – those zealous to push the issue of parliamentary reform – more likely to laud the French over the British constitution, or to expose in public the hope that events in France, including military victories, would be the agency occasioning parliamentary reform in Britain? How democratic were they, and what price were they willing to pay to see such principles introduced? Unquestionably the Society of the Friends of the People, formed in April 1792 at Lord Porchester's house,[60] did far more to break the Whig party apart than the split between Burke and Fox. For most Whigs, in 1791–2, thought the views of the Revolution of both Fox *and* Burke as too extreme, as well as too publicly expressed.

It was Charles, Earl Grey, later the hero of the 1832 Reform Act, there-fore, rather than Burke or Fox, who 'drove the anti-Reform section under the Duke of Portland to concert measures with Pitt against their fellow Whigs'.[61] What, then, did Grey imagine he was doing in leading the Foxites[62] in this direction? What animated Grey was, in part, the exultation, even the insolence, of youth; he was twenty-five when the Bastille fell. But Grey did acknowledge Fox's leadership of the party, and the SFP did not, in its call for restoring freedom of elec-tion, a more equal representation of the people, and more frequent elections, go beyond what the reformers of the early and mid-1780s (including of course Pitt) had proposed.[63] Stressing that 'our opin-ions neither possess the advantage, nor are liable to the objection of novelty', the SFP couched its claims in terms of restoration rather than innovation, much less revolution (and the original uppercase words are significant):

We say that the Reforms we have in view are not innovations. Our intention is not to change, but to restore; not to displace, but to reinstate the Constitution upon its true principles and original ground ... WE DENY THE EXISTENCE OF ANY RESEMBLANCE WHATEVER BETWEEN THE CASES OF THE TWO KINGDOMS; AND WE UTTERLY DISCLAIM THE NECESSITY OF RESORTING TO SIMILAR REMEDIES.[64]

Throughout the spring of 1792 this was the theme constantly reit-erated by the SFP. Distancing itself from both Paine and the older Society for Constitutional Information, which argued for universal male suffrage (when Major John Cartwright joined the SFP five of its leading members resigned in protest), the SFP stressed that man was 'the creature of habit as well as reason'. Thus it was

therefore our bounden duty to propose no extreme changes, which, however specious in theory, can never be accomplished with-out violence to the settled opinions of mankind, nor attempted without endangering some of the most estimable advantages which we confessedly enjoy.[65]

As the debate in 1792 began to turn upon the issue of the implica-tions for the system of property ownership of an extension of the franchise,[66] the SFP insisted that 'we shall be perfectly satisfied with the decision of an equal representation – that when we speak of liberty and equality, we by no means intend *civil rights* to be mistaken for *civil distinctions*'.[67] Only on one occasion did it appear to distance itself substantially from the Whig party as such, and this was in the proclamation of the Southwark branch (possibly paraphrasing Paine) that

> we are wearied with the unmeaning names of WHIG and TORY, and of MINISTERIAL and OPPOSITIONAL parties, and having often – too often, been deceived by both, we can no longer implicitly confide in either. We will THINK for ourselves; we will study our own Rights, and we will leave to the INS and the OUTS all that idle quibble of debate which only serves to amuse and deceive the nation, and to hold it alternately the prey of COURT and PARTY INTRIGUES.[68]

In its enemies' eyes the threat the SFP posed, then, lay chiefly in its timing, and the possibility that it might be usurped by a radical faction,[69] rather than its programme. Substantively Grey wished to go no further than household suffrage, well short of John Cartwright, never mind the London Corresponding Society. Its membership fee was set at two and a half guineas for residents (though branches in Holborn and Southwark asked 9s. and 6s. respectively).[70] Pitt's retort that Grey sought to 'overthrow the whole system of government' was sociological rather than theoretical. What he really meant was that the SFP, if successful in whipping up outdoor agitation, might well engender such an alteration. The key problem, again, was that to support the Revolution seemed to entail embracing the application of its principles to Britain.[71] The London Corresponding Society had been founded only a few months earlier; and there was a clear danger that Grey's use of overly elastic principles would fuel more popular ambitions. Grey said that he was 'not a friend to Paine's doctrines,' but also insisted that he was 'not to be deterred by a name from acknowledging that I consider the rights of man as the foundation of every government'.[72] Such statements were the reason why Fox supported Grey even if he would not join the SFP. His opposition to it would have probably prevented the split in the party, since this was the chief reason why a coalition with Pitt did not take place in the summer of 1792, everything else being, in Pitt's words, 'entirely forgotten'.[73]

For the same reasons which saw Fox marginalised in this period, the SFP saw its strategy fail. Attacked by Paine for its moderation,[74] alienated from the mainstream Whigs, derided by the Pittites as Jacobin, it met last in May 1795, after a year's inactivity, only to suspend its activities for good.

How did one of Burke's original targets, the Revolution Society, led by 'Citizen' (Earl) Stanhope, handle these controversies? The mere fact of its correspondence with members of the National Assembly had aroused Burke's ire, but led the Society in turn to publish a full account of its communications, in both French and English, to alleviate any further suspicions and to refute the charge of the *Reflections* and the *Appeal* that it sought 'the subversion of nothing short of the *whole* Constitution'.[75] Though the Society had, at its famous meeting of 4 November 1789, declared its 'firm attachment to the civil and religious principles which were recognized and established', it recognised that in a zealous attachment to liberty France might be overtaking Britain:

> BRITAIN has undoubtedly every since the aera of its Revolution been a most distinguished and favoured kingdom, and held out to the world an example of national dignity and happiness derived from the possession of liberty, which has instructed other kingdoms. But our regard to truth requires us, at the same time that we thus boast, to acknowledge that now the time seems to be arrived when we shall lose this honourable distinction. France is taking the lead; and Britain will be left behind, if not provoked by the example of France to correct abuses that are every day growing more palpable; and, in particular, to substitute for its present partial and imperfect Representation as our brethren in France are likely to enjoy.[76]

This formulation could be construed either as a plea for restoration or a proposal to innovate. The Society insisted that 'The precedent set by our Ancestors a Century ago cannot but appear now more glorious to us than ever', but also that 'never till now, never till the happy aera of the French Revolution have we seen reason and the unalienable rights of mankind so completely triumph over Despotism and arbitrary Power'. More than the SFP, the Revolution Society sought to link the revolutions of 1688 and 1789: 'as *you*, perhaps, have profited from the example of our Ancestors, so shall we from *your* late glorious and splendid actions'. But it did so only rarely using the language of the *imitation* of France, and even here imitation was construed as encouraging a return to original principles in Britain: 'We hope to profit ourselves from your successful exertions in favour of Freedom; and that an imitation of your splendid actions may soon enable us to purify our own Government'.[77]

Yet occasionally, by the spring of 1791, the Revolution Society departed from such cautious formulations. In one letter it described the American constitution as 'the best Constitution known to civilized nations'. In another it seemed to give a priority to alteration over purification:

> Hitherto the superiority of our Constitution, over those of the rest of Europe, has extremely attached the majority of our countrymen to its forms, and they have tolerated its *faults*, from affection to its *excellencies*. But you have now given us such convincing practical instructions on the true formation of Governments, that we are persuaded, all our Fellow Citizens will soon be inspired with as ardent a desire of *improving* their own, as they formerly have been of *preserving* it.[78]

In three other respects, too, the Revolution Society was unwhiggish in its emphases. It was willing, if only rarely, to praise Paine's *Rights of Man*,[79] a distancing from which was generally now regarded as the *sine qua non* of Whig self-definition. It also invoked the British republican tradition, praising Harrington's *Oceana* as 'an excellent model of a commonwealth' (though the highest encomium was for 'The most valuable improvement ever made in the Representative System', the indirect election of national legislative representatives).[80] And it spoke from time to time that quasi-millennial, quasi-Quakerish language which linked the French Revolution to the cause of universal peace and brotherhood, thus shifting the political terms of reference dramatically:

> We joyfully anticipate the period when the World shall be *one* Family, without Tyrants, without Slaves, without Persecution, and without War. ... thus proving to the World, that Men, whom the folly of antiquity has called *natural* enemies, may unite in 'the

natural bond of brotherhood,' and strive together for the amelioration of human nature.[81]

* * *

Conclusion

The issue of political consistency, as we have seen, was central to the dispute between Burke and leading members of the Whig party, as well as the Whigs and some of those to their left. Which Whigs, then, were finally 'unwhigg'd' by their support for or opposition to the French revolution? Burke's opponents certainly felt that he had abandoned the 'Old Whig' standard by the eloquence of his defence of the despotic French *ancien régime*.[82] Burke as clearly thought himself within the old Whig camp, and many of his nineteenth-century interpreters agreed. The Foxites sought to remain Whigs, including within this definition the possibility of limited parliamentary reform, but discountenancing more extreme measures of reform. In the democratic application of the term, Fox was not a 'republican'; this even Burke conceded. Nor were the Foxites. Some, but few, of the 'new Whigs', may have been, depending on how the term was defined. But were they then still 'Whigs'? To prefer the French to the British constitution was clearly to 'unwhig' oneself; to sympathise with the revolution was not, unless (which was Burke's view) such sympathy combined with a contempt for the British constitution which invited a 'tacit' imitation of 'French' principles. This, as we have seen, was usually understood to mean 'innovation' or 'improvement' upon the British constitution. But it could also mean the wish to introduce constitutional changes described by some as 'British', such as an 'equal' suffrage, but understood by others as 'French'. But to seek universal manhood suffrage, and even equal electoral districts, was not, as such unwhiggish, though the timing of such demands was often seen to be. To be a 'radical' reformer – the term is just emerging to define this strand of opinion[83] – did not as such unwhig oneself. To agitate outside the party and outside of parliament, as the SFP did, was not necessarily unwhiggish; to elect members from plebeian societies to a 'convention' was. To criticise the monarch, the lords, and parliamentary corruption was not necessarily unwhiggish; to call for their replacement by a republic was. To praise the French republic's resistance to invaders who sought to restore absolutism was not necessarily unwhiggish; even to condemn the war as misguided and unjust after 1793 was not unwhiggish. To correspond with members of the National Assembly (before the war) did not as such, as we have seen, invite an unfavourable comparison of the British with the French constitution, though it might. To conspire with France to secure Britain's defeat, during the war, was, of course, simply treason. Yet while there was a grey area – ignoring the pun – between sympathy and conspiracy, such subtleties were increasingly lost as the war of opinion progressed. Later generations of Whigs could afford a more latitudinarian view of the Revolution; Macaulay, for instance, wrote that 'it is our deliberate opinion that the French Revolution, in spite of all its crimes and follies, was a great blessing to mankind'.[84] But throughout the 1790s and well beyond, such generosity proved too costly; for, paradoxically, the Revolution may well, rather than advancing the cause of parliamentary reform in Britain, have set it back for several decades.

Chapter Seven: William Godwin
The Enquiry Concerning Political Justice *(1793) and the Origins of Philosophical Anarchism*

Life and Background

Born in Wisbech in East Anglia on 3 March 1756, William Godwin was the seventh in a family of 13 children, whose father was a strict minister in a small Baptist sect, the Sandemanians. This group, followers of John Glas, upheld three ideals which Godwin would later develop in a secular manner in his chief work, the *Enquiry Concerning Political Justice* (1793): that belief in God must be wholly reasonable; that property should be subject to the needs of the congregation of the Church; and that the decisions of the Church should be unanimous, and reached through rational discussion.[1] After becoming a Sandemanian minister in 1778, Godwin abandoned his beliefs, and left the church to become a historian and novelist. *Political Justice*, now usually described as the founding text of British philosophical anarchism, brought Godwin immediate fame, and he helped, by swaying public opinion, to defeat the government's prosecution of leading radicals in 1794. Despite the success of his first major novel, *Caleb Williams* (1794), he failed to develop his literary career in the atmosphere of anti-Jacobin repression, and died in relative obscurity in 1836. The account of his ideas in this chapter will survey the chief doctrines of *Political Justice*, some crucial shifts in Godwin's thought in the later 1790s, and the development of his reputation in this period.

118

The Central Doctrines of the Enquiry Concerning Political Justice

Composed between September 1791 to January 1793, Godwin's *Political Justice* was to become the most sophisticated and far-reaching critique of the social and political status quo of its time.[2] Extending the anti-statist elements in Paine, Rousseau, Swift and others, and exuding a Spartan disdain for opulence and luxury, *Political Justice* proposed reverting to a relatively primitive subsistence economy without a centralised government, where individual independence would be maximised. More than any other response to the main issues debated in this period, *Political Justice* represented the most optimistic, utopian strand of the radical enlightenment in Britain, particularly in its quasi-Rousseauist form.[3] Although *Political Justice* is a complex work which explores many aspects of both the revolutionary debate and political thought more widely, five chief themes merit particular scrutiny here: (1) Godwin's theory of justice; (2) his plea for a simple, decentralised or 'anarchist' society which maximises independence; (3) his critique of existing political institutions, including democracy, and of patriotism as their moral justification; (4) his theory of property; (5) his account of the prospect of eventual human perfectibility.

Godwin's Theory of Justice

In his own time, Godwin was better known as the promoter of a system of moral philosophy which stressed the need for 'universal benevolence', or charity towards all, than for his anti-statist ideas. Yet this benevolence was to be applied in a peculiarly selective fashion. Godwin's moral philosophy offered a secular, utilitarian account in which public and private duty were met by a single, compelling injunction always to act with the aim of maximising the happiness of all, notably by assisting virtuous individuals. This was for Godwin to be contrasted to the Christian idea of loving one's neighbour equally, 'my neighbour's moral worth, and his importance to the general weal' being 'the only standard to determine the treatment to which he is entitled'.[4] If individuals were bound by a stern injunction to promote the public good, no gratitude was required for benefits so bestowed as a consequence of necessary duties. Nor, correspondingly, were concepts of abstract, conflicting or discretionary universal rights commensurate with this ideal; we see what a distance Godwin has moved from Paine.[5] Deference within a society of ranks, rather, where grovelling ingratiation to superiors was the norm, had to be supplanted by a rational ideal of moral progress, where respect was paid not to wealth and station, but genuine worth. And, consequently, too, private and domestic affections, where feeling and loyalty were given priority over the dictates of reason, were to be super-seded by universal benevolence.

Godwin's account of justice thus distinguished between the types of persons to whom we might owe obligations or assistance. In his famous example in which I can only rescue one of two persons from a fire, utility dictates saving the more eminent:

> In a loose and general view I and my neighbour are both of us men; and of consequence entitled to equal attention. But, in reality, it is probable that one of us is a being of more worth and importance than the other. A man is of more worth than a beast; because, being possessed of higher faculties, he is capable of a more refined and genuine happiness. In the same manner the illustrious archbishop of Cambray was of more worth than his valet, and there are few of us that would hesitate to pronounce, if his palace were in flames, and the life of only one of them could be preserved, which of the two ought to be preferred.[6]

This conception of intellectual elitism would appeal to many of Godwin's followers, and would remain in various guises a central theme in nineteenth-century British thought, notably in Carlyle, Mill, Ruskin and Arnold, as the decline of aristocratic predominance increasingly demanded that leadership be exercised by some other group. Yet this ideal as such, it would appear, could for Godwin be developed in any type of society. Why, then, did he come to contend that only where individual independence was maximised could justice develop most fully? And why was this only possible in circumstances of the greatest simplicity?

Godwin's 'Anarchism'

In order to understand what drove Godwin towards what would later be called anarchism,[7] we must appreciate the degree to which he felt that government had a negative influence on both individual inde-pendence and personal morality. Godwin clearly indicates in the first edition of *Political Justice* the centrality of the study of politics to moral improvement:

> If it could be proved that a sound political institution was of all others the most powerful engine for promoting individual good, or

on the other hand that an erroneous and corrupt government was
the most formidable adversary to the improvement of the species, it
would follow that politics was the first and most important subject of
human investigation.[8]

Part of the original aim in writing *Political Justice*, Godwin tells us,
was to correct the 'errors and imperfections'[9] of Montesquieu in *The
Spirit of the Laws* (1748); in other words, to deny that climate and geog-
raphy were primarily causal in explaining behaviour. In the early
stages of society, Godwin acknowledged, physical causes had been
more powerful than moral. With the progress of society, however,
ideas of political liberty circulated more widely, and – truth being
omnipotent and government founded upon opinion – freedom
increased, its extension being hindered only by the ability of despotic
governments to distort and suppress the truth. Hence general
experience confirmed 'the comparative inefficacy of climate, and the
superior influence of circumstances political and social'.[10]

Amongst these circumstances, then, which factors were of greatest
importance? Godwin's own conclusion was that government was an
extraordinarily powerful factor in moulding human character. As the
second edition of *Political Justice* stressed, 'it insinuates itself into our
personal dispositions, and insensibly communicates its own spirit to
our private transactions'.[11] But Godwin further deduced that this influence was primarily negative. Though he agreed with Montesquieu that
pure democracies could flourish in small states, he does not however
seem to have arrived at a much more 'anarchist' conclusion prior to
sometime in 1792. 'Of the desireableness of a government in the utmost
degree simple', Godwin wrote in the preface to the first edition, '[I]
was not persuaded but in consequence of ideas suggested by the
French Revolution'.[12] In his diary, 'Execution of Louis' stands out
starkly beneath the date, 21 January 1793. Godwin had finished
Political Justice only four days earlier.[13]

The chief source for Godwin's embrace of decentralised simplicity
was his early reading of Rousseau rather than, as Élie Halévy once suggested, Paine.[14] In a manuscript note Godwin claimed that 'Rousseau
discovered the omnipotence of politics *en fait du mal, pas en fait du
bien*'. Rousseau was thus

the greatest of all philosophers. He opened the career, and prepared the way, for all that has since been done in France, by establishing
the thesis – That the moral man is the offspring of sensation – and

infusing this corollary – That the vices of individuals arise out of the vices of governments.[15]

Rousseau had been the first to teach

that the imperfections of government were the only perennial source of the vices of mankind ... that government, however formed, was little capable of affording solid benefit to mankind.[16]

Although he had read many of Rousseau's works prior to the composition of *Political Justice*, Godwin returned to a number of them as he wrote, paying particularly close attention to the *Discourse on the Origins of Inequality*, Rousseau's brilliant and compelling account of the loss of human freedom.[17] Here the ideas referred to by Godwin as 'confederate action' and 'co-operation', play a central role. In Rousseau's eyes

as the bonds of servitude are formed merely by the mutual dependence of men on one another, and the reciprocal needs that unite them, it is impossible to make any man a slave, unless he first be reduced to a situation in which he cannot do without the help of others.

Independent man knew only a few cases 'in which mutual interest might justify him in relying upon the assistance of his fellows'. This dependency was itself one of the origins of property:

from the moment one man began to stand in need of the help of another, from the moment it appeared advantageous to any one man to have provisions for two, equality disappeared, property was introduced, work became indispensable, and vast forests became smiling fields, which man had to water by the sweat of his brow, and where slavery and misery were soon seen to germinate and grow up in the crops.[18]

Rousseau's conception of dependence – at least in Godwin's interpretation – is thus closely linked to his idea of the development of the division of labour. One of the great safeguards of virtue in the ancient republics was that:

Citizens were neither lawyers nor soldiers nor priests by profession; they performed all these functions as a matter of duty. That is the real secret of making everything proceed toward the common goal, and of preventing the spirit of faction from taking root at the expense of patriotism, so that the hydra of chicanery will not devour a nation.[19]

All of this Godwin took very much to heart, although his proposals for the abolition of the division of labour are ultimately rather different from Rousseau's. The most important connection between them in this regard, however, was Godwin's acceptance of Rousseau's essential preference for 'a society in which, each being equal to his occupation, no one should be obliged to commit to others the functions with which he was entrusted'.[20] Rousseau's only mistake, as far as Godwin was concerned, was that he 'substituted as the topic of his eulogium, the period that preceded government and laws, instead of the period that may possibly follow upon their abolition'.[21]

Establishing Godwin's debt to Rousseau does not, however, clarify why he concluded that, as the second edition put it, 'all confederate action is in the nature of government', and that 'all government corresponds, in a certain degree, to what the Greeks denominated a tyranny'.[22] This is the true root not merely of Godwin's anti-statism, but the specifically individualist nature of Godwin's 'anarchism'. Dependency, politics, and all forms of co-operation are identified in Godwin: individuals act upon each other when collected together in a manner normally associated with states, that is to say, in a word, repressively, the strong always dominating and manipulating, outwitting and imposing their opinions upon, the weak. This is the key question for understanding why Godwin turned against 'government' in the abstract, for all forms of 'dependency' were now seen by him as partaking in the nature of 'government'.

Godwin's notion that 'everything that is usually understood by the term co-operation is, in some degree, an evil' rests upon the idea (later developed by J.S. Mill) that 'individuality is of the very essence of intellectual excellence'.[23] A man could be thus 'neither great nor wise, but in proportion as he is independent'.[24] In contemporary political thought political independence was generally supposed to rest upon having sufficient property, which permitted independent and virtuous judgement. Godwin reduces this maxim to an epistemological maxim as such: the cultivation of truth requires, most essentially, that we think for ourselves. Knowledge for Godwin is primarily the product of individual rational reflection, and only secondarily a social construct. Our proneness to rely upon and defer to others rather than thinking for ourselves meant that the progress of individual knowledge necessitated as little interference from the opinions of others as possible. Hence the primacy of private judgement, the great Protestant Dissenting doctrine upholding the domain of individual conscience in religious matters, remains absolute. (And the case can be made for seeing moral self-direction as central not merely to later anarchist thought,[25] but liberalism more broadly.) Godwin thought some incidental modification of opinions, tempers, and habits was inevitable, and here sincerity, a republican as well as Dissenting virtue, became 'the most powerful engine of human improvement', intimately connected with 'inno-cence, energy, intellectual improvement, and philanthropy'.[26] But to preserve such independence of opinion a minimal uniformity of activ-ity must be ensured. Common labour, common meals, and all other forms of 'supererogatory co-operation' ought to be avoided, and Godwin seems to have thought that machinery would be invented with this exact purpose in mind.[27] Marriage, as the most immediate form of communal relationship, was similarly condemned. This extreme form of individualism thus took Godwin a great distance from Rousseau.

But in the absence of centralised forms of coercion, how could such a society function? To a substantial degree public order would be derived from the reciprocal moral control of public opinion. This was the true rationale for small states:

> To govern individuals in a petty and limited circle is easy. They may be governed, if sufficient judgment be exercised on the subject, by reason alone. But it is far otherwise with nations, with millions of men united under a single head. In a petty and limited circle, all exercise an inspection over all. There are no deeds that are concealed: the general censure or applause, follows immediately in the rear of every action that is performed. But in nations of men there is no eye pene-trating enough to detect every mischief in its commencement: craft is successful in escaping those consequences which justice would annex to injury. Men take pleasure in this species of dexterity, and the web of society is rent by the sallies of wantonness.[28]

Thus while natural independence, more merely doing as we please, 'without being accountable to the principles of reason', was 'highly detrimental to the general welfare', Godwin supported 'moral depend-ence', 'a censure to be exercised by every individual over the actions of another, a promptness to enquire into and judge them'. A 'general inspection that is exercised by the members of a limited circle over the conduct of each other' was reasonable; only 'all watchfulness that proposes for its object the calling in of force as the corrective of error' was invidious. Every individual thus would live under the public eye, constantly prey to the disapprobation of his neighbours, 'a species of coercion not derived from the caprice of men, but from the system of the universe', which would 'inevitably oblige' any malefactor 'either to reform or to emigrate'.[29]

Reversion to a simpler society also implied renouncing a complex division of labour. There would be no need for specialised professions (doctors, lawyers, ministers, soldiers, etc.) who acted against the general human interest. Doctors, for example, were known to prolong the illness of their patients for financial reasons, and all who were not cultivators forced others, as such, to provide their subsistence for them, thus depriving the majority of the leisure required for intellectual cultivation.[30] Godwin was particularly damning respecting the professional soldier:

> The man that is merely a soldier must always be uncommonly depraved. War, in his case, inevitably degenerates from the necessary precautions of a personal defence into a trade, by which a man sells his skill in murder, and the safety of his existence, for a pecuniary recompense. The man that is merely a soldier ceases to be, in the same sense as his neighbours, a citizen. He is cut off from the rest of the community, and has sentiments and a rule of judgment peculiar to himself. He considers his countrymen as indebted to him for their security; and by an unavoidable transition of reasoning, believes that, in a double sense, they are at his mercy.[31]

Thus no standing or professional army would be possible, or necessary, in a just and enlightened society.

Godwin's Critique of Existing Political Institutions

Much of *Political Justice* consists of a methodical and telling condemnation of the corruptions of existing political institutions. Godwin's arguments against both monarchy and aristocracy, and notably their tendency 'to undermine the virtues and the understandings of their subjects', were familiar to many readers by 1793. What is more surprising, and what links Godwin to, for instance, Tocqueville's account of republican practices in *Democracy in America*, as well as the later nineteenth-century anarchists, is his critique of representative democracy. He was willing to concede that, of all forms of government, democracy

> restores to man a consciousness of his value, teaches him, by the removal of authority and oppression, to listen only to the suggestions of reason, gives him confidence to treat all other men with frankness and simplicity, and induces him to regard them no longer as enemies against whom to be upon his guard, but as brethren whom it becomes him to assist.[32]

Nonetheless democracy generated a crucial defect: the tendency for tumult and confusion to arise when issues are submitted to the citizens at large. The only remedy for this was delegation or representation, which principle Godwin defends in certain circumstances. As long as mankind are imperfect, the first principle of government is 'having some man, or body of men, to act on the part of the whole'. Delegation, moreover, does not necessarily violate the principle that it is the business of every man to exercise his own judgement in all things, for there was no exact parallel between the individual judging cases which are 'truly his own', and examining those which are commonly estimated to be a concern of all. Thus

> the individuals to whom the delegation is made are either more likely, from talents or leisure, to perform the same function in the most eligible manner, or there is at least some public interest requiring that it should be performed by one or a few persons, rather than by every individual himself ... all contest as to the person who shall exercise a certain function and the propriety of resigning it is frivolous the moment it is decided how and by whom it can most advantageously be exercised. It is of no consequence that I am the parent of a child when it has once been ascertained that the child will live with greater benefit under the superintendence of a stranger.[33]

Voting after all discussions, however, commonly ruined whatever intellectual improvements the process of give and take might provide. Debates were also prone to descend into haranguing rants in which 'the orator no longer enquires after permanent conviction, but transitory effect. He seeks rather to take advantage of our prejudices than to enlighten our judgement'. Subtle arguments were reduced to clumsy but recognisable slogans to make voting possible, and then, by a 'flagrant insult upon all reason and justice', truth was decided by a mere majority labouring under the fatuous delusion of their collective wisdom. If the vote was by secret ballot this further encouraged dissimulation. Leaders with followers to humour lost their moral bearings and intellectual energy, moreover. Drawn into the mass, even 'men of the most elevated genius dwindle into vulgar leaders when they become involved in the busy scenes of public life'. The factionalism of parties and cabals, where loyalty was rewarded before principle, would disappear 'in a country where opposition of sentiments, and a struggle of interests, were not allowed to assume the formalities of distinct institutions'. For all of these reasons, national assemblies should be employed as sparingly as possible, preferably only during extraordinary emergencies.[34] Finally, Godwin also rejected the doctrine of patriotism, or love of country, the basis of most previous republican conceptions of public duty, as too limited, opting instead for universal benevolence:

> The love of our country has often been found to be a deceitful principle, as its direct tendency is to set the interests of one division of mankind in opposition to another, and to establish a preference built upon accidental relations and not upon reason. ... A wise and well informed man will not fail to be the votary of liberty and justice. ... But his attachment will be to the cause, as the cause of man, and not to the country.[35]

Godwin's Theory of Property and Account of Luxury

The theory of property outlined in book eight of *Political Justice* would remain amongst the most influential sections of the book.[36] In it, particularly in the first edition, Godwin was primarily concerned to argue that inequality of property was the greatest source of social evil, crime, and selfishness. Nothing was 'more pernicious to the human mind than the love of opulence', and the effects of luxury were the principal reason why a simpler society was preferable.[37] Here Godwin developed the idea of a simple society in which all were cultivators, deriving their own subsistence from the land, and distributing any surplus produce according to need, without exchange as such. If the poor were now enslaved in order to furnish luxuries to the rich, the ideal society would see superfluity banished. Thus 'the necessity for the greater part of the manual industry of mankind would be superseded; and the rest, being

amicably shared among the active and vigorous members of the community, would be burthensome to none'. Labour could accordingly be
reduced to a few hours per day, and free time devoted to intellectual
pursuits.[38] Inequality of property was at present a primary cause of war
and selfish behaviour. If all provided plenty for themselves, however,
sharing

> alike the bounties of nature, these sentiments would inevitably
> vanish. No man being obliged to guard his little store, or to provide,
> with anxiety and pain, for his restless wants, each would lose his
> individual existence in the thought of the general good. No man
> would be an enemy of his neighbour, for they would have no subject
> of contention; and of consequence, philanthropy would resume the
> empire which reason assigns her.[39]

In the present, however, how should property be most justly managed? As in the Sandemanian church in which he had been raised,
Godwin insisted in his chapter on justice that all property was held as
a 'trust' over which we are merely stewards:

> my neighbour is in want of ten pounds than I can spare. There is no
> law of political situation that has been made to reach this case, and
> to transfer this property from me to him. But in the eye of simple
> justice, unless it can be shown that the money can be more benefi-
> cially employed, his claim is as complete as if he had my bond in his
> possession, or had supplied me with goods to the amount.[40]

Yet while the first edition of *Political Justice* was being composed,
Godwin became concerned that he might be seen to be promoting an
indiscriminate charity, by giving our surplus wealth to relieve the wants
of all the poor. This might be erroneous on at least two counts: it conflicted with his original theory of justice, by which we should help those
most likely to contribute to social progress to a greater degree, not on
the basis of need as such; and that merely giving the poor money as such
might not be the best means of aiding the ultimate goal of maximising
individual independence. In Book Eight, thus, he considered amongst
other objections the view 'that we find among different men very different degrees of labour and industry, and that it is not just they should
receive equal reward'.[41] This problem he clearly found puzzling for a
considerable period of time, for there were various amendments made

in this respect in both the second (1795) and third (1798) editions of the text. In the final analysis, Godwin acknowledged that some inequality of property ownership was justifiable on the basis of merit, or 'the particular object of utility any individual is engaged in promoting'.[42] At the same time, however, he maintained that providing the poor with money as such was indeed insufficient: what was requisite was to provide them with the means of feeding themselves. This, as we will see below, would become the starting point for Malthus's *Essay on Population*. Moreover, Godwin also reinforced a right to private property (in view of accusations of being a 'leveller') which left the wealthy a duty – but a discretionary rather than an absolute duty – to assist the poor, and gave the poor no absolute right to any substantial share of the property of the rich as such, only an imperfect or passive claim. By 1798, thus, the doctrine that that property therefore belongs 'to him who most wants it, or to whom the possession of it will be most beneficial'[43] was replaced by the view that all have 'a right to that, the exclusive possession of which being awarded to him, a greater sum of benefit or pleasure will result than could have arisen from its being otherwise appropriated'.[44] 'Want', as such, was now clearly subordinated to utility.

Godwin's Conception of Perfectibility

Finally, *Political Justice* became well known for Godwin's proposal that mankind were capable of an indefinite improvement. Reason might eventually come to govern the passions, including sexual desire, thus obviating the objection that over-population would rapidly destroy the plenty of a primitive society. Machines might be devised, like a self-moving plough, which could lighten still further the burden of labour, though how such technological complexity was to be combined with minimal co-operation and extensive decentralisation was problematic. Mind, in short, Godwin asserted, quoting Benjamin Franklin, might one day reign supreme over matter.[45] Rarely have the prospects of reason been invested with such confidence.

The Enquirer *(1797) and Godwin's Later Views: Doubts Respecting Simplicity*

In rewriting *Political Justice* for the second and third editions (1796, 1798), Godwin made a number of important alterations in his argument which clearly reflect his response to the revolution debate.[46]

In the second edition, with his friend John Thelwall's activities particularly in mind, he strengthened his argument against violent revolutionary change and mass political activity, and stressed that progress would occur as 'rational enquirers' ascertained political truths through cultivated intercourse. He now increasingly gave greater credence to the feelings, as opposed to reason, as the basis of voluntary action.[47] The method of *Political Justice*, he now argued, as it had been outlined in the first edition, was 'incommensurate to our powers':

> that the cause of political reform, and the cause of intellectual and literary refinement, are inseparably connected; those who would promote reform must be found amiable in their personal manners, and even attached to the cultivation of miscellaneous enquiries.[48]

In an essay entitled 'Of Politeness' in *The Enquirer: Reflections on Education, Manners, and Literature* (1797), Godwin now acknowledged that 'men of bold temper ... smitten with a love for the sublimer virtues' were often accused of being enemies of politeness.[49] But he now said that if moral behaviour included the consultation of 'the transitory feelings of his neighbours' as well as 'exerting oneself for multitudes', lesser moralities, being 'of incomparably more frequent demand' could exert great social good.

Such conclusions clearly entailed a revision of the doctrine of universal benevolence. The 'intellectual eye of man', (here Godwin perhaps echoed Burke's appeal to our 'little platoon')[50] was described as perhaps

> formed rather for the inspection of minute and near, than of immense and distant objects. We proceed most safely, when we enter upon each portion of our process, as it were, de novo, and there is danger, if we are too exclusively anxious about consistency of system, that we may forget the perpetual attention we owe to experience, the pole-star of truth. An incessant recurrence to experiment and actual observation, is the second method of investigating truth, and the method adopted in the present volume.[51]

By the end of the 1790s this concession of the contingency of perception and knowledge upon immediate experience had persuaded Godwin that *Political Justice* was erroneous in several of its chief principles. Reflecting in 1800 on these mistakes, Godwin acknowledged that

> Too much stress is ... laid in the *Enquiry Concerning Political Justice*, on the inferences from the doctrine of necessity. That doctrine may perhaps be beneficially applied toward extirpating the odious sentiment of revenge, and moderating the fury of political and private animosities. But we live in a world of delusion; we appreciate persons and things, not by an impartial standard, but from their nearness to ourselves: nor is this by any means without its use.[52]

When he came sometime in this period to draw up notes for possible further revisions of *Political Justice*, Godwin's self-judgement was even harsher, though he clearly wished to reconcile benevolence with his new theory. In a note entitled 'Claims of the Individual', he wrote of the 'miserable nature of benevolence' where 'self mixes in all our actions':

> I should neither accumulate money, nor benefit my neighbour, if I did not find a personal gratification in these actions ... Benevolence is the love of my neighbour, and, as this passion is neither the first in our history, nor the most congenial to the minds of man, we should admit no opportunity to cultivate it [sic] ... We should begin with ourselves and our own personal sphere, for this our own nature obliges us to do: but we should go on, for of this we are capable, to see things as they are, and to put ourselves in the place of a superhuman spectator of moral concerns ... The first tendency of the human mind is to be affected by present and sensible attractions and disgusts. By habits, civilisation and education, we become capable of foresight, of being affected by absent objects and in the proportion of our calculations respecting them. The man who approaches most nearly in his feelings to the regarding an object in the same manner, whether (near) or present is most intellectual in his character, most judicious in his conduct, and most likely to secure to himself a permanent happiness. He is also a man of the greatest civilisation.[53]

These themes also led by 1798 to a wholesale re-evaluation on Godwin's part of his opposition to luxury in the first edition of *Political Justice*. What 'simplicity' meant for Godwin in 1793, as we have seen, was primarily simplicity of manners, which ought ideally to rest upon simplicity of social organisation. Upon this matter both Dissenters and republicans were perfectly agreed, since both (Godwin assumed) promoted frankness and sincerity as the most appropriate behaviour. And it was to meet this end, among others, that property was eventually to become more equal. 'Simplicity of manners' was in turn juxtaposed to the corruption and artificiality of manners imposed by the diffusion of luxury – itself the product of a vastly unequal distribution of property – throughout society. Nonetheless Godwin was well aware that the ideal of cultivated and polished manners was associated (for example in Hume, its greatest populariser), with a highly unequal society and mixed (if not absolute) monarchy, not with a republic or simple society of any type. The virtues of simplicity, frankness and sincerity thus collided with the image of a highly cultivated, artistically sensitive society of refined behaviour, and with Godwin's more general goal of intellectual cultivation.

What evidence is there that Godwin became aware of such a conflict? In the first edition of *Political Justice*, Godwin included two chapters which dealt specifically with the subject of luxury, book 1, chapter 8, 'Of the Objection to These Principles from the Influence of Luxury', respecting political institutions; and book 8, chapter 3, 'Of the Objection to These Principles from the Admirable Effects of Luxury', in regard to property. In the first instance his concern was to argue that a nation which had already experienced the widespread effects of luxury could nonetheless undergo a moral regeneration. This notion had been 'partly founded upon the romantic notions of pastoral life and the golden age'. But, Godwin insisted,

> Innocence is not virtue. Virtue demands the active employment of an ardent mind in the promotion of the general good. No man can be eminently virtuous who is not accustomed to an extensive range of reflection. He must see all the benefits to arise from a disinterested proceeding, and must understand the proper method of producing those benefits. Ignorance, the slothful habits and limited views of uncultivated life, have not in them more of true virtue, though they may be more harmless, than luxury, vanity, and extravagance.[54]

The alterations to Godwin's views in Book 8 indicate a shift in his conception of luxury. In 1793 Godwin had included in chapter 1 of book 8 his 'Estimate of Luxury – Its Pernicious Effects on the Individual Who Partakes Of It'. This had been primarily concerned to refute the Mandevillian paradox of 'private vices, public benefits' and its corollary, that we should praise the prodigal who spent his wealth employing thousands 'to procure dainties for his table, who unites distant nations in commerce to supply him with furniture, and who encourages the fine arts and all the sublimities of invention to furnish decorations for his residence'. Godwin furnished a number of moral grounds for rejecting trade of this type. But he answered this specific objection by arguing that the real issue at the heart of the luxury debate was that population growth might be impeded by the circulation of luxury goods and their attendant vices. But he resolved this problem by suggesting that if sufficient motives could 'be furnished to excite men to agriculture, there is not doubt, that population may be carried on to any extent that the land can be made to maintain'.[55]

By 1798 Godwin's argument had altered markedly. Now, ignoring the problem of population growth, he focused upon the proposition that 'elegance of taste, refinement of sentiment, depth of penetration, and largeness of science' were not merely 'the noblest ornaments of man'. They were also 'connected with inequality; they are the growth of luxury ... To this cause we are indebted for the arts of architecture, painting, music and poetry ... In a state of equality we must always have remained, and, with equality restored, we must again become, barbarians'.[56] Godwin's response to this objection was to contend that the choice was not between a reversion to savagery and the refinement of the few but slavery of the many in contemporary society. A state of luxury and inequality might 'perhaps' have been 'necessary to pass in order to arrive at the goal of civilization'. But if so, it was not 'necessary to its support. We may throw down the scaffolding, when the edifice is complete'. The love of distinction and other forms of motivation would ensure that 'he who has tasted the pleasures of refinement and knowledge will not relapse into ignorance'. Luxury, moreover, Godwin now insisted, could be understood as a vice if it entailed 'something which is to be enjoyed exclusively by some, at the expense of undue privations, and a partial burthen upon others'.[57] If, however, it were defined as the provision of 'every accommodation which is not absolutely necessary to maintain us in sound and healthful existence ... the procuring and communicating luxuries may then be virtuous' because 'the end of virtue is to add to the sum of pleasurable sensation ... we ought not to study that we may live, but to live that we may replenish existence with the greatest number of unallayed, exquisite and substantial enjoyments?'[58]

Utility, with luxury now defined as an essential component in human happiness, seemed to have won the day. If, as Godwin claimed, such enjoyments could be achieved with only half an hour's labour per day, the remaining time would be spent 'not probably in idleness, not all men, and the whole of their time, in the pursuit of intellectual attainments'. Instead they might devote themselves as well to the production of those 'accommodations … which will give us real pleasure, after the insinuations of vanity and ostentation shall have been dismissed'. Godwin even acknowledged that 'a considerable portion of time would probably be dedicated, in an enlightened community, to the production of such accommodations'. Such labour would be seen as voluntary, even as 'a source of amusement and variety'. Consequently, it appeared 'that a state of equality need not be a state of Stoical simplicity, but is compatible with considerable accommodation, and even, in some sense, with splendour; at least, if by splendour we understand copiousness of accommodation, and variety of invention for the purposes of accommodation'. No reversion to simplicity, as such, was thus necessary.[59] This is not to argue that Godwin renounced all desire to see society considerably more simplified, only that he now saw this problem as considerably more complex than he had in 1793, and was aware of how his original position had been both interpreted and misinterpreted. But we can see clearly how mistaken it is to identify the ultimate social vision of the *Political Justice* of 1796 and 1798 with, for example, the pastoral imagery of one of his early novels, *Imogen*, or even Godwin's account of simplicity in 1793.

The Reception of Political Justice

That *Political Justice* met with critical acclaim is clear. It quickly sold as many as four thousand copies, no mean achievement for a three guinea work of moral philosophy which William Pitt thought too expensive to merit prosecution.[60] Its themes were taken up in a variety of works, including at least one literary utopia of note.[61] A few years after its publication a sympathetic account of Godwin noted that

within a few weeks of the appearance of that work, his immediate object, the acquisition of fame and its consequent power in the application of his talents, was obtained. He was not merely made known to the public, but was ranked at once among men of the highest genius and attainments … the work … was scarcely published when it was everywhere the theme of popular conversation and praise. Perhaps no work of equal bulk ever had such a number of readers; and certainly no book of such profound inquiry ever made so many proselytes in an equal space of time.[62]

To the young solicitor Henry Crabb Robinson the work 'had an excellent effect on my mind – it made me feel more generously ... His idea of justice I adopted and still retain', adding that *Political Justice* 'gave a turn to my mind, and in effect directed the whole course of my life ... [but] which, after producing a powerful effect on the youth of that generation, has now sunk into unmerited oblivion'.[63]

William Hazlitt's comments are also well known:

No work in our time gave such a blow to the philosophical mind of the country ... Tom Paine was considered for the time as a Tom Fool to him, Paley an old woman, Edmund Burke a flashy sophist. Truth, moral truth, it was supposed, had here taken up its abode; and these were the oracles of its thought.[64]

Why was *Political Justice* so attractive? The last part of Hazlitt's comment gives us a good indication of how *Political Justice* was read by many amongst the younger, literate middle classes, particularly the 'inferior votaries of literature' contemptuously dismissed by the *Anti-Jacobin Review*.[65] It was seen as a moralizing text, 'a metaphysical and logical commentary on some of the most beautiful and striking texts of Scripture'.[66] Another reader commented that

it is impossible to ascend into the region of Mr. Godwin's speculations without improvement of the heart and enlargement of the understanding, and without carrying with us into the world we are obliged to act in, something to purify our conduct and ameliorate our condition.[67]

Godwin's impact on the plebeian reform movement was more limited. But he certainly influenced John Thelwall, who described *Political Justice* as 'the most extensive plan of freedom and innovation ever discussed by any writer in the English language'.[68] Thelwall read excerpts from the work on coercion and punishment to a London Corresponding Society meeting in 1794. He also lectured on the abuse of the professions,[69] and was even quoted as asserting that there was no necessity for law,[70] and that gratitude was no virtue,[71] since individuals should act always according to the dictates of social duty. These were all themes prominently associated with Godwin. He was less enthused when Godwin attacked his behaviour as a lecturer in 1795, however.[72]

The most famous of those to fall for any length of time under Godwin's intellectual spell were the poets Coleridge and Southey, whose 'pantisocracy' project for establishing a colony in Virginia based upon community of property and collective intellectual inquiry certainly owed something to Godwin.[73] Besides applauding Godwin's opposition to violence, another budding poet, William Wordsworth, was particularly struck by his interpretation of the philosophy of necessity, and his opposition to ideas of free will; Hazlitt reported him saying, 'Throw aside your books of chemistry ... and read Godwin on necessity' to a young student in the Temple.[74] What seems to have most enthused him was the notion that the enlightenment of all mankind would gradually take place through the progress of reason and dissemination of truth, and that necessity invalidated the notions of individual guilt, crime, and desert. Such views, along with his general exaltation of the individual, in fact, seemingly attracted most of Godwin's young devotees. But Wordsworth would eventually turn sharply against Godwin's individualism, seeing in it a mirroring of the 'reckless competition and race for wealth' commended by the political economists, as Leslie Stephen later put it.[75]

Coleridge was also taken by the doctrine of necessity, Godwin's notion of perfectibility, the notion of vice as the product of circumstances, and the subordination of the individual to the public good and the possibility of disinterested behaviour. He was certainly attracted to Godwin's intellectual elitism, which doubtless influenced his own later doctrine of the leading role to be played by a new 'clerisy', which in turn would be taken up by J.S. Mill.[76] What most distressed him about Godwin, however, was his utilitarianism, the condemnation of private affections, which Coleridge felt underpinned wider forms of benevolence, and especially, Godwin's opposition to Christianity. To Coleridge, belief in God was not only in itself right; it also enjoined vital social duties which otherwise were not sufficiently obligatory.[77] (Other potential Godwinians, such as Charles Lamb and Robert Southey, who 'all but worshipped' Godwin,[78] were also repelled by his seeming atheism and thus drawn away from his system generally.)[79] Coleridge's economic ideas also show a clear

Godwinian debt, however, not only in the 1790s, when he denigrated luxury, urged a fairer division of labour, and condemned all who oppressed the lower orders, but also after 1815, when, with Southey, he became a major critic of the evils of the commercial and manufacturing system.

Conclusion

As we saw above (Ch. 4), reactions to Godwin must be seen in the context of the emergence of the issue of 'levelling', or social equality, during the first stage of the debate over the revolution. Well after the controversy over Paine's *Rights of Man* had died down, accusations of primitivism were – with rather more justification – being made against Godwin by his critics, some of whom would continue to charge him with promoting a 'brutal stage of savage equality' where 'independence' merely disguised the rule of the strongest,[80] and only profound ignorance would result.[81] Such charges doubtless help to explain some of the essential changes in Godwin's approach to luxury, and would, as we will see (below, conclusion) form the starting point for Malthus's famous assessment of Godwinian utopianism in the *Essay on Population*.

Chapter Eight: John Thelwall
Luxury, Property and the Rights
of Labour

Introduction

After Paine fled to France in late 1792, the leading republican writer
in Britain was John Thelwall. Born in Covent Garden on 27 July 1764,
Thelwall was apprenticed as a silk-mercer and tailor, and was then a
student of divinity, medicine and law. The author of *Poems on Various
Subjects* (1787), and later friend of Coleridge and Wordsworth, Thelwall
moved from a youthful Toryism towards radical principles, and
became a lecturer, journalist, and political pamphleteer. He joined
the London Corresponding Society in late 1793, and was tried for
treason in 1794, but acquitted after six months' imprisonment.[1] Though
he resumed lecturing, harassment forced him to retreat to rural Wales
in 1797. He later became a successful lecturer on elocution, and
re-entered radical politics as editor of the *Champion* newspaper from
1818–21. He died on 17 February 1834.

Republicanism, Poverty and Luxury: Thelwall's Intellectual
Development and Significance

The salient quality in Thelwall's thought was a shift in the mid-1790s,
parallel to that of Paine and Godwin, towards seeing property rights as
central to radical argument, and away from a classical republican, and
especially Rousseauesque, solution to the need to reconcile inequality
of property with political virtue by resisting refinement and luxury.

138

Politically, Thelwall, like many radicals, early concluded that the French revolution presented a grand opportunity to purge corrupt British morals and politics, and to renew both civic and private virtue through moral and political reform. By 1794, Thelwall was wholeheartedly committed to the principles of universal suffrage and annual parliaments.[2] In much he happily followed Paine, whose works, a spy reported, he once said 'alone contained the true principles of government'.[3] Like Paine, he considered that pure democracy was practicable only in small states. A modern republic meant 'a government so constituted and organised that the whole body of the people may convey their will to the heart and centre of government, and by means of representatives and properly appointed officers, conduct the business of the country according to the general voice of the people'.[4] Politically, Thelwall remained devoted to

> one grand principle, namely, that the people are the fountain of all power, honour, trust and distinction – that they have the absolute right of choosing the representatives that are to make their laws, and of cashiering not only those representatives whenever they have forfeited their confidence, but all such officers and magistrates, also, as by their arbitrary proceedings or corrupt practices impede the due execution of those laws. A principle like this, if followed through all its conclusions, must shortly annihilate all party. It is not possible, if you admit so broad a principle, for any combination of families, however great or powerful ... to grasp and monopolize all power in their hands, as they now do.

'The quick rotation of magistracy and subjection' was thus 'the very soul of the republican system'.[5] Thelwall's political agenda also included the creation of a civic militia instead of a standing army; the abolition of the slave trade; the reduction of the national debt and reform of the funding system; and the ending of all unfair forms of taxation. Only by such reforms could good institutions be constructed, and civic virtue be reinforced, for 'liberty and good laws' alone made 'good men'.[6]

The maintenance of civic virtue, however, also required for Thelwall a relative equality of property, and this in turn implied, Thelwall thought, in the early 1790s, a restriction of commerce and the luxury trade in particular. More than anything else, it was increasing poverty in the mid-1790s which altered the framework of political debate. By 1795, and for much of the next decade, near-famine conditions and rising food prices generated a growing number of disturbances aimed at preventing speculators from withholding grain from the market until prices rose. As the burden of the poor's rate grew heavier, landlords complained bitterly that they were forced to shoulder this considerable tax by themselves. Merchants, meanwhile, contended that famine could be forestalled only by leaving the market alone, for even if speculators did profit by hoarding grain, their actions at least ensured that some food was always held in reserve. (This view was succinctly expressed in Burke's *Thoughts and Details on Scarcity*, 1795).[7]

Until the mid-1790s, Thelwall was highly critical of commerce, and affected a deeply rural and pastoral, Rousseauesque, as well as classical, orientation. The growth of commerce and luxury, that 'opiate of the soul', as he put it in 1794, with the increasing selfishness and rapacity of the rich, had debased political institutions and manners, weakened the national fibre, and lessened that love of liberty which alone protected a free nation.[8] His hand never far from a history of ancient Greece or Rome, Thelwall in the early 1790s in particular often harkened back to the simple manners and staunch patriotism of their heroic ages. But the republican virtue of the ancients might, he hoped, be wedded to the more cosmopolitan and peaceable vision which the phrase 'universal benevolence' conjured up for many reformers in this period.

Until about 1795, Thelwall's ideas about commerce were thus certainly closer to the neo-classical republicanism of Burgh, and to the Rousseauist pastoralism of Godwin (in 1793) and his followers, than to Paine. In the three volumes of his poetry and narrative published as *The Peripatetic* in 1793, Thelwall adopted the device of a ramble through London and elsewhere to comment on social conditions. He warned that commerce was a 'doubtful' and 'partial' good which often fostered war, spread 'the poison'd stream of luxury', and 'Fatten'st a few upon the toils of all'. He lamented that amidst 'Grandeur and Opulence', the poor man was ignored, and too often driven from 'his cottage, from his little garden, and his bubbling spring, to seek, perhaps, a miserable habitat in the smoky confines of some increasing town'. How could a country like Britain be termed 'wealthy', he demanded, when the majority of its inhabitants could afford meat barely once a week? Thelwall regretted that the concentration of landed wealth had curtailed the rental of small allotments. Once master and labourer had been 'near enough to a level to sympathise in each other's misfortunes; and the reciprocity of kindness might rationally be expected'. Now 'the system' threw 'every advantage into the hands of the wealthy few, at the expence of the entire depression of the many'.[9]

Some of this hostility to commerce Thelwall retained well into the mid-1790s. In a poem entitled 'To Luxury', written in 1794, he condemned its 'noxious weeds'. In 'To Simplicity of Manners', he praised 'those ancient Manners – simple and severe', which Sparta in particular had cherished.[10] These alone, Thelwall believed, upheld that political virtue without which no free state could long survive. And they were compatible solely with a far more egalitarian society than nearly any which had existed in Europe since the rise of feudalism. Individual reformation of manners, he hoped, would commence a new era of self-restraint. In his London lectures of 1795–6, Thelwall thus powerfully exhorted his listeners to

> labour to abolish luxury ... Let us in our own houses, at our own tables, by our exhortations to our friends, by our admonitions to our enemies, persuade mankind to discard those tinsel ornaments and ridiculous superfluities which enfeeble our minds, and entail voluptuous diseases on the affluent, while diseases of a still more calamitous description overwhelm the oppressed orders of society, from the scarcity resulting from this extravagance. Thus let us administer to the relief of those who, having the same powers of enjoyment with ourselves, have a right to, at least, an equal participation of all the necessaries of life, which are the product of their labour.[11]

He also reminded the London Corresponding Society that 'a love of virtuous poverty' was amongst the indispensible prerequisites of a people 'desiring to obtain or to preserve the blessings of liberty'.[12]

But it was no longer solely the domain of citizenship and the reform of political corruption which interested Thelwall by the mid-1790s. Thelwall remained anxious about the economic burdens which the 'inordinate taxation' of a corrupt state imposed upon the poor, and even estimated that four-fifths of the labourer's product went towards 'the support of placemen, pensioners, and other tools of corruption'.[13] Increasingly, however, he also considered relations between employer and employee in the sphere of civil society as crucial to any examination of the issue of wealth and poverty. By 1796, Thelwall began to see the profits of rapacious employers as a key cause of poverty, and to conceive of justice increasingly in terms of fair wages, rather than solely the accession of political rights.[14] Simultaneously, he began to accept commerce to a much greater degree than formerly. He now began to plead for an end of scarcity by establishing universal freedom of trade in surplus produce. At the same time, his attitudes towards trade and luxury became markedly more sophisticated. Any reversion towards 'simplicity', in particular, Thelwall now began to see as neither possible nor necessary. Against a scheme strongly reminiscent of Godwin's position in the first edition of the *Enquiry Concerning Political Justice*, for reducing human labour to half an hour daily by abolishing luxuries and producing only necessities, thus, Thelwall now conceded, as Godwin would do in the *Enquirer* a year later, that buildings, books, paintings and the like were advantageous, provided they did not grind the poor down. Though he still feared its effect on manners, Thelwall now saw the crucial problem of luxury as lying less in its tendency to engender moral and political corruption than in its exacerbation of social inequality. (We have seen that Godwin was edging towards a similar stance at about the same time). 'Commerce', he now submitted, 'uncorrupted by monopolizing speculation', was 'one of the greatest advantages that result from social union'. When conducted 'on liberal and equal principles', it could help eradicate narrow patriotic chauvinism, 'and convince us that we ought to extend the narrow sphere of our affections'. Commerce had been vital in breaking the stranglehold of feudal tyranny, and could do much to secure future peace. Thelwall's shift in concerns, thus, was towards the monopolistic results of commerce and away from the moral effects of luxury.[15] Hence he now began to scrutinise carefully the origins and nature of modern trade, and to grapple with the problem of poverty from an urban, political and economic more than a narrowly moral perspective. The result would be his claim that not only were liberty and opulence compatible, but that their reconciliation could be achieved while promoting much greater social equality.

Though it clearly had other causes, including a probable re-reading of Paine's *Rights of Man*, this new sophistication in Thelwall's views, and his manifest optimism about commerce, certainly resulted in part from his close scrutiny of the *Wealth of Nations* at this time. He now paid greater heed to the categories of political economy, and notably the all-important language of 'productive and unproductive labour', than any other radical in this period.[16] Examining in several lectures the causes of the dearness and scarcity of provisions in 1795, a near-famine year, Thelwall agreed with Smith that 'real wealth' consisted only in 'the quantum of real necessaries and comforts'. He praised 'the fair, the just, and rational system of commerce' which exported a surplus only after home demands had been met, and whose advantage was that it helped 'prevent excessive want and scarcity'. 'My idea of the first and genuine principles of just government, with respect to agriculture', he proposed, was 'to produce the largest quantity of the necessaries of life, and to promote the most equal distribution of those articles'. This implied that the interest of the domestic consumer should be placed above profits from foreign trade in food. The object of agriculture ought not 'to be commerce, but the comfort and accommodation of the people', which were being disregarded by 'monied speculators'. This would help to avoid the extreme inequality which characterised the present commercial system. Instead, society should be linked by 'imperceptible gradations of rank, where step rises above step by slow degrees' until all were 'connected together by inseparable interests'. This gentle hierarchy was superior even to any 'golden age of absolute equality'. But such an ideal was unattainable where monopoly existed. Speculation, 'the over eager pursuit of opulence among one class of the people', had eradicated the moral advantages of a 'fair and equitable process of exchange'.[17] But levelling the existing system of ranks was no answer either, and community of goods he elsewhere referred to as 'a wild and absurd scheme' impracticable on a large scale.[18] As Thelwall told a huge crowd in late 1795:

> Equality of property … is totally impossible in the present state of the human intellect and industry, and if one of you once could be reduced to attempt a system so wild and extravagant, you could only give to rascals and cut-throats an opportunity, by general pillage and assassination, of transferring all property into their own hands, and establishing a tyranny more intolerable than anything of which you now complain.[19]

Instead, Thelwall insisted, what he sought was an equality of rights, 'the equality which protects the poor against the insults and oppressions of the rich, as well as the rich against the insults and invasions of the poor'.[20]

This embracing of 'fair' commerce entailed a new look at luxury. Referring in October 1795 to a plan by an African colonisation projector, the Swedenborgian C.B. Wadstrom, which proposed supplying individuals only according to their real, rather than their 'artificial' wants, Thelwall agreed – and his readiness to pose the question in these terms is notable – that this addressed 'the important dilemma of simplicity or luxury'. But it is clear that his sympathy towards simplicity was undergoing a vital shift. Taking a very different tack from his position in 1793, he argued at length that commercial luxury did not inevitably corrupt any nation. Athenian republicanism, for example, sprang from a 'generous and magnanimous virtue' which a commercial nation like Athens might also possess. But it could do so only where greater independence resulted from individuals reaping 'the profits of their individual exertions'. This alone aided 'the general happiness and welfare', and might therefore be derived from trade as well as landownership. The chief flaw in modern commerce was thus that the necessaries of life, especially grain, had become objects 'not of open traffic, but of commercial speculation'. True freedom of trade would lower prices to the point where only 'a living profit' would be attained, which was in the general interest. But commercial freedom in a republic also required civil and political liberty, which in turn rested on 'a simplicity of manners, a fortitude of character, and a pure and generous system of morality'. These, Thelwall confessed, were more often found at present in largely agricultural countries like Switzerland. Earlier republics, like ancient Greece, had possessed them only because commerce had increased the independence of all by being

> made to produce equal advantage to every citizen of the community. Every man participated not only in the labour, but in the profit ... the rich merchant, the great landed proprietor, and higher classes of society, are enabled to enjoy more luxuries, and live in great pomp, the tendency of the laws and institutions of society ought to be such, that the labourer also will have his proportion of the advantage, eat with more comfort, sleep in a better cabin, and be enabled to give his offspring a better education, and a better knowledge of their rights and duties.[21]

Virtuous Poverty Abandoned: The Rights of Nature Against the Usurpations of Establishments *(1796)*

The problem was how to accomplish this in a vastly more unequal modern society. In *The Rights of Nature Against the Usurpations of Establishments* (1796), Thelwall outlined how the majority might share in the advantages of commerce, and achieve opulence without necessarily sacrificing virtue, albeit at the expense of simplicity. Though the two were likely unaware of each other's tracts, Thelwall like Paine now thought that demands for both greater social equality and increasing opulence could be reconciled by enriching the labouring classes.[22] In his 1795 lectures, and at one of the great London Corresponding Society meetings that year, Thelwall stressed that the standard of living of the poor, but also of tradesmen, shopkeepers, ploughmen and mechanics, had been falling steadily. The cause lay in 'the corruption that has poisoned the government and constitution of this country', with 'the luxury and splendour of political plunderers' coming from the oppression of the so-called lower orders, which allowed greedy monopolisers and forestallers to thrive. Thelwall's chief concern here was to tie economic discontent to the necessity for political reform. 'If you had not a system of borough-mongering corruption – that is to say, a system of political monopoly', he insisted, 'there could be no mono-poly of trade, much less of the necessaries of life; and above all, the price of labour would keep pace with the price of these necessaries'. In the *Rights of Nature*, his central premise was that every man and woman had

a sacred and inviolable claim, growing out of the fundamental maxim, upon which alone all property is supported, to some com-forts and enjoyments, in addition to the necessaries of life, and to some 'tolerable leisure for such discussion, and some means of such information', as may lead to an understanding of their rights; with-out which they can never understand their duties.[23]

Thelwall's aim here was to give the poor and labouring classes greater independence. But, while Paine's redistributive plans assumed an essentially static economy, and focussed on taxing landed wealth, his own ideal was more dynamic and commercially oriented. Society had the duty 'not merely to protect, but to improve the physical, the moral, and intellectual enjoyments ... of the whole population of the state. It ought to expand the faculties, encrease the sympathies, harmonise the passions, and promote the general welfare'.[24]

This claim was defended in *The Rights of Nature* in four ways. Firstly, Thelwall proposed that 'man has naturally an equal claim to the ele-ments of nature', of which light, air and water in particular remained in common. ('Naturally' here meant man taken as an 'abstraction', devoid of social and political ties, with natural rights being deter-mined by man's wants, faculties, and means). This implied that each person additionally possessed 'a right to exercise his faculties upon those powers and elements, so as to render them subservient to his wants, and conducive to his enjoyments'. Since all rights entailed a reciprocal duty to secure the identical rights of others, those who monopolised the means of support violated such rights.[25] Thelwall's first rights claim was thus that since this natural inheritance was shared by all in the state of savagery, society must compensate for its subsequent loss.[26] This parallels a similar argument by Paine in *Agrarian Justice*,[27] and thus echoed, albeit in a quite secular form, the familiar natural law doctrine concerning the Creation and God's intention that the earth be used for the support of all its inhabitants.

Thelwall's conclusion regarding common property rights was reached by reviewing the progress of society through the savage, pastoral and agricultural stages. He concurred with the widespread view that property in herds alone had existed in the pastoral state, with land having been appropriated only after agriculture had made considerable headway.[28] Thereafter, Thelwall stressed, property ought always to be the 'fruit of useful industry; but the means of being usefully industrious are the common right of all'. This clearly implied a right to labour and to receive a reasonable reward therefrom.[29] The state of cultivation was admittedly an immense improvement upon the ruder stage. But the appropriation of land by 'moral and political expediency', not merely occupancy or a right derived from labour, ended the relatively equal distribution of property which had long prevailed.[30] Afterwards, the invention of primogeniture and governmental protection of privilege and wealth further divided society into proprietor and labourer, with the few monopolising the benefits of the majority's labour. (Broadly speaking Thelwall here followed a Harringtonian view of the primacy of property ownership in the evolution of society, though he warned against applying it too rigidly.)[31] Reinstating an equality of landed property was to Thelwall clearly impossible. The question, therefore, was what rights propertyless labourers now possessed. And these, he contended, rested on 'the triple basis of nature, of implied contract, and the principles of civil association'.[32]

Naturally, labourers were 'men', and as such heirs to 'the common bounties of nature'. But at birth, each found 'his inheritance is alienated, and his common right appropriated'. Individuals of course retained the right to the 'advantages' of their industry when employed on the common elements of nature. But now such opportunities were rare: proprietor and labourer were far from equal, and society was thus 'responsible ... for an equivalent for that which society has taken away'. The permanent possession of land was rooted in mere expediency, especially the generally acknowledged tendency of private ownership to stimulate production. But labourers, Thelwall argued, had (on the basis of an unexplored principle of reciprocity) the right to receive as much in return as they had given to society, as well as to employ their faculties beneficially. Any unjust agreement 'extorted by the power of an oppressor' for inadequate wages was thus morally and politically void, the genuine basis of property being labour alone.[33]

Thelwall thus proposed a redistribution of property, firstly, on the basis of compensation for the loss of natural inheritance; and secondly, with reference to a reciprocal reward all labourers merited through their contribution to society. Thelwall's third argument for redistribution rested on the notion of an 'implied compact' tacitly entered into by all upon leaving the state of nature, but now relevant to any agreement between labourer and employer.[34] This is an interesting use of a social contract argument usually applied only to the problem of consent and political legitimacy, and demonstrates the importance of political models to explanations of economic oppression in this period. An original agreement of this type, Thelwall claimed in his most striking argument, conceded to the labourer a right to the produce of his or her employer proportionate to the latter's profit. This contract was 'implied in the very distinction of labourer and employer ... by the reason of the thing, and the rules of moral justice', specifically because capital could not be productive without labour, nor vice-versa. Moreover, its general ground was further supported by the widely accepted notion that civil association was constituted for the general good, mankind having abandoned natural society for 'the comforts and abundance of all'. Agricultural cultivation also occurred by common labour alone. Tyranny by the wealthy few, thus, was 'not a compact of civil association, but a wicked and lawless anarchy' which violated 'the very nature' of the tenure of the property-holder by substituting usurpation and plunder for legitimate possession. To Thelwall, moreover, the labourer had the right not merely to maintenance, but the education of his family, and their participation in 'all the sweets of polished society'. Natural rights, crucially, were thus not fixed in Thelwall's view, but could encompass the greater needs which social evolution fuelled. Consequently 'natural' entitlements had expanded, and now included the produce of commerce and manufacturing as well as agriculture.[35] And it was the recognition of such rights alone which legitimated any further expansion of a capitalist economic system.[36]

We see here how important for Thelwall, as well as other natural law writers, a claim to recall the original intention of the founders of civil society was. To Grotius, for example, the defense of rights of necessity, in other words of the poor to take food in the face of starvation, assumed that those who first appropriated property reserved such a right. This hypothetical intention indeed obviated the need for firmer discussions of any original contract. For Pufendorf, a 'tacit compact' accompanied the introduction of private property. For Locke, such a contract recognised the original mixing of labour with raw materials which founded property.[37] As Istvan Hont has emphasised, the more 'negative community' theorists (who believed individual appropriation was consistent with an original community of property) stressed a gradual and historical emergence of private property, the less likely was any reliance upon a contract. (The need to assume such a compact Hutcheson, for example, denied.)[38] But for Thelwall, the 'implied contract' which supported a proportionate right to profits played a crucial role, and established that the relation of capital to labour was as important as the rules of civil association.

Thelwall's first two arguments clearly parallel the principles of both 'progress' and of 'social duty' which Paine defended in *Agrarian Justice*.[39] Thelwall, too, made much of the idea that compensation for the loss of a natural inheritance justified greater equality of property. What was particularly distinctive to *The Rights of Nature*, however, and what most clearly yoked it to the cause of commercial progress, was the claim that the labourer possessed a right to a proportion of the employer's profits, because society rested upon common labour. Here Paine, while agreeing that 'personal property is the effect of society', instead proposed that a fixed sum be paid to all as restitution for their loss of land.[40] Appropriately given his greater stress on the labour basis of property, Thelwall through the rule of proportionate advantage instead considered the problem of how to regulate wages generally. This represented a critical shift away from previous republican treatments of the limitation of landed property by an agrarian law, and towards a focus on commercially-generated forms of inequality. Now Thelwall felt it possible to insist, quite dramatically given his earlier hostility to luxury as such, that he 'would extend civilisation: I would increase refinement' while meeting the demands of social justice.[41]

Given its importance to his argument, Thelwall's rule of proportionate advantage merits closer examination. In keeping with his dictum that society should not merely protect but improve the welfare of all, Thelwall's juristic strategy can be understood as seeking to socialise existing theories of property rights by construing all property relationships as occurring between consenting equals, albeit possessing unequal property, rather than between master or servant.[42] This invoked a familiar natural law concern for the interdependence of all ranks, and the duties of the wealthy towards the poor. But we can also term Thelwall's emphasis here a radical republican interpretation of jurisprudential discussions of contract – an extension of 'politics' into 'society' – and a strategy which was impossible without both the demand for political equality and a Lockean and Smithian stress on the role of labour in production.

Thelwall's account thus relied heavily upon a reinterpretation of the nature of contractual relations. His claim that all property was essentially social in nature, and specifically that all cultivation rested on social labour, can be construed as a reworking of the early eighteenth-century natural law truism that the chief advantage of society, lay, as Hutcheson put it, in the division of labour and the increasing expertise and production it encouraged.[43] And this of course was also one basis of Smith's commercial sociability.[44] But Thelwall applied the idea of sociability rather differently in *The Rights of Nature*. Most importantly, by adverting to the equal contributions of both capital and labour, he clearly conceived of the relationship of master to servant (the core of most previous descriptions of wage relations) not solely in terms of a contractual compromise of interests. This implied, as Burke, for example, contended, that once a wage had been settled, no further conflict of interests remained between employer and employee.[45] Instead, while Thelwall, echoing Smith, remained enough of an individualist to insist that 'whatever can be done by an individual is always better done single-handed, than when the same thing is attempted by several persons combined together',[46] he evidently concluded here that all labour relations should be understood in terms of the law of partnership and the pursuit of common gain. This he presumed to be that part of the 'implied contract' which justified proportionate advantage in dividing profits. This also involved the restitution of what Thelwall took to be natural equity, whose protection Grotius and others had also described as one of the goals of the original establishment of private property.[47]

Wage labour, thus, was no longer to be defined solely by the market, that is, by the usefulness of the labour and the number of labourers, as Grotius' disciples like Thomas Rutherforth insisted. This premise permitted the payment of mere subsistence wages, indeed less if charity supplemented wages, as it commonly did. Instead, wage labour embodied not merely a 'contract for mutual benefit' (to use Rutherforth's phrasing), as the hire of labour had been construed previously. Rather, it entailed a full partnership governed by the rules of 'comparative share' or proportionate gain. This for Thelwall was the only form of contractual relationship fully compatible with the general obligation to mutual advantage of the social compact (which writers like Rutherforth admitted should not be violated in such contracts).[48] This was the meaning of the assertion that the 'implied contract' rested on the principles of civil association generally, for the state of nature was left only for common, not particular advantage.[49] And this was clearly the only construction of economic activity compatible with republicanism, in Thelwall's view.

The key problem here was of course the question of what right we have to use the 'property' (which for Thelwall crucially included labour) of others for our own profit. In Pufendorf, for example, probably the best known natural law writer in eighteenth century Britain, we find a plea both for a 'just equality' in contractual relationships, and, more specifically, the injunction that in partnerships 'when any Labour is bestow'd in the Improvement of any Commodity, which is put in by another, he is suppos'd to have such a Share in the Thing it Self, as is proportionable to the Improvement it has received'. But Pufendorf admitted that many types of 'accessional advantages' added value to commodities, which nonetheless belonged to the property owner and not the labourer. And this, of course, was the usual understanding of the wage-labour relationship.[50] But partners, the natural law writers agreed, were entitled to a return from any enterprise proportionate to their contribution, whether this be in labour or capital.[51]

Thelwall evidently envisioned every employment contract in these terms, and thus extended the rule of proportionate advantage to all. While agreeing that the genuine basis of property was labour, however, he put forward no claim for 'the whole produce of labour'. (Charles Hall, we will see, would take this up a few years later.) Instead, he argued for reciprocal, proportionate rights based upon the constitution of society for the benefit of all. These rested, as we have seen, on common rights to both a reasonable reward for labour and 'the means of being usefully industrious', as well as equivalency rights based upon the implicit contract and the constitution of society as a collective enterprise.[52] Thelwall did not, therefore, merely echo jurisprudential discussions of the poor's right to subsistence. Virtually every natural law commentator had conceded that the poor had the right to be supported through their labour and to some share of the social surplus in times of necessity.[53] But while writers like William Ogilvie acknowledged a claim to the improvements of landed property, the natural law tradition recognised a right to a proportionate return of all property to be generated not in a relation of servitude, but only as a consequence of partnership. A key example was where one individual lent money to another to profit from, and was thereby entitled to a share of the profit.[54] Nor did Thelwall therefore attempt to revive a 'moral economy' of just prices and fair wages, since wages were now to be proportionate to profit, not to the cost of living. Instead he proposed a new vision of economic justice which assumed an expanding economy, centered on the contractual relations between worker and employer, and did not merely expect economic grievances to be removed by the alleviation of unduly heavy taxation.[55]

The *Rights of Nature* thus heralded that ideal of co-operative partnership between labour and capital which some socialists found an attractive alternative to both capitalism and communism in the following century, and which even such a dedicated laissez-faire liberal as John Stuart Mill, finally, was to settle upon as the most satisfactory solution to the problem of class inequality and the degenerate, selfish character which he conceded commercial society almost universally created.[56] Its central themes foreshadow that emphasis on 'fair exchange' within a socialist market system which some of Robert Owen's followers, notably William Thompson, found appealing.[57] Thelwall's assessment of the results of machinery, especially its tendency 'to furnish a cheaper substitute for manual labour' and to 'accelerate the progress of accumulation' in the hands of the capitalist, strikingly anticipates the central themes of Owenite economic thought. So, too, does his growing sense that the labouring classes were becoming ever more 'subject to the whole Corporation of Employers, instead of an individual proprietor', and that the increasing concentration of wealth was creating a three-class system of 'monied speculators', 'drones' (the aristocracy) and 'the poor hard-working drudges' (the labouring classes).[58] This account of wage-labour in an industrial economy shows how far the discourse on political rights of the early 1790s had shifted towards an economic focus by the end of the decade. Thelwall's observations were intended to be extended in further lectures on the mercantile, manufacturing, and funding systems, which unfortunately were never given. Nor, with his retirement from politics, did Thelwall build upon the prescient comments he made on the cotton industry in Manchester, where Owen was employed, in 1797, when, gathering details on the new manufactories, Thelwall noted that 'Machinery that brings a multitude to labour in one spot, bad. Regulations possible'.[59]

Conclusion

Thelwall's last major contribution to the debates of the 1790s was, appropriately enough, an attack upon Edmund Burke's final tirade against the revolution, *A Letter to a Noble Lord* (1796). Here Burke, in a virulent assault upon the aristocratic reformers, actually mentioned Thelwall's lectures, expressing the hope that no Lord would attempt to augment his education there.[60] Thelwall's response, *Sober Reflections on the Seditious and Inflammatory Letter of the Right Hon. Edmund Burke to a Noble Lord* (1796), linked the ferocity of Burke's reaction to the reformers to his profiting from aristocratic patronage and a government pension. Burke himself, Thelwall asserted, was a mere a 'high-toned aristocrat', willing to manipulate any cause to serve his own ends, and not therefore inconsistent in his seeming sympathy for the American revolution and opposition to the French. Such rancour as Burke manifested against those nobles who sympathised with reform, warned Thelwall, threatened finally to undermine all respect for 'rank, fortune, and hereditary station'. It might indeed bring about a far more complete social revolution than even most of the reformers sought. For Burke, in impugning the origins of the title from which the Duke of Bedford's estate originated, had also recalled the massacres, murders, venality and corruption which paved the way for the ennoblement of many an ambitious commoner. Thelwall then turned to the causes of the war; to Burke's role in fomenting the reaction against reform; to the sources of the Terror in France; and to the role of 'philosophy' in fomenting the revolution. Thelwall's defence here of the revolution's central principles, 'equal rights and equal laws', was, he insisted, unrelated to what 'a few ruffians' had perpetrated by dictatorial means. We can see clearly here, thus, the distance between Thelwall and Robespierre, despite the former's momentary sympathy for the Jacobins, and how far the causes of the Terror lay for him in the rapine, oppression and tyranny of 'the old despotism' rather than the principles of the revolution itself.[61] This was Thelwall's final substantial critique of 'the oligarchy of the rotten borough-mongers'. It is a stalwart defence of the principles from whose profession he was finally forced to retreat, but which he would reassert with renewed vigour when public sympathy for political reform revived some twenty years later.

Conclusion

The Aftermath

War, intimidation, the exile and emigration of large numbers of reformers, and a markedly 'anti-Jacobin' shift in public opinion combined to repress radical sentiment in Britain for at least a decade. When parliamentary reform finally occurred in 1832, some of the actors of the 1790s, notably Earl Grey, but also former members of the London Corresponding Society, like Francis Place and Thomas Hardy, played important roles. Political unrest and intellectual dissent were never wholly suppressed during the intervening period, however. At the end of the 1790s nationalism would ally dramatically with radical principles to produced the short-lived, bloody rebellion of 1798 in Ireland,[1] where the French Revolution had been described as 'universally popular' and Paine's doctrines had been welcomed even more fervently than in England.[2] Naval mutinies at Spithead and the Nore in 1797, and the activities of genuinely subversive underground groups like the United Englishmen, were met in part by a massive volunteer movement which armed the gentry and yeomanry against enemies both foreign and domestic.[3] Smouldering embers of radical and utopian sentiment were also still evident after 1795, as we have seen, which may be as closely associated with Godwinism as with Paineite radicalism. These were met by a new wave of loyalist propaganda, spearheaded by the longest-running and most successful loyalist periodical, *The Anti-Jacobin Review* (1799–1821). Alarmed by evidence that 'doctrines of Infidelity have been extensively circulated among the lower orders',[4] notably through the sale of *The Age of Reason* among London Corresponding Society members, a campaign commenced against religious scepticism as the original, underlying cause of the Revolution, popularised by two books

154

in particular, the Abbé Barruel's *Memoirs Illustrating the History of Jacobinism* (4 vols, 1797), and *Proofs of a Conspiracy against All the Religions and Governments of Europe* (Edinburgh, 1797), by an Edinburgh professor, John Robison.[5] This was linked to a burgeoning Evangelical movement for the moral reformation of the upper and middle classes in particular, led by William Wilberforce and Hannah More, whose success has been interpreted as one of the chief long term consequences of the French Revolution for British society.[6]

By way of conclusion, this section explores two new trends of thought respecting the central issues of the revolutionary debate which occurred around 1800, which were to have a crucial bearing on how the debates of the 1790s would be understood for much of the nineteenth century. The first concerns Thomas Robert Malthus's approach to the rights of the poor in the *Essay on Population* (1798); the second, Charles Hall's critique of republicanism in his *The Effects of Civilization on the People in European States* (1805).

Epilogue: Exit Strategies

Godwin and Malthus

Though its title implies a scholarly intervention in a burgeoning demographic debate, the publication of Thomas Robert Malthus's *Essay on Population* in 1798 was widely read as marking an extraordinarily powerful condemnation of social and political reformers of all types, and especially the most extreme egalitarians, associated with Godwin in Britain and Condorcet in France.[7] Indeed, for nearly a century, the *Essay* was to be invoked constantly as having refuted for good the prospect of any serious amelioration in the condition of the working classes. The reason for this lies in Malthus's shifting of the entire terrain of the revolutionary debate from issues of civil and political rights, and the consequences of constitutional alterations, to the question of the right of charity of the poor from their wealthier neighbours, and the human, rather than the institutional, source of poverty itself, in unrestrained sexual passion.

A Church of England clergyman isolated in a remote Surrey parish for some ten years after his ordination in 1788, Malthus had evidently nonetheless followed the revolutionary debate with some care. One conclusion he had reached summed up, as we have seen, a leading loyalist allegation: as he wrote to Godwin, 'Great improvements may

take place in the state of society, but I do not see how the present form
or system can be radically and essentially changed, without a danger
of relapsing again into barbarism'.[8] Much more dramatically, however, he also contended that the Godwinian, and indeed every other,
egalitarian system, exhibited one fatal flaw: the greater the superfluity
of the means of subsistence possessed by the working classes, the
faster would population grow, until the pressure of overpopulation
would reintroduce poverty. Indeed in 'a state of great equality and
virtue, where pure and simple manners prevailed, and where the
means of subsistence were so abundant that no part of the society
could have any fears about providing amply for a family', population
would increase at rate 'much greater than any increase that has hitherto been known'.[9]

As a general principle, then, the power of population was 'indefinitely greater than the power in the earth to produce subsistence for
man'.[10] It was pointless, Malthus insisted to Godwin, alleging that reason would dictate a restriction of population in such circumstances:

> The prudence which you speak of as a check to population ... implies
> a foresight of difficulties; and this foresight of difficulties almost nec-
> essarily implies a desire to remove them ... With the present acknowl-
> edged imperfections of human institutions, I by no means think that
> the greatest part of distress felt in society arises from them. The very
> admission of the necessity to prudence, to prevent the misery from
> an overcharged population, removes the blame from public institu-
> tions to the conduct of individuals.[11]

If poverty resulted from lack of individual moral restraint resulting
in unsupportably large families, how then could the poor be assisted?
Malthus's own starting point had been a debate with his father over
Godwin's approach to this issue in *The Enquirer*. Here, in the essay, 'Of
Avarice and Profusion', Godwin had contended that while the pro-
fuse man might be 'actuated by motives the most consonant to justice
and virtue', neither giving money to the poor, nor indeed employing
them as such, unproductively, was in fact the best means of assisting
them.[12] Instead, the rich should employ the poor cultivating new
land, in order to augment agricultural produce, with the ultimate aim
of securing their independence. Curiously, thus, Malthus's starting
point was quite similar to Godwin's view, indeed even with the general

tenour of Godwin's (and even more Paley's) utilitarianism.[13] He agreed that

> If I turn up a piece of uncultivated land, and give him the produce, I then benefit both him, and all the members of the society, because what he before consumed is thrown into the common stock, and probably some of the new produce with it. But if I only give him money, supposing the produce of the country to remain the same, I give him a title to a larger share of that produce than formerly, which share he cannot receive without diminishing the shares of others.[14]

Yet Malthus extended the logic of this argument even further, and shifted the ground of the argument from an emphasis on intellectual contributions to society to economic productivity. If the aim of charity was, like that of the system of production generally, to maximise economic output, then charity should be extended only to those who were capable of making a contribution to this output. Although he had not mentioned Paine in the first edition of the *Essay*, Malthus in 1803 lamented the 'mischiefs occasioned by Mr. Paine's Rights of Man', which he attributed largely to the fact that Paine had 'shewn himself totally unacquainted with the structure of society, and the different moral effects to be expected from the physical difference between this country and America'. Whatever rights existed, he continued, 'there is one right, which man has been generally thought to possess, which I am confident he neither does, nor can, possess, a right to subsistence when his labour will not fairly possess it'. No person, thus, had 'any claim of right on society for subsistence, if his labour will not purchase it'.[15] No 'right to charity' consequently existed, separate from the ability and willingness of the poor to make a contribution to common produce. In a startling passage inserted in the second edition of the *Essay* (1803), but excised from later editions, Malthus asserted that he who could not

> get subsistence from his parents on whom he has a just demand, and if the society do not want his labour, has no claim of *right* to the smallest portion of food, and, in fact, has no business to be where he is. At nature's mighty feast there is no vacant cover for him. She tells him to be gone, and will quickly execute her orders, if he do not work on the compassion of some of her guests.[16]

Not only did the poor not possess a right to charity, thus: assisting them with money was counterproductive, since it encouraged population growth, as well as, on a sufficiently large scale, an increase in the price of food. Godwin's great error – but it was the core assumption of all the radical reformers – had been 'attributing almost all the vices and misery that are seen in civil society to human institutions'. In fact, thought Malthus, perhaps echoing Burke, 'though human institutions appear to be the obvious and obtrusive causes of much mischief to mankind; yet, in reality, they are light and superficial, they are mere feathers that float on the surface, in comparison with those deeper seated causes of impurity that corrupt the springs, and render turbid the whole stream of human life'.[17] The true cause of poverty, then, lay in unrestrained sexual desire, and in the incapacity of reason to govern the passions. These produced a general tendency for population growth to outstrip mankind's ability to provide an adequate subsistence. This argument against perfectibility was not novel; it had been suggested by Robert Wallace forty years earlier.[18] But this expression of it was enormously influential. Sixty years before the appearance of Darwin's *Origin of Species*, which was much indebted to Malthus, the *Essay* described the mass of humanity as little better than animals, and condemned large numbers who 'in the great lottery of life, have drawn a blank',[19] to suffer from want, and to have their numbers restricted by disease, famine and war rather than prudential restraint. The sole remedy was to reduce relief to the 'idle and provident' to the 'very scanty' level, and never more than the worst-paid common labour, with the eventual aim of abolishing the system of poor relief.[20] We know how deeply this message was driven home from many accounts; Thomas Wedgewood insisted to his friend the reformer Thomas Poole in 1803, for instance, that the latter study the second edition of the *Essay* because it was 'too sanguine about bettering the condition of the Poor'.[21] And when Britain's poor laws came to be reformed in 1834 with the aim of making relief as stringent as possible, Malthus was widely regarded as the architect of the change.

To those who accepted such arguments the vapid optimism of the radical Enlightenment was now exploded. Whether government was republican or monarchical mattered little so far as the condition of the poor was concerned. Within a generation Malthus' *Essay* was described as forming 'the groundwork of the reasonings of all intelligent men, on the affairs of mankind'.[22] United with the burgeoning evangelical movement, which laid great stress on the primacy of Original Sin, the

Essay dealt a blow to the language of rights from which it has scarcely fully recovered. It would be some eighty years before public opinion would shift against the thrust of Malthus's conclusions, and even then its place was taken by 'the theory of natural selection as applied to society ... as the great intellectual stand-by of all opponents of social justice'.[23] Every subsequent utopia would have to come to terms with the tyranny of blind, unstoppable instinct Malthus had divulged. And yet, ironically, as we have seen, Malthus's starting point parallels Godwin's theory of justice: we must not assist others equally, but in proportion to their contribution to the common good.

Charles Hall and the Origins of Socialism

The work of an obscure London physician, *The Effects of Civilization on the People in European States* (1805), has often been identified with the origins of British socialism.[24] Its main contention was that the general course of 'civilization' (the growth of science, conveniences, and luxuries) was to reduce the mass to poverty and to deprive them of their 'original share of things'.[25] Hall's starting point, the loss of originally equal property rights, was thus similar to Paine and Thelwall's, and he had some correspondence with Thomas Spence over their proposals.[26] But he was the first republican to detail at length what he saw as the dual effects of manufacturing on this process (a start had been made by Ferguson as well as Thelwall[27]), both directly through the new forms of work in manufactories, and indirectly by further depriving labourers of their right to part of the produce of the soil. And Hall offered the most extensive defense of an anti-commercial republic of this period, going even beyond Spence in his desire to eradicate inequalities of personal as well as landed property, and unlike Godwin and Thelwall, remaining unflinchingly opposed to commercial society.[28] A brief examination of Hall's ideas thus enables us to see how the turn towards a discussion of property rights in *Agrarian Justice* and the writings of Godwin and Thelwall would form the starting point for a post-war generation engaged for the first time in the serious analysis of the system of commerce and then, by 1815, industry, which would soon be more widely termed capitalism.

The thrust of both Hall's account of the existing system and his critique of republicanism lay in his definition of wealth, as the possession of those things which could obtain and command the labour of man, or in a word, 'power'. Hume, Smith, and other defenders of commercial society had failed to foresee that while feudalism might be abolished, it had been replaced by a 'new species of dependence of the lower order on the rich, which is established in its stead, in most civilized states'. Smith had famously warned in book five of the *Wealth of Nations* that if a narrow division of labour were allowed to be extended indefinitely among the working classes, with no mitigating circumstances, an extreme 'mental mutilation', or dehumanisation through repetitive labour, would result.[29] For Hall, taking this idea as his starting point, as later writers like Marx and Ruskin would do, this was exactly what the future boded. Manufactures, moreover, would increasingly draw employment from agriculture, and thus reduce food production, engender scarcity, and diminish the size of the population. Having initially helped to break up the landed monopoly of the aristocracy by encouraging the exchange of land for other commodities, the new industrial processes now threatened to forge an even greater dependency for the poor, crowning a new tyranny which was primarily economic in nature.[30] Hall can still be understood as upholding the Harringtonian doctrine that power followed the distribution of property in society. Economic power, in his eyes, automatically entailed other types of social and political control. The wealthy were an aristocracy who held the reins of legislative, judicial, ecclesiastical and other forms of power regardless of governmental form (and this argument continued to shock many contemporary republicans until the existence of distress and growing inequalities in the United States became widely known).[31]

Central to this account was the new role played by the possessor of capital, the manufacturer or 'capitalist', as he was just now coming to be called.[32] Those whose wealth was mobile and based on credit or money alone, rather than land, had always been an object of suspicion to republican writers, for their loyalties could be as fluid as their wealth, and patriotism usually gave way to self-interest.[33] To Hall, the capitalist's power lay partly in his ability to command the necessaries of life, since landowners desired refined commodities and saw manufacturers and tradesmen merely as 'agents ... to whom they delegate a portion of their authority; that is, they make over to them, as it were, a part of the necessaries of life, which their estates produce; the disposal of which gives them the command over the labour of the poor'.[34] The abstract nature of Hall's definition of wealth, and his virtual reduction of all forms of labour to labour power, allowed him to treat for the first time all forms of wealth as aspects of a single, systematic, relationship of labourer to non-labourer. All capital, 'the wealth with which any business is carried on', thus was 'power over the labour of the poor', with even holders of stock having power over the future labour of the poor.[35] Rather than integrating societies by mutually fulfilling needs, as commercial republicans like Paine contended, trade merely exacerbated the conflict of interest between rich and poor. The interest of buyer and seller was 'in every case, opposite', the buyer seeking to give as little, the seller to get as much, as possible. In keeping with his definition of wealth, Hall defined rich and poor as merely buyers and sellers of labour, and estimated that the poor received only about a ninth of the value of their labour after rent, profit and taxes had been subtracted. This effort to measure what proportion of the product of labour was received by the labourer was indisputably a crucial turning point in modern social theory. Previously, most republicans had emphasised that the burden of taxation of corrupt governments was the chief source of economic distress, and invoked the loss of their inheritance of the common earth in order to re-assert the rights of the poor. Now, contractual and economic relations were increasingly central to the new radical analysis of poverty, though competing theories were by no means simply swept aside.[36] With Hall's definition of commercial antagonism, and of the fundamentally irreconcilable interests of rich and poor, the language of class confrontation, so central to most forms of nineteenth century radicalism, was essentially in place. Of course, 'classes', if no longer 'ranks' and 'estates', were still designated as useful producers/ useless consumers and productive/unproductive labourers, rather than defined more sociologically.[37] Yet this was very close to the language of socialism which emerged fifteen years later.[38] To anticipate Owen's views, Hall's assumptions lacked only a description of opposing interests as 'competition', a greater stress on sociability as the goal of society, and the aim of communal production as well as ownership.

In this account the specific form of government under which the poor lived was thus of only marginal interest. Paine had relied strongly on the vitality of democratic control and the American model. Spence had asked 'what does it signify whether the form of government be monarchical or republican while estates can be acquired?', but had worried only about the effects of an inequality of landed property.[39] Hall even more emphatically dismissed even popular political control, the great goal of every radical reformer, as irrelevant. Thus he was the first notable British republican writer to criticise the 'rising aristocracy of the American States', seeing the effects of wealth here as 'more obvious', since wealth here 'universally ... puts power into the hands of those that have it'. Perhaps influenced by radical criticisms of the growing inequality of the Federalist era, this began a profoundly important critique of the United States as a model for the great inequalities inherent in, not incidental to or avoidable by, modern commercial republicanism generally. This negative image would remain crucial to socialist arguments throughout the nineteenth century and beyond. The great ideal of the late eighteenth century, the American revolution, was already cast into doubt. Yet as Britain was to continental liberals, America remained, despite French developments, a republican example of great importance to all European radicals, as it had been to Paine and Thelwall, for a lengthy period to come.[40]

To counter the growing power of the capitalist, Hall therefore wished, in a Rousseauesque vein, to defend the poor's right to return to agriculture. With Paine and Thelwall, he agreed both that God had intended the land for the common good of his creatures, and argued (against Hume, Paley and Blackstone) that all retained some right to part of it. Land had originally been held in common, and mankind had been born inalienably 'equal and independent of each other', at least in the sense of possessing an equality of rights. To eliminate existing inequalities, Hall hence proposed an agrarian law. If each family held about 36 acres, it could subsist on the produce of its own labour without being able to accumulate too much.[41] By abolishing primogeniture and heavily taxing refined manufactures, capital would be driven back into agriculture. As much machinery would remain as was valuable for coarse manufactures alone. A great increase of agricultural labour would dramatically raise farm production and allay any future threat of famine. When all laboured only for their own families, moreover, laws would be few and foreign trade minimal; we are not far from the Godwinian autarky of 1793. Leisure would thus be available for the mental improvement of the majority, though Hall thought a few select persons might preserve languages, the arts and sciences, and was far less interested in intellectual attainments than Godwin (of works of art he thought there were 'too many already'). Here simplicity thus primarily ensured social justice and self-sufficiency, rather than, as for Godwin, sincerity of manners and intellectual independence. Like many such republicans, Hall pointed out that greater equality of property had resulted under the Jewish and Spartan constitutions and in the Jesuit colony in Paraguay.[42]

Conclusion: The Prelude to Modern Liberty and Equality

Despite the restoration of the Bourbon monarchy the century after 1815 witnessed the continuing destruction of feudal institutions across Europe. With this came the concomitant growth, albeit unevenly, of greater social equality. Notwithstanding notable setbacks, there followed the gradual acceptance, in the second half of the twentieth century, of representative democratic institutions wedded to social democratic systems of welfare which substantially mitigate the effects of poverty, and have become definitive of the European model of modernity. This particular reconciliation of the ideals of liberty and equality, more egalitarian than, for instance, the model popularised by the United States, where liberty is given greater priority over equality of condition, represents perhaps the most enduring legacy of the French Revolution. (Fraternity, the third in the unholy trinity of republican virtues, has always gotten shortest shrift.) Modern ideals of social equality are not Rousseauist or primitivist, though throwbacks, notably in the case of the Khmer Rouge under Pol Pot, have occurred. Instead, they are compatible with a highly developed system of luxury and international trade, and tend to be associated with political apathy rather than any muscular conception of political virtue. Modern bourgeois liberty rests upon formal political equality and notional popular sovereignty. Monarchy where existent is politically insignificant, and territorial aristocracies have all but vanished. If we have not supplanted religion with the worship of Reason, nonetheless the unfreedom of feudalism is now little tolerated anywhere. In its stead rather, we embrace that universal, self-conscious desire for liberty of which, of all of those who translated the principles of the French Revolution into the language of philosophy, Hegel remains the most profound interpreter, reminding us that, by contrast to the near-enslavement of most of humanity throughout human history, the dawning of modern liberty represents indeed a startling, blissful, even sublime moment of the consciousness of freedom.

In the nineteenth century demands for political liberty in Europe were thus also accompanied by a desire for substantially greater social equality, but this equality was generally understood as compatible both with considerable wealth and a system of economic competition. In this sense, while scholars have tended to side with Burke as inhabiting 'an intellectual sphere altogether superior to that in which Paine was able to rise' whose 'speculative power' was 'superior to Paine's meagre philosophy',[43] it was the Paineite, rather than the loyalist, case which won the day. Yet the Burkeian argument that lawless insubordination might evolve into more systematic terror remained a stern warning that democracy could degenerate into a tyranny not merely of the milder Tocquevilleian type, in which excessive individualism undermines the bonds of community, but something akin to twentieth century totalitarianism, in which we recognise Hitler and Stalin as the incalculably more murderous successors of Danton and Robespierre. (But this bloodthirstiness owes nothing to 'Enlightenment' and everything to the irrationalist obsessions with identities based on class, race, and nation.) Yet to treat the grand contest of ideas of the 1790s as now completed, and only of antiquarian interest, is to fail to recognise the persistence of substantial inequality of women, of poverty on a large scale, of recurrent periods of increasing concentration of wealth, and of the repeated failure of democracy to take root successfully in many nations. If obsequious peasants no longer bow before haughty peers, Marx would remind subsequent generations that unfreedom could assume novel forms in bourgeois Europe. And we need little reminding of the still extraordinary degree to which dictatorship, oppression and intolerance flourish elsewhere. The debate of the 1790s thus reveals the basic parameters between which we continue to assess the capabilities, hopes, and potential of modern societies. Liberty, desirable as an end in itself, may yet undermine equality, also a desirable end, and vice versa; the trick is to get the balance right. Readers of these debates today will position themselves between these parameters as they please, but cannot fail to recognise not only that the conflict of principles they represent is as relevant today as ever, but that, as the combatants of the 1790s realised, a capacity to engage in rational political argument as such is a central component of freely evolving societies.

Notes

Chapter One: Introduction

1. Lord Acton. *Lectures on the French Revolution* (Macmillan & Co., 1910), p. 1.
2. Slavery was abolished in the French colonies in 1794 but reintroduced by Napoleon in 1802.
3. Notably Jacob Talmon. *The Origins of Totalitarian Democracy* (New York, Praeger, 1960).
4. For a slightly later assessment of this theory, see Henry Brougham. *Historical Sketches of Statesmen Who Flourished in the Time of George III* (3 vols, 1843), vol. 3, pp. 1–7.
5. Francis Jeffrey. *Contributions to the Edinburgh Review* (2nd edn, 3 vols, 1846), vol. 3, pp. 210–11.
6. Thomas Carlyle. *The French Revolution. A History* (3 vols, 1898), vol. 1, p. 12.
7. For a judicious near-contemporary assessment of the causes of the Revolution, see [Samuel Bailey]. *Questions in Political Economy, Politics, Metaphysics, Polite Literature, and Other Branches of Knowledge* (1823), pp. 186–7.
8. Thomas Carlyle. *The French Revolution. A History* (3 vols, 1898), vol. 1, p. 11.
9. Henry Cockburn. *Life of Lord Jeffrey* (2 vols, 1852), p. 126. For a recent survey of developments in the period see Jennifer Mori. *Britain in the Age of the French Revolution* (Harlow, Longman, 2000).
10. Henry Cockburn. *Memorials of His Time* (1856), p. 45.

11. John Oswald. *Review of the Constitution of Great-Britain,* in Gregory Claeys, ed. *Political Writings of the 1790s* (8 vols, Pickering & Chatto, 1993), vol. 3, p. 437.

12. On the 1790s as originating socialism, see, for example, Anton Menger's influential *The Right to the Whole Produce of Labour* (Macmillan, 1899). For the liberal origins of the welfare state, see, for example, my *Thomas Paine: Social and Political Thought* (Unwin Hyman, 1989). On the origin of the modern idea of poverty see especially J.R. Poynter. *Society and Pauperism: English Ideas on Poor Relief, 1795–1834* (Routledge & Kegan Paul, 1969), and Gertrude Himmelfarb. *The Idea of Poverty. England in the Early Industrial Age* (Faber, 1984). On the 1790s and the origins of liberalism, see especially John Burrow. *Whigs and Liberals. Continuity and Change in English Political Thought* (Oxford, Clarendon Press, 1988), and Stefan Collini, Donald Winch and John Burrow. *That Noble Science of Politics. A Study in Nineteenth Century Intellectual History* (Cambridge, Cambridge University Press, 1983).

13. Works covering various parts of the terrain include: William Laprade. *England and the French Revolution 1789–1797* (Baltimore, Johns Hopkins University Press, 1909); Walter P. Hall. *British Radicalism 1791–1797* (New York, Columbia University Press, 1912); Philip Anthony Brown. *The French Revolution in English History* (Allen & Unwin, 1918); James Boulton. *The Language of Politics in the Age of Wilkes and Burke* (Routledge & Kegan Paul, 1963); R.R. Fennessy. *Burke, Paine and the Rights of Man* (The Hague, Martinus Nijhoff, 1963); Clive Emsley. *British Society and the French Wars 1793–1815* (Macmillan, 1979); Günther Lottes. *Politisches Aufklärung und plebejisches Publikum. Zur Theorie und Praxis des englischen Radikalismus im späten 18. Jahrhundert* (Munich, Oldenbourg, 1979); Colin Jones, ed. *Britain and Revolutionary France* (Exeter: University of Exeter, 1983); Seamus Deane. *The French Revolution and Enlightenment in England 1789–1832* (Cambridge, MA, Harvard University Press, 1988); Barton R. Friedman. *Fabricating History: English Writers on the French Revolution* (Princeton, Princeton University Press, 1988), Stephen Prickett. *England and the French Revolution* (Macmillan, 1989); H.T. Dickinson, ed. *Britain and the French Revolution 1789–1815* (Macmillan, 1989); Ceri Crossley and Ian Small, eds. *The French Revolution and British Culture* (Oxford, Oxford University Press, 1989); Mark Philp, ed. *The French Revolution and British Popular*

Politics (Cambridge, Cambridge University Press, 1991), and H.T. Dickinson. *The Politics of the People in Eighteenth-Century Britain* (Macmillan, 1995).

14. On Ireland see Hugh Gough and David Dickson, eds., *Ireland and the French Revolution* (Dublin, Irish Academic Press, 1990). A dated survey of Scottish developments is Henry Meikle. *Scotland and the French Revolution* (Glasgow, James Maclehose, 1912).

15. A good starting point, here, however, is Gary Kelly. *The English Jacobin Novel 1780–1805* (Oxford, Clarendon Press, 1976).

16. For the background to this debate, see Christopher Berry. *The Idea of Luxury: A Conceptual and Historical Investigation* (Cambridge, Cambridge University Press, pp. 126–76, and generally Donald Winch. *Riches and Poverty: An Intellectual History of Political Economy in Britain, 1750–1834* (Cambridge, Cambridge University Press, 1996).

17. *The Correspondence of William Augustus Miles on the French Revolution* (2 vols, 1890), vol. 1, pp. 267–8.

18. The case for the threat of revolution, classically presented in E.P. Thompson's *The Making of the English Working Class* (Harmondsworth, Penguin Books, 1977), is re-stated in Roger Wells. *Insurrection: The British Experience 1795–1803* (Stroud, Alan Sutton. 1983). The evidence favouring stability is given in Ian Christie. *Stress and Stability in Late Eighteenth-Century Britain: Reflections on the British Avoidance of Revolution* (Oxford, Oxford University Press, 1985). See also Edward Royle. *Revolutionary Britannia? Reflections on the Threat of Revolution in Britain, 1789–1848* (Manchester, Manchester University Press, 2000).

19. Benjamin Disraeli. *Parliamentary Reform* (1867), p. 422.

20. See Gladstone's protest thereon, in Herbert Woodfield Paul. *The Life of William Ewart Gladstone* (Smith, Elder & Co., 1901), pp. 260–1.

21. Frederic Harrison. *The Meaning of History* (1894), p. 182.

22. The 'republican' or civic humanist view is best represented by J.G.A. Pocock (e.g., *Virtue, Commerce and History*, Cambridge, Cambridge University Press, 1985, pp. 215–310), the 'liberal' on the American side by Joyce Appleby (e.g., 'Liberalism and the American Revolution', *New England Quarterly*, 49, 1976, 3–26), and the British, Isaac Kramnick ('Religion and Radicalism. English Political Theory in the Age of Revolution', *Political Theory*, 5, 1977, 505–34, and 'Republican Revisionism Revisited', *American*

Political Science Review, 87, 1982, 629–64), reprinted in Isaac Kramnick. *Republicanism and Bourgeois Radicalism. Political Ideology in Late Eighteenth-Century England and America* (Ithaca, Cornell University Press, 1990).

23. For example, Adam Smith, *The Wealth of Nations* (Oxford, Oxford University Press, 1976), vol. 1, pp. 86, 91.

24. See Ch. 4.

25. [Samuel Romilly]. *Thoughts on the Probable Influence of the French Revolution on Great-Britain* (1790), p. 1.

26. Henry Meister. *Letters Written During a Residence in England* (1799), pp. 29–30. On early press reaction see K. Schweizer and R. Klein. 'The French Revolution and Developments in the London Daily Press to 1793', *Publishing History*, 18 (1985), 85–97.

27. *Memoirs of Charles James Fox* (2 vols, 1853), vol. 2, p. 341.

28. *Political Writings of the 1790s*, vol. 3, p. 67.

29. Ibid., vol. 1, p. 156. Christie was editor of the *Analytical Review* (1788–99), an important Dissenting journal. For its view of the Revolution, see Brian Rigby. 'Radical Spectators of the Revolution: The Case of the *Analytical Review*', in Ceri Crossley and Ian Small, eds. *The French Revolution and British Culture* (Oxford, Oxford University Press, 1989), pp. 63–83.

30. *An Enquiry into the Present Alarming State of the Nation* (1793), p. iii.

31. Mark Wilks. *The Origin and Stability of the French Revolution. A Sermon* (2nd edn., Norwich, 1791), p. 6. A similar view of 1688 is evident in James Peddie. *The Revolution the Work of God, and a Cause of Joy* (Edinburgh, 1789). See generally Clarke Garrett. *Respectable Folly. Millenarians and the French Revolution in England and France* (Baltimore, Johns Hopkins University Press, 1975).

32. George Dyer. *The Complaints of the Poor People of England* (1793), p. 83.

33. *Political Writings of the 1790s*, vol. 1, p. 363.

34. A good popular expression of this is in [E.H. Iliff]. *A Summary of the Duties of Citizenship! Written Expressly for the Members of the London Corresponding Society* (1795), p. 22.

35. Thomas Paine. *Address and Declaration of the Friends of Universal Peace and Liberty* (1791), p. 2.

36. 'With an enthusiasm bordering upon frenzy did the Dissenters view this event', commented one observer (David Rivers. *Observations on the Political Conduct of the Protestant Dissenters*, ?1799, p. 28). The author of this tract, which summarises the case for seeing the

Dissenters as active supporters of the Revolution, was himself a former Nonconformist minister. But astute commentators recognised that most of the Dissenters were 'neither Tories nor Republicans, but friends to the principles of the Revolution' (*Anecdotes of the Life of Richard Watson, Bishop of Llandaff*, 2 vols, 1818, vol. 1, p. 421). On some reactions of Dissenters, see John Creasey. 'Some Dissenting Attitudes Towards the French Revolution', *Transactions of the Unitarian Historical Society*, 13 (1966), 155–67.

37. The third of the population who were poor in France, most notably, had sunk closer to Irish than English depths. Unlike Britain, most of the judgeships in France were sold openly. The nobility, which numbered some 120–350,000, owned up to a third of the land, had feudal rights over the rest, owned most heavy industry, and received as much as a quarter of the Church's revenues. The Gallic Church itself owned about 10 per cent of the land. But the national debt in Britain was often calculated at twice that of France. On British reactions to the American Revolution in Britain see John Derry. *English Politics and the American Revolution* (J.M. Dent, 1976), Colin Bonwick. *English Radicals and the American Revolution* (Chapel Hill, University of North Carolina Press, 1977), and H.T. Dickinson. '"The Friends of America": British Sympathy with the American Revolution', in Michael T. Davis, ed. *Radicalism and Revolution in Britain, 1775–1848* (Macmillan, 2000), pp. 1–29.

38. The Society of the Friends of the People would claim that 154 persons returned a majority of MPs to the Commons. See Ch. 6.

39. On British radicalism in this period and immediately beforehand, see C.B. Roylance Kent. *The English Radicals. An Historical Sketch* (1899); George Veitch. *The Genesis of Parliamentary Reform* (Constable, 1913); Ian Christie. *Wilkes, Wyvill and Reform. The Parliamentary Reform Movement in British Politics 1760–1785* (Macmillan, 1962); E.P. Thompson. *The Making of the English Working Class* (Victor Gollancz, 1963); Eugene Black. *The Association. British Extraparliamentary Political Organization 1769–1793* (Cambridge, MA, Harvard University Press, 1963); Carl Cone. *The English Jacobins. Reformers in Late 18th Century England* (New York, Charles Scribners, 1968); Gwyn Williams. *Artisans and Sans-Culottes. Popular Movements in France and Britain during the French Revolution* (New York, W.W. Norton, 1969); Albert Goodwin. *The Friends of Liberty. The English Democratic Movement in the Age of the French Revolution* (Hutchinson,

1979); and H.T. Dickinson. *British Radicalism and the French Revolution 1789–1815* (Oxford: Basil Blackwell, 1985).

40. There were few theoretical treatments of the Revolution prior to this. A notable exception is [Charles Hawtrey]. *On Liberty and the Revolution in France* (Oxford, 1790).

Chapter Two: Edmund Burke

1. Burke had recently gambled much on the King's mental breakdown, only to see George III recover in 1789. He had begun a personal crusade against Warren Hastings's government of British India, the impeachment proceedings of which, beginning in 1786, quickly bogged down and eventually came to nothing. These disappointments clearly had some bearing on his position respecting the Revolution. Considerable weight can also be placed on strained relations between Burke and Sheridan over the Regency Crisis, which led each to interpret the Revolution differently and had produced an open feud by February 1790, when Burke broke from Sheridan during his speech on the Army Estimates. See L.G. Mitchell. *Charles James Fox and the Disintegration of the Whig Party 1782–1794* (Oxford, Oxford University Press, 1971), pp. 155–6.

2. *The Correspondence of Edmund Burke* (9 vols, Cambridge, Cambridge University Press, 1968), vol. 6, pp. 44–5.

3. Ibid., p. 47.

4. He continued: 'I certainly think that all Men who desire it, deserve it. It is not the Reward of our Merit or the acquisition of our Industry. It is our Inheritance. It is the birthright of our Species' (Ibid., vol. 6, p. 41; November 1789).

5. Already in November 1789, for instance, Burke wrote to Lord Fitzwilliam that 'As to France, if I were to give way to the speculations which arise in my mind from the present State of things, and from the Causes which have given rise to it and which now begin to be unfolded, I should think it a country undone; and irretrievable for a very long Course of time' (Ibid., p. 36).

6. *The Speeches of the Right Honourable Edmund Burke* (4 vols, 1816), vol. 3, p. 461.

7. *The Correspondence of Edmund Burke*, vol. 6, p. 96 (26 February 1790).

8. Ibid., p. 80.

9. Reprinted in Gregory Claeys, ed. *Political Writings of the 1790s* (8 vols, Pickering & Chatto, 1993, vol. 3, pp. 3–22). On Burke's views of Price see Frederick Dreyer. 'The Genesis of Burke's Reflections', *Journal of Modern History*, 50 (1978), 462–79, and generally R.R. Fennessy, *Burke, Paine, and the Rights of Man* (The Hague, Martinus Nijhoff, 1963), ch. 6. On Price see D.O Thomas. *The Honest Mind. The Thought and Work of Richard Price* (Oxford, Clarendon Press, 1977), and Henri Labourcheix. *Richard Price as Moral Philosopher and Political Theorist* (Oxford, Voltaire Foundation, 1982).

10. See *Political Writings of the 1790s*, vol. 3, p. 16.

11. A similar debate had long existed about whether William the Conqueror had inherited or seized the English throne, which foreshadowed some of these themes. For a summary of this question see, for example, Robert Brady. *An Introduction to the Old English History* (1684). On the context of this interpretation of 1688, see Gerald Straka. 'Sixteen Eighty-Eight as the Year One: Eighteenth-Century Attitudes towards the Glorious Revolution', *Studies in Eighteenth-century Culture*, vol. 1 (1971), pp. 143–67; H.T. Dickinson. 'The Eighteenth-Century Debate on the "Glorious Revolution"', *History*, vol. 61 (1976), pp. 28–45; Lois G. Schwoerer. 'The Contributions of the Declaration of Rights to Anglo-American Radicalism', in Margaret Jacob and James Jacob, eds. *The Origins of Anglo-American Radicalism* (George Allen & Unwin, 1984), pp. 105–24; and Mark Francis and John Morrow. 'After the Ancient Constitution: Political Theory and English Constitutional Writings, 1765–1832', *History of Political Thought*, vol. 9 (1988), pp. 283–302.

12. *The Correspondence of Edmund Burke*, vol. 6, p. 83.

13. 'In reality, my Object was not France, in the first instance, but this Country' (ibid., p. 141). Burke also privately lumped the reformers together not only with the National Assembly, but also 'their allies the Indian delinquents', in other words his opponents in the Hastings impeachment (ibid., p. 91). Several of these, notably George Rous and John Scott, wrote replies to the *Reflections*.

14. *The Correspondence of Edmund Burke*, vol. 6, p. 95.

15. Burke. *Speeches* (4 vols, 1816), vol. 3, p. 455.

16. Edmund Burke. *Reflections on the Revolution in France*, ed. J.G.A. Pocock (Indianapolis, Hackett Publishing Company, 1987),

p. xxx. See further Pocock. 'Edmund Burke and the Redefinition of Enthusiasm: The Context as Counter-Revolution,' in Francois Furet and Mona Ozuf, eds. *The French Revolution and the Creation of Modern Political Culture* (Oxford, Pergamon Press, 1989), pp. 19–43.

17. Some saw religion this as the main theme of the work. See, for example, [William Petty]. *Temperate Comments Upon Intemperate Reflections* (1791), pp. 36–49. Burke most notably equated Price with the regicide preacher Hugh Peters (*Reflections on the Revolution in France* (1790), p. 13). On Burke and Ireland see Michael Fuchs. *Edmund Burke, Ireland, and the Fashioning of the Self* (Oxford, Voltaire Foundation, 1996), and Luke Gibbons. *Edmund Burke and Ireland* (Cambridge, Cambridge University Press, 2003).

18. Alfred Cobban. 'Edmund Burke and the Origins of the Theory of Nationality,' *Cambridge Historical Journal*, 2 (1926–8), 37.

19. 14 March 1790. *The Correspondence of Edmund Burke*, vol. 6, p. 103.

20. *The Correspondence of Edmund Burke*, vol. 6, p. 160n. This occasioned Tooke's toast, 'If Mr Burke be ever prosecuted for such a libel on the Constitution, may his impeachment last as long as that of Mr Hastings', which was withdrawn after much opposition. But Lord John Russell was so incensed at this, and a second toast, 'May the Parliament of Great Britain become a National Assembly', that he reportedly cut his name out of the membership book of the Club, from which Lord Stanhope also withdrew (*Life and Letters of Sir Gilbert Elliot*, 1874, vol. 1, pp. 364–5). Later Whigs often considered that it was this 'extravagant veneration for all established rites and ceremonies in religion' that was the prime motive for his shift of view (Lord Holland. *Memoirs of the Whig Party* (2 vols, 1862), vol. 1, p. 5). Holland wrote that 'Till the ecclesiastical revenues were suppressed, Burke was far from disapproving the French Revolution. But what conclusion, against the sincerity of his opinions, is to be drawn from the fact? An extravagant veneration for all established rites and ceremonies in religion appears to have been a sentiment long and deeply rooted in his mind. It arose, indeed, from a conviction of the necessity of some establishment to the preservation of society, and the necessity of some outward show and pomp to the maintenance of that establishment, rather than from any strong predilection for particular tenets. Mr. Fox has more than once assured me, that in his invectives against Mr. Hastings' indignities to the Indian Priesthood, he spoke of the piety of the Hindoos with admiration, and of their holy religion

and sacred functions with an awe bordering on devotion. The seizure of the property of the Clergy, in France, might then excite alarm in breasts less predisposed to sensibility on such subjects. It was, in the judgment of many, an outrageous violation of property; when, therefore, it professed to be the result of a philosophy which denied the usefulness of all ecclesiastical institutions, rather than the desperate resource of an exhausted exchequer, it suggested a train of apprehensions in the mind of Mr. Burke, who, from the habitual tenor of his opinions, was prepared to receive such impressions' (Holland. *Memoirs of the Whig Party*, 1862, vol. 1, p. 6.)

21. *The Correspondence of Edmund Burke*, vol. 6, p. 126.
22. Edmund Burke. *The Works of the Right Honourable Edmund Burke* (12 vols, 1899), vol. 3, p. 263, vol. 4, p. 17. On the background and development of these ideas, see most recently Jennifer Walsh. *Edmund Burke and International Relations: The Commonwealth of Europe and the Crusade against the French Revolution* (Macmillan, 1995). Earlier accounts include Peter Stanlis. 'Edmund Burke and the Law of Nations', *American Journal of International Law*, 47 (1953), 397–413, James F. Davidson. 'Natural Law and International Law in Edmund Burke', *Review of Politics*, 21 (1959), 483–94, and R.J. Vincent. 'Edmund Burke and the Theory of International Relations,' *Review of International Studies*, 10 (1984), 205–18.
23. Thomas Carlyle. *The French Revolution. A History* (3 vols, 1898), vol. 2, p. 228.
24. *The Works of the Right Honourable Edmund Burke*, vol. 3. p. 274.
25. Edmund Burke. *Reflections on the Revolution in France* (1790), p. 7.
26. Ibid.
27. For this parallel, see, for example, *Reflections on the Irish Conspiracy* (1797), pp. 116–19, [David Rivers]. *Cursory Remarks on Paine's Rights of Man* (1792), p. 14. On the continuity of natural rights ideas from the American Revolution to this period see David Ritchie. *Natural Rights* (Swan Sonnenschein, 1903), pp. 3–19.
28. *The Works of the Right Honourable Edmund Burke*, vol. 3. p. 282.
29. See J.G.A. Pocock. 'The Political Economy of Burke's Analysis of the French Revolution', *Historical Journal*, vol. 25 (1982), pp. 331–49, and Pocock's introduction to his edition of the *Reflections* (Hackett Publishing Company). On Burke as an economist see Donald Winch. *Riches and Poverty: An Intellectual History of Political Economy in Britain, 1750–1834* (Cambridge, Cambridge University Press, 1996), pp. 166–220, and George Fasel. '"The Soul

That Animated": The Role of Property in Burke's Thought', *Studies in Burke and His Time*, 17 (1976), 27–41.

30. Thomas Carlyle. *The French Revolution* (3 vols, 1898), vol. 3, pp. 314–15.

31. *The Works of the Right Honourable Edmund Burke*, vol. 3, p. 306.

32. Ibid., p. 309.

33. Ibid., pp. 310–11.

34. Ibid., pp. 311–12.

35. E. Burke, *Reflections on the Revolution in France* (1987), pp. 35–46, 51–55. For a summary of disagreements about Burke's theory of rights see Michael Freeman, *Edmund Burke and the Critique of Political Radicalism* (Oxford, Basil Blackwell, 1980), pp. 85–93. A longer account is Burleigh Wilkins, *The Problem of Burke's Political Philosophy* (Oxford, Clarendon Press, 1967), pp. 163–246, which argues that Burke continued to believe in natural rights.

36. *The Works of the Right Honourable Edmund Burke*, vol. 6, p. 333.

37. Ibid., vol. 2, p. 254.

38. Ibid., p. 437.

39. Ibid., vol. 3, pp. 310–11.

40. *The Speeches of the Right Honourable Edmund Burke* (4 vols, 1816), vol. 3, p. 476.

41. Ibid., vol. 4, p. 51.

42. He commented privately that 'It is not calling the landed estates, possessed by old prescriptive rights, the "accumulations of ignorance and superstition", that can support me in shaking that grand title, which supersedes all other title, and which all my studies of general jurisprudence have taught me to consider as one principal cause of the formation of states; I mean the ascertaining and securing prescription. But these are donations made in "ages of ignorance and superstition". Be it so. It proves that these donations were made long ago; and this is prescription; and this gives right and title' (*The Correspondence of Edmund Burke*, vol. 6, p. 95). On Burke's conception of reason generally see Francis P. Canavan. *The Political Reason of Edmund Burke* (Durham, Duke University Press, 1960). In this sense Burke has often been seen as an opponent of utilitarianism; see, for example, Thomas Macknight. *History of the Life and Times of Edmund Burke* (3 vols, 1860), vol. 3, pp. 341–2, James MacCunn. *The Political Philosophy of Edmund Burke* (Edward Arnold, 1913), pp. 9, 49, but also 98.

43. See Iain Hampsher-Monk. 'Rhetoric and Opinion in the Politics of Edmund Burke', *History of Political Thought*, 9 (1988), 455–84.

44. For the natural law view of Burke see Peter Stanlis. *Edmund Burke and the Natural Law* (Ann Arbor, University of Michigan Press, 1958), and for emphases on utility and prescription, Paul Lucas. 'On Edmund Burke's Doctrine of Prescription; Or, An Appeal from the New to the Old Lawyers', *Historical Journal*, vol. 11 (1968), pp. 35–63, J.R. Dinwiddy. 'Utility and Natural Law in Burke's Thought: A Reconsideration', *Studies in Burke and His Time*, vol. 16 (1974), pp. 105–28, and F.P. Lock. *Burke's Reflections on the Revolution in France* (London, George Allen & Unwin, 1985), pp. 90–4.

45. In one of the few documented instances where an effigy of Burke was burnt by radicals, it carried two signs: 'Edmund Burke, the Irish Pensioner' and 'I hate the Swinish Multitude' (*Derby Mercury*, no. 3172, 31 January 1793, p. 1). Pamphlets appeared with titles like *An Address to the Hon. Edmund Burke from the Swinish Multitude*. The phrase was still recalled twenty-five years later (cf. Samuel Bamford. *Passages in the Life of a Radical and Early Days* (2 vols, 1894), vol. 2, p. 334).

46. Burke later communicated to the Queen by cypher, c. 17 August 1791, warning her 'For Gods sake have nothing to do with Traitors', and recommending no compromise on any issue (*The Correspondence of Edmund Burke*, vol. 6, pp. 349–52).

47. *The Works of the Right Honourable Edmund Burke*, vol. 3, pp. 331–2.

48. Ibid., pp. 345–6.

49. Ibid., p. 359.

50. Ibid., p. 397.

51. Ibid., p. 492.

52. On contemporary criticisms see especially Carl B. Cone, 'Pamphlet Replies to Burke's *Reflections*', *The Southwestern Social Science Quarterly*, 26 (1945), 22–34, and my 'The *Reflections* Refracted: The Critical Reception of Burke's *Reflections on the Revolution in France* during the early 1790s,' in John Whale, ed. *Edmund Burke's Reflections on The Revolution in France* (Manchester, Manchester University Press, 2000), pp. 40–59, and F.P. Lock. *Burke's Reflections on the Revolution in France* (George Allen & Unwin, 1985), pp. 132–65.

53. Charles Knight. *Passages of a Working Life* (3 vols, 1864), vol. 1, pp. 37–8. The King presumably ordered a copy personally.

54. At a levée on 3 February 1791 which Burke attended with the Duke of Portland the King complimented him highly on the work.

55. *The Correspondence of Edmund Burke*, vol. 6, p. 219.

56. Earl Stanhope. *Life of the Right Honourable William Pitt* (3 vols, 1861), vol. 2, p. 245.

57. *The Correspondence of Edmund Burke*, vol. 6, pp. 155–6.

58. James Prior. *Life of the Right Honourable Edmund Burke* (1854), p. 315.

59. *Extracts from the Journals and Correspondence of Miss Berry* (1866), vol. 1 p. 251 (8 Nov. 1790). She noted elsewhere that 'To do the book full justice, it is not necessary to agree with it in all points. To say nothing of its eloquence, it has that merit in a sovereign degree without which no book can thoroughly charm me, that of making me love the author. His ideas on religion I did really take notice of, as being finely expressed' (*The Berry Papers*, ed. Lewis Melville, John Lane, 1914, p. 35).

60. He added that 'One would think that the author of such a work would be called to the government of his country by the combined voice of every man in it. What shall be said of the state of things when it is remembered that the writer is a man decried, persecuted and proscribed; not being much valued even by his own party, and by half the nation considered as little better than an ingenious madman!' (*Correspondence of Edmund Burke and William Windham*, 1910, p. 23)

61. James Prior. *Life of the Right Honourable Edmund Burke* (1854), p. 316.

62. *The Journal and Correspondence of William, Lord Auckland* (1861), vol. 2, p. 377–8.

63. *The Correspondence of Edmund Burke*, vol. 6, p. 193n.

64. *The Autobiography of Edward Gibbon* (J.M. Dent, 1932), p. 178; *The Letters of Edward Gibbon* (3 vols, Cassell & Co., 1956), vol. 3, p. 216. On the background to Gibbon's views see J.G.A. Pocock. *Barbarism and Religion* (2 vols, Cambridge, Cambridge University Press, 1999).

65. *The Farington Diary*, (8 vols, Hutchinson & Co., 1922), vol. 4, p. 22.

66. Francis and Windham both received advance copies from Burke on 27 October.

67. *The Correspondence of Edmund Burke*, vol. 6, p. 89. Privately it was reported that Francis said that 'Burke, was a man who truly & propheticaly foresaw all the consequences which would arise from the adoption of the French principles, – but said Sir Francis, Burke wrote with so much passion, so much vehemence, that instead of convincing He created doubts in the minds of his readers, who hesitated to believe a man so carried away by his feelings.' (*The Farington Diary*, vol. 1, p. 271).

68. Burke's retort on this point (20 February 1790) was: 'I really am perfectly astonished how you could dream, with my paper in your hand, that I found no other cause than the beauty of the queen of France (now, I suppose, pretty much faded) for disapproving the conduct which has been held towards her, and for expressing my own particular feelings. I am not to order the natural sympathies of my own heart, and of every honest breast, to wait until all the jokes of all the anecdotes of the coffee-houses of Paris, and of the dissenting meeting-houses of London, are scoured of all the slander of those who calumniate persons, that, afterwards, they may murder them with impunity'.

And further: 'I tell you again, that the recollection of the manner in which I saw the queen of France, in the year 1774, and the contrast between that brilliancy, splendour, and beauty, with the prostrate homage of a nation to her, and the abominable scene of 1789, which I was describing, did draw tears from me and wetted my paper. These tears came again into my eyes, almost as often as I looked at the description; they may again' (*The Correspondence of the Right Hon. Edmund Burke*, 3 vols., 1844, vol. 3, pp. 137–9).

69. *Memoirs of Sir Philip Francis* (2 vols, 1867), vol. 2, p. 282.

70. *Life and Letters of Gilbert Elliot, First Earl of Minto* (3 vols, 1874), vol. 1, pp. 369–70. Samuel Parr noted that 'I am most fixedly and most indignantly on the side of Mr. Sheridan and Mr. Fox against Mr. Burke. It is not merely French politics that produced this dispute; they might have been settled privately. No, no, there is jealousy lurking underneath; jealousy of Mr. Sheridan's eloquence; jealousy of his popularity; jealousy of his influence with Mr. Fox; jealousy, perhaps, of his connection with the Prince' (Thomas Moore. *Memoirs of the Life of the Right Honourable Richard Brinsley Sheridan*, 2 vols, 1826, vol. 2, p. 128). See Ch. 6.

71. Edmund Burke. *The Works of the Right Honourable Edmund Burke*, vol. 5, p. 6: 'In my journey with them through life, I met Mr. Fox in my road; and I travelled with him very cheerfully, as long as he appeared to me to pursue the same direction with those in whose company I set out. In the latter stage of our progress a new scheme of liberty and equality was produced in the world, which either dazzled his imagination, or was suited to some new walks of ambition which were then opened to his view'.

72. Ibid., vol. 3, p. 236.

73. Earl Stanhope. *Life of the Right Honourable William Pitt* (4 vols, 1861), vol. 2, p. 97.

74. See, for example, John Derry. *Charles James Fox* (B.T. Batsford, 1972), p. 305.

75. Edward Lascelles. *The Life of Charles James Fox* (Oxford, Oxford University Press, 1936), p. 228. Fox told Burke that 'The king, it seems, was represented to have used some expressions favourable to Mr. Fox. In order, therefore, to secure himself in his situation, the minister was asserted to have given out the watch-word, that Mr. Fox was by principle a republican; and it was supposed that, in pursuance of this plan, he instigated Mr. Burke to the discussion. Mr. Burke undeceived his friend, by relating the fact as it was' (*Speeches of the Right Honourable Edmund Burke*, vol. 4, p. 2).

76. Duke of Buckingham and Chandos. *Memoirs of the Court and Cabinets of George III* (2 vols, 1853), vol. 1, p. 54. But the Prince himself Burke thought 'deeply concerned that the ideas of an elective crown should not prevail. He had experienced, and you had all of you fully experienced, the peril of these doctrines on the question of the Regency' (*The Correspondence of Edmund Burke*, vol. 7, p. 58).

77. *The Journal and Correspondence of William, Lord Auckland* (4 vols, 1861), vol. 2, p. 252.

78. *The Correspondence of Edmund Burke*, vol. 6, p. 272.

79. Ibid., p. 274.

80. '... while I lament the Miseries too frequently attendant even upon well-conducted Revolution, I can not but rejoice that so large a Portion of my Fellow Creatures have, at any rate short of Destruction, been emancipated from a Tyranny grievous indeed, and which, spite of the boasted, tho', as I have always thought, superficial and unreal Suavity of Manners, was the more oppressive, as, by the unchecked Despotism of a widespread Nobility, it was brought even to the Door of every Individual', (to Richard Burke, 9 August 1791, *The Correspondence of Edmund Burke*, vol. 6, p. 332).

81. Burke in August 1791 said that 'I believed, as he did, that inwardly even Fox did not differ from me materially, if at all; and that I was sure the rest for the far greater Number heartily agreed and without any limitation. The misfortune was that so many good and weighty men, thinking the same way, should, upon grounds of mistaken prudence, suffer themselves to be added to the weight

of a scale to which they did not belong' (*The Correspondence of Edmund Burke*, vol. 6, p. 336). And there is evidence for this. Fox in 1790 denied that his view on France meant that he was 'a friend to democracy': 'He declared himself equally the enemy of all absolute forms of government, whether an absolute monarchy, an absolute aristocracy, or an absolute democracy. He was adverse to all extremes, and a friend only to a mixed government, like our own, in which, if the aristocracy, or indeed either of the three branches of the constitution, were destroyed, the good effect of the whole, and the happiness derived under it, would, in his mind, be at an end' (*The Speeches of the Right Honourable Charles James Fox*, 6 vols, 1815, vol. 4, p. 52).

82. In mid-1791 Burke commented that 'The supper at Brookes's was a sort of Academy for these Doctrines. Individuals, little courted before, were separately talked over, and, as it were, canvassed. I found, that the Prince of Wales, to Whose very existence the principles of that Book were necessary, was very early led to take, and to express, no small dislike to them; and to abstain even from expressions of common politeness on the Pamphlets being presented to him. If I had not receivd very particular intelligence of all these manouvres, to the moment of the explosion in Parliament, yet the face of things, and the extraordinary change in Persons, could have left no Doubt in my Mind upon the subject' (*The Correspondence of Edmund Burke*, vol. 6, p. 273).

83. Edmund Burke. *The Works of the Right Honourable Edmund Burke*, vol. 4, p. 167.

84. Ibid., p. 69.

85. Edmund Burke. *The Speeches of the Right Honourable Edmund Burke*, vol. 4, p. 92.

86. Ibid., p. 73.

87. Edmund Burke. *The Works of the Right Honourable Edmund Burke*, vol. 4, pp. 166–7, 189.

88. Edmund Burke. *The Speeches of the Right Honourable Edmund Burke*, vol. 4, p. 165.

89. Earl of Malmesbury. *Diary and Correspondence of James Harris, First Earl of Malmesbury* (3 vols, 1844), vol. 2, p. 453.

90. 'The success of this last Pamphlet is great indeed. Every one tells me, that it is thought much better than the former. I have no Objection to their thinking so – but it is not my opinion. It may however be more useful. Not one word from one of our party.

They are secretly galled. They agree with me to a title – but they dare not speak out for fear of hurting Fox' (*The Correspondence of Edmund Burke*, vol. 6, p. 360).

91. 30 September 1791, *The Correspondence of Edmund Burke*, vol. 6, p. 417.

92. *The Correspondence of Edmund Burke*, vol. 6, pp. 418–19. 'Jacobites', after *Jacobus*, the Latin for 'James', were supporters of the Stuart dynasty after the 'Glorious Revolution' of 1688–9 had deposed James II.

93. 'Thoughts on French Affairs', *The Works of the Right Honourable Edmund Burke*, vol. 4, p. 324.

94. *The Correspondence of Edmund Burke*, vol. 6, p. 420.

95. Lord John Russell, ed. *Memorials and Correspondence of Charles James Fox* (4 vols, 1854), vol. 2, p. 360.

96. *Correspondence of the Right Honourable Edmund Burke* (4 vols, 1844), vol. 3, p. 395; *The Correspondence of Edmund Burke*, vol. 6, p. 422.

97. Ibid., vol. 7, pp. 54–5.

98. Ibid., p. 150.

99. Fanny Burney. *Diary and Letters of Madam D'Arblay* (3 vols, 1876), vol. 3, p. 419.

100. *The Correspondence of Edmund Burke*, vol. 7, p. 192.

101. To Lord Ossory, ibid., vol. 7, p. 196.

102. For example, William Augustus Miles. *The Correspondence of William Augustus Miles on the French Revolution* (2 vols, 1890), vol. 2, p. 343.

103. Edmund Burke. *The Works of the Right Honourable Edmund Burke*, vol. 5, p. 18.

104. Ibid., p. 43.

105. Ibid., p. 49.

106. Ibid., vol. 1, p. 458.

107. Croly wrote that Burke was the 'restorer of Whiggism to the principles of its ancient and better days' (George Croly. *Memoir of the Political Life and the Right Honourable Edmund Burke*, 1840, vol. 1, p. 291). Portland noted that when anyone criticized the *Reflections* to him, he told them that he had recommended it to his sons as containing the true Whig creed (Portland to Dr French Laurence, 29 August 1791, Portland MSS, at Nottingham, quoted in *The Correspondence of Edmund Burke*, vol. 6, p. 161n.).

108. Of Paine he was scathing: 'He is utterly incapable of comprehending his subject. He has not even a moderate portion of learning of any kind. He has learned the instrumental part of literature, a style, and a method of disposing his ideas, without having ever made a previous preparation of Study or thinking for the use of it' (*The Correspondence of Edmund Burke*, vol. 6, pp. 303–4).

109. George Pellew. *The Life and Correspondence of the Right Hon. Henry Addington*, 1847, vol. 2, p. 241. See Burke's letter to Mackintosh, in *Memoirs of the Life of the Right Honourable Sir James Mackintosh* (1836), vol. 1, pp. 88–90.

110. *Political Writings of the 1790s*, vol. 1, p. 271.

111. *Memoirs of the Life of the Right Honourable Sir James Mackintosh* (1836), vol. 1, p. 91.

112. William Smyth. *Lectures on History* (2nd series, 3 vols, 1842), vol. 3, pp. 1–26.

113. *The Speeches of the Right Honourable George Canning* (3rd edn., 1836), vol. 5, p. 451.

114. But Brougham continued that 'That Mr. Burke did, however, err, and err widely in the estimate which he formed of the merits of a restored Government, no one can now doubt. His mistake was in comparing the old régime with the anarchy of the Revolution; to which not only the monarchy of France but the despotism of Turkey was preferable. He never could get rid of the belief that because the change had been effected with a violence which produced, and inevitably produced the consequences foreseen by himself; and by him alone, therefore the tree so planted must for ever prove incapable of bearing good fruit' (Henry Brougham. *Contributions to the Edinburgh Review*, 1856, vol. 1, pp. 280–1).

115. Henry Brougham. *Historical Sketches of Statesmen who Flourished in the Time of George III* (1839), vol. 1, p. 157, 160.

116. William Hazlitt. *Political Essays* (1819), p. 264.

117. Both cited from James Sack. 'Edmund Burke and the Conservative Party in the Nineteenth Century', in Ian Crowe, ed. *Edmund Burke. His Life and Legacy* (Four Courts Press, 1997), p. 77. See also J.J. Sack. 'The Memory of Burke and the Memory of Pitt: English Conservatism Confronts Its Past, 1806–1829', *The Historical Journal*, 30 (1987), 623–40. I here draw upon my 'The Nineteenth Century Appraisal of Burke's *Reflections*: From Sir James Mackintosh to John Morley' (forthcoming).

118. T.E. Kebbel. *History of Toryism* (1886), p. 398.
119. James Sack. 'Edmund Burke and the Conservative Party in the Nineteenth Century', in Ian Crowe, ed. *Edmund Burke. His Life and Legacy* (Four Courts Press, 1997), pp. 80, 83. Elsewhere, however, Sack makes the claim that the *Reflections* was one of two texts (the other being Richard Musgrave's *Memoirs of the Different Rebellions in Ireland*, 1801) to define the 'British Right' in the nineteenth century (*From Jacobite to Conservative. Reaction and Orthodoxy in Britain*, c. *1760–1832*, Cambridge, Cambridge University Press, 1983, p. 96.
120. Keith Feiling. *Toryism. A Political Dialogue* (1913), p. 39. But Burke is later here also bracketed with 'all the great Tory writers' such as Bolingbroke and Coleridge (p. 142).
121. Henry Montagu Butler. *The Character of Edmund Burke. An Oration Delivered in the Hall of Trinity College* (Cambridge, 1854), pp. 14–15.
122. John Morley. *Edmund Burke. A Historical Study* (1867), p. 45.

Chapter Three: Thomas Paine

1. Thomas Paine. *Rights of Man*, ed. G. Claeys (Indianapolis, Hackett Publishing Company, 1992), p. 31. Subsequent references are to this edition.
2. Ibid., pp. 125–6. On the American model in Paine see, most recently, Harvey J. Kaye. *Thomas Paine and the Promise of America* (New York, Hill & Wang, 2005).
3. Ibid., pp. 14–15.
4. The phrase was a favourite of Bentham's; cf. Jeremy Bentham. *The Book of Fallacies* (1824), p. 390.
5. Thomas Paine. *Rights of Man*, p. 24. On the development of these themes from this period onwards, see A. Taylor. *Down With the Crown. British Anti-Monarchism and Debates about Royalty since 1790* (Reaktion Books, 1999).
6. Ibid., pp. 37–8.
7. 'That whenever any Form of Government becomes destructive of these ends, it is the Right of the People to alter or to abolish it, and to institute new Government'. A good brief survey of the background to these ideals is J.H. Burns. 'The Rights of Man since the Reformation: An Historical Survey', in Francis Vallat, ed.

An Introduction to the Study of Human Rights (Europa Publications, 1971), pp. 16–30.

8. Thomas Paine. *Rights of Man*, p. 39.

9. Ibid., pp. 15, 40, 110. On Paine's controversy with the Abbé Sieyès respecting the need for a republic see *The Writings of Thomas Paine*, ed. Moncure Conway (4 vols, New York, G.P. Putnam's Sons, 1902–8), vol. 3, pp. 1–10, and for the context, Sieyès. *Political Writings*, ed. Michael Sonenscher (Indianapolis, Hackett Publishing Company, 2003).

10. A. J. Ayer. *Thomas Paine* (Secker & Warburg, 1988), p. 91; Gwyn Williams. *Artisans and Sans-Culottes. Popular Movements in France and Britain during the French Revolution* (New York, W.W. Norton, 1969), p. 7; Thomas Paine. *Rights of Man*, p. 124.

11. Thomas Paine. *Rights of Man*, p. 127.

12. Ibid., p. 135.

13. Ibid., pp. 135–42.

14. This interpretation is defended in my *Thomas Paine*, chapter three.

15. Paine said elsewhere of Rousseau that he had demonstrated 'a loveliness of sentiment in favor of liberty, that excites respect, and elevates the human faculties … without describing the means of possessing it' (Paine. *The Writings of Thomas Paine*, vol. 2, p. 334.) He cited the *Social Contract* only once (ibid, vol. 3, p. 104), in October 1792.

16. Thomas Paine. *Rights of Man*, pp. 172–3.

17. On Paine's economic ideas generally see Joseph Dorfman. 'The Economic Philosophy of Thomas Paine', *Political Science Quarterly*, 53 (1938), 372–86, and William Christian. 'The Moral Economics of Tom Paine,' *Journal of the History of Ideas*, 54 (1973), 367–80.

18. See generally Gareth Stedman Jones. *An End to Poverty? A Historical Debate* (Profile Books, 2004), pp. 110ff.

19. Thomas Paine. *Rights of Man*, pp. 200–219.

20. See Robert Falk. 'Thomas Paine: Deist or Quaker?', *Pennsylvania Magazine of History and Biography*, 62 (1938), 52–63, and Harry Hayden Clark, 'An Historical Interpretation of Thomas Paine's Religion', *University of California Chronicle*, 35 (1933), 56–87, both of which argue against Conway's biography of Paine in particular, and more generally Franklyn R. Prochaska. 'Thomas Paine's *The Age of Reason* Revisited', *Journal of the History of Ideas*, 33 (1972), 561–76, Richard H. Popkin. '*The Age of Reason* versus *The Age of Revelation*: Two Critics of Tom Paine: David Levi and Elias Boudinot', in

J.A. Leo Lemay, ed. *Deism, Masonry and the Enlightenment* (Newark, University of Delaware Press, 1987), pp. 158–70, and Jack Fruchtman, Jr. *Thomas Paine and the Religion of Nature* (Baltimore, Johns Hopkins University Press, 1993). On Paine's own conception of his indebtedness to the Quakers see *The Complete Writings of Thomas Paine* (ed. P. Foner, 2 vols, New York, Citadel Press, 1945), vol. 2, pp. 53, 56–60, 83, 86. Paine may also have preached as an itinerant Methodist minister. See George Hindmarsh. 'Thomas Paine and the Methodist Influence', *Bulletin of the Thomas Paine Society*, vol. 6 (1979), pp. 59–78. For contemporary rumours that Paine had been an itinerant preacher, see David Rivers. *Observations on the Political Conduct of the Protestant Dissenters* (?1799), p. 35.

21. 'The Age of Reason', ibid., vol. 1, pp. 464, 474, 493, 520, 529. On the text and reactions to it see Franklyn Prochaska, 'Thomas Paine's *The Age of Reason* Revisited', *Journal of the History of Ideas*, 33 (1972), 561–76.

22. Graham Wallas. *The Life of Francis Place* (4th edn, George Allen & Unwin, 1925), p. 20.

23. Thomas Paine. *Complete Writings*, vol. 1, pp. 482–4, 486, vol. 2, p. 731. On the background to this conception see Ursula Vogel. 'When the Earth Belonged to All: The Land Question in Eighteenth-Century Justifications of Private Property', *Political Studies*, 36 (1988), 102–22.

24. Ibid., vol. 1, pp. 498, 503, 599, 498, vol. 2, pp. 90, 920, 305, 752, 816, 748–56. For Paine's view of Newton see vol. 1, p. 164.

25. Ibid., vol. 2, p. 731.

26. See, for example, Hugo Grotius. *De Jure Belli ac Pacis*, (1625) (Clarendon Press, 1925), vol. 2, pp. 188–9, and for commentary, Istvan Hont. 'The language of sociability and commerce: Samuel Pufendorf and the theoretical foundations of the "Four-Stages Theory"', in Anthony Pagden, ed. *The Languages of Political Theory in Early-Modern Europe* (Cambridge, Cambridge University Press, 1987), pp. 253–76, reprinted in Istvan Hont. *Jealousy of Trade. International Competition and the Nation State in Historical Perspective* (Cambridge, MA, Harvard University Press, 2005), pp. 159–84.

27. Thomas Paine. *Complete Writings*, vol. 1, p. 611, vol. 2, p. 274.

28. Thomas Paine. *Rights of Man*, p. 39.

29. Philip Foner, Paine's leading modern editor, has even contended that 'Paine supported the communistic aspects of Babeuf's theories'

which he saw as 'correctly aimed at the removal of social inequalities in property' (*Complete Writings*, vol. 1, p. 607). This view is mistaken because it confuses Paine's arguments with his actual program. For Babeuf's views see R.B. Rose. *Gracchus Babeuf. The First Revolutionary Communist* (Stanford University Press, 1978), esp. pp. 230–2, and generally R.B. Rose. *The Enragés: Socialists of the French Revolution?* (Cambridge, Cambridge University Press, 1965), esp. pp. 89–91, for contemporary French discussions of the Agrarian Law. On the general political milieu in which Paine was writing in this period see Isser Woloch. *Jacobin Legacy. The Democratic Movement under the Directory* (Princeton, Princeton University Press, 1970).

30. Thomas Paine. *Complete Writings*, vol. 1, pp. 606–7.

31. Ibid., pp. 609–10, 619.

32. Ibid., pp. 610–11.

33. See, for example, Hugo Grotius. *De Jure Belli ac Pacis*, vol. 2, p. 186, Samuel Pufendorf. *De Jure Naturae et Gentium* (1672) (Clarendon Press, 1934), p. 537. Only a few late eighteenth-century writers contested the 'negative community' conclusion, namely William Ogilvie, to some extent Robert Wallace, Thomas Reid and Thomas Spence. See W. Ogilvie. *An Essay on the Right of Property in Land* (1781), p. 11 ('the earth having been given to mankind in common occupancy, each individual seems to have by nature a right to possess and cultivate an equal share'); Robert Wallace. *Various Prospects of Mankind, Nature, and Providence* (1761), pp. 38–40, 66; Thomas Spence. *The Rights of Man* (4th edn., 1793), pp. 21–2; Thomas Spence. *The Rights of Infants* (1797). See generally my *Machinery, Money and the Millennium: From Moral Economy to Socialism, 1815–1860* (Princeton, Princeton University Press, 1987), pp. 1–33, and on the development of the four-stages theory, Ronald Meek. *Social Science and the Ignoble Savage* (Cambridge, Cambridge University Press, 1976). On discussions of property prior to this period generally see also Paschal Larkin. *Property in the Eighteenth Century* (Cork, Cork University Press, 1930), Thomas Horne. *Property Rights and Poverty: Political Argument in Britain, 1605–1834* (Chapel Hill, University of North Carolina Press, 1990), which focuses mainly on rights to charity rather than to the produce of labour, Alan Ryan. *Property and Political Theory* (Oxford, Basil Blackwell, 1984), chs. 1–2, and Stephen Buckle. *Natural Law and the Theory of Property. Grotius to Hume* (Oxford, Clarendon Press, 1991).

34. Thomas Paine. *Complete Writings*, vol. 1, p. 611.

35. Ibid., pp. 612–13, 621.

36. *Collected Writings*, vol. 2, p. 580.

37. On the development of radicalism from 1800–32 see Simon Maccoby. *English Radicalism 1786–1832* (George Allen & Unwin, 1955); A.W. Smith. 'Irish Rebels and English Radicals 1798–1820', *Past and Present*, vol. 7 (1955), pp. 78–85; N.C. Miller. 'John Cartwright and Radical Parliamentary Reform, 1808–1819', *English Historical Review*, vol. 83 (1968), pp. 705–28; T.M. Parsinnen. 'Association, Convention and Anti-Parliament in British Radical Politics 1771–1848', *English Historical Review*, vol. 88 (1973), pp. 504–33; E.P. Thompson. *The Making of the English Working Class* (Penguin, 1977); Iowerth Prothero. *Artisans and Politics in Early Nineteenth Century London* (Dawson, 1979); John Belchem. 'Republicanism, Popular Constitutionalism, and the Radical Platform in Early 19th Century Britain', *Social History*, vol. 6 (1981), pp. 1–32; J.A. Hone. *For the Cause of Truth. Radicalism in London 1796–1821* (Oxford, Clarendon Press, 1982); W. Rubinstein. 'The End of "Old Corruption" in Britain 1780–1860', *Past and Present*, vol. 101 (1983), pp. 55–86; Craig Calhoun. *The Question of Class Struggle. Social Foundations of Popular Radicalism during the Industrial Revolution* (Oxford, Basil Blackwell, 1984); John Belchem. *'Orator' Hunt. Henry Hunt and English Working Class Radicalism* (Oxford, Clarendon Press, 1985); Gregory Claeys. *Citizens and Saints. Politics and Anti-Politics in Early British Socialism* (Cambridge, Cambridge University Press, 1989); and James A. Epstein. *Radical Expression. Political Language, Ritual and Symbol in England 1790–1850* (Oxford, Oxford University Press, 1994).

38. British Library Add. MSS. 27818, fols. 72–3.

39. *Sherwin's Political Register*, 17 May 1817, p. 111.

40. See Francis Thackeray. *Order vs. Anarchy, Being a Reply to Thomas Paine's Attack upon the British Constitution, Entitled 'The Rights of Man'* (1831).

41. *Flower's Political Review and Monthly Magazine*, May 1808, p. 331.

42. See Edward Royle. *Victorian Infidels. The Origins of the British Secularist Movement 1791–1866* (Manchester, Manchester University Press, 1974), and Edward Royle. *Radicals, Secularists and Republicans. Freethought in Britain, 1866–1915* (Manchester, Manchester University Press, 1980).

43. Max Beer. *The Pioneers of Land Reform* (G. Bell & Sons, 1920), p. vi.
    Cf. the illuminating comment by the conservative W.H. Mallock
    respecting Henry George that 'The statements which he makes
    with such frequency, with regard to God and God's intentions,
    and which form the practical fulcrum of his reforming lever, are
    part of the stock-in-trade of the whole democratic school, and it
    is hardly too much to say that no revolutionary appeal to the
    people ever is made, or can be made, without them' (*Studies in
    Contemporary Superstition*, 1895, p. 218).

Chapter Four: Mary Wollstonecraft

1. 'On the Admission of Women to the Rights of Citizenship',
   written in 1790.
2. This trend is increasingly acknowledged in recent studies, for
   example, Virginia Sapiro. *A Vindication of Political Virtue. The
   Political Theory of Mary Wollstonecraft* (Chicago, University of
   Chicago Press, 1992), p. xxv. An earlier version of this section was
   presented at the University of Hull in 1998. I am grateful to
   Cambridge University Press for permission to reprint part of
   it here.
3. An exception is Mitzi Meyers. 'Reform or Ruin: "A Revolution in
   Female Manners"', in Harry Payne, ed. *Studies in Eighteenth Century
   Culture*, vol. 11 (1982), pp. 199–216, which stresses (203) the prox-
   imity of some of Wollstonecraft's views and those of, for example,
   the evangelical reformer Hannah More. On the general context,
   see especially Maurice J. Quinlan. *Victorian Prelude. A History of
   English Manners 1700–1800* (New York, Columbia University Press,
   1941), pp. 40–102, Muriel Jaeger. *Before Victoria. Changing Standards
   & Behaviour* (Chatto & Windus, 1956), pp. 118–38; Joanna Innes.
   'Politics and Morals: The Reformation of Manners Movement in
   Late Eighteenth-Century England', in Eckhart Hellmuth, ed.
   *The Transformation of Political Culture. England and Germany in the
   Late Eighteenth Century* (Oxford, Oxford University Press, 1990),
   pp. 57–118, and G.J. Barker-Benfield. *The Culture of Sensibility. Sex
   and Society in Eighteenth-Century Britain* (Chicago, University of
   Chicago Press, 1992), especially pp. 359–68, which assumes
   Wollstonecraft to have been central to the 'gendering' of sensibility

in this period, though it does not look closely at the relationship between the texts examined here.

4. *Vindication of the Rights of Woman* (1792) (*The Works of Mary Wollstonecraft*, William Pickering, 1989, vol. 5, pp. 65–266), p. 66. All subsequent references will be to this edition, which contains both texts under discussion. For commentary, see also Barbara Taylor's introduction to her edition of the second *Vindication* (E.P. Dent, 1992).

5. Godwin later described her religious ideas as 'almost entirely of her own creation' (*Memoirs of the Author of a Vindication of the Rights of Woman*, Penguin Books, 1987, p. 215). Claire Tomalin, for example, stresses of Wollstonecraft's religious views that she, with many other radical Dissenters, was not much concerned with church attendance, but 'retained a tenuous but stubborn belief in God' (*The Life and Death of Mary Wollstonecraft*, Meridian Books, 1974, p. 76). Her brief account of the second *Vindication* (pp. 103–7) similarly ignores the continuing significance of Wollstonecraft's religious views. Two recent full-scale studies of Wollstonecraft's thought do not go far to clarifying the central religious context of the second *Vindication*. See Gary Kelly. *Revolutionary Feminism., The Mind and Career of Mary Wollstonecraft* (Macmillan, 1992), pp. 107–39, which focuses on the question of manners; and Virginia Sapiro. *A Vindication of Political Virtue. The Political Theory of Mary Wollstonecraft* (Chicago, University of Chicago Press, 1992), which though it pays closer heed to the issue of Wollstonecraft's religious views (see esp. pp. 44–52), does not take up the view expounded here. Little attention is paid to religion, much less its implications for Wollstonecraft's view of rights, in any edition of the second *Vindication*, for example, in Miriam Kramnick's Penguin edition (1978) or Barbara H. Solomon and Paula S. Berggren, eds. *A Mary Wollstonecraft Reader* (Mentor, 1983) or Ulrich H. Hardt, ed. *A Critical Edition of Mary Wollstonecraft's Vindication of the Rights of Woman* (Whitson Publishing Company, 1982). Moreover, the theme is virtually ignored even in such well-known and wide-ranging accounts of Wollstonecraft's ideas as: Carolyn W. Korsmeyer's 'Reason and Morals in the Early Feminist Movement: Mary Wollstonecraft', reprinted in *A Vindication of the Rights of Woman*, ed. Carol H. Poston (Norton Books, 1988), pp. 285–97; Elissa S. Guralnick. 'Radical Politics in Mary Wollstonecraft's *A Vindication of the Rights of Woman*', ibid., pp. 308–17; 'Mary Wollstonecraft Stoic Liberal-Democrat',

Canadian Journal of Political and Social Theory, 1 (1977), 59–74; G.J. Barker-Benfield. 'Mary Wollstonecraft: Eighteenth Century Commonwealthwoman'. *Journal of the History of Ideas*, 50 (1989), 95–115; and Anca Vlasopolos. 'Mary Wollstonecraft's Mask of Reason in *A Vindication of the Rights of Woman*', *Dalhousie Review*, 60 (1980), 462–71. See also Mervyn Nicholson. 'The Eleventh Commandment: Sex and Spirit in Wollstonecraft and Malthus', *Journal of the History of Ideas*, 51 (1990), 401–21. See also Carol Kay. 'Canon, Ideology, and Gender: Mary Wollstonecraft's Critique of Adam Smith', *New Political Science*, 15 (1986), 63–76. A recent account improving greatly on this lack of treatment is Barbara Taylor. *Mary Wollstonecraft and the Feminist Imagination* (Cambridge, Cambridge University Press, 2003). The general religious context is explored in Ursula Henriques. *Religious Toleration in England 1787–1833* (Routledge & Kegan Paul, 1961), Roland Stromberg. *Religious Liberalism in Eighteenth-Century England* (Oxford, Oxford University Press, 1954), Richard Barlow. *Citizenship and Conscience. A Study in the Theory and Practice of Religious Toleration in England During the Eighteenth Century* (Philadelphia, University of Pennsylvania Press, 1962), Knut Haakonssen, ed. *Enlightenment and Religion. Rational Dissent in Eighteenth Century Britain* (Cambridge, Cambridge University Press, 1996), and B. Young. *Religion and Enlightenment in Eighteenth-Century Britain: Theological Debate from Locke to Burke* (Oxford, Clarendon Press, 1998).

6. Wollstonecraft. *Works*, vol. 5, p. 7. For commentary on the first *Vindication* see especially Mitzi Meyers. 'Politics From the Outside: Mary Wollstonecraft's First *Vindication*', *Studies in Eighteenth Century Culture*, 6 (1977), 113–32, G.J. Barker-Benfield. 'Mary Wollstonecraft: Eighteenth Century Commonwealthwoman', *op. cit.*, and Gary Kelly. *Revolutionary Feminism., The Mind and Career of Mary Wollstonecraft* (Macmillan, 1992), pp. 84–106.

7. Ibid., pp. 8–9. A good general treatment of Wollstonecraft's view of sensibility is Mary Poovey. 'Mary Wollstonecraft: The Gender of Genres in Late Eighteenth-Century England', *Novel: A Forum on Fiction*, 15 (1982), 111–26.

8. Wollstonecraft. *Works*, vol. 5, p. 9.

9. Ibid., p. 10.

10. Ibid., pp. 7, 201. On the development of ideas of politeness see Lawrence Klein. *Shaftesbury and the Culture of Politeness: Moral Discourses and Cultural Politics in Early Eighteenth-Century England*

(Cambridge, Cambridge University Press, 1994), and Jenny Davidson. *Hypocrisy and the Politics of Politeness: Manners and Morals from Locke to Austen* (Cambridge, Cambridge University Press, 2004).

11. David Hume. *Essays Moral, Political and Literary* (1903 edn.), pp. 127–8, 120, 278. Wollstonecraft quotes Hume on character (*Works*, vol. 5, p. 124).

12. For Burgh, for example, see his *An Account of the First Settlement ... of the Cessares* (1764), reprinted in my *Utopias of the British Enlightenment* (Cambridge, Cambridge University Press, 1994), pp. 111–20. Godwin was later insistent that what he termed this 'occasional harshness and ruggedness of character' in the second *Vindication* was much modified in the latter years of her life (*Memoir of Mary Wollstonecraft*, Constable & Co., 1928, p. 84.)

13. Wollstonecraft. *Works*, vol. 4, pp. 32–3.

14. Ibid., vol. 1, p. 61.

15. Ibid., vol. 7, p. 66.

16. Ibid., pp. 109, 370.

17. Ibid., p. 314.

18. Hannah More. *The Works of Hannah More* (11 vols, 1830), vol. 11, pp. 36–7.

19. The standard survey of the origins of this movement is Ford K. Brown. *Fathers of the Victorians. The Age of Wilberforce* (Cambridge, Cambridge University Press, 1961).

20. William Paley. *The Works of William Paley* (5 vols, 1837), vol. 1, p. 189.

21. Wollstonecraft. *Works*, vol. 5, pp. 166–7.

22. Ibid., pp. 10–11.

23. Ibid., p. 14.

24. Ibid., p. 16.

25. Ibid., p. 23.

26. Ibid., p. 22.

27. Ibid., p. 24.

28. Ibid., pp. 34, 39. An account which treats this theme as central to the first Vindication is Gary Kelly. *Revolutionary Feminism. The Mind and Career of Mary Wollstonecraft* (Macmillan, 1992), p. 96.

29. Wollstonecraft. *Works*, vol. 5, pp. 40–1.

30. Ibid., pp. 105, 52, 55, 57.

31. Ibid., pp. 18, 21. Wollstonecraft's brief review of Price's *A Discourse on the Love of Our Country* (Works, vol. 7, pp. 185–7) is however laudatory.

32. Wollstonecraft. *Works*, vol. 5, p. 58.
33. William Godwin. *Memoirs of Mary Wollstonecraft* (Constable & Co., 1928), p. 54.
34. Wollstonecraft. *Works*, vol. 5, p. 114.
35. Ibid., pp. 157, 23.
36. Ibid., pp. 249, 221, 66–7.
37. Ibid., p. 256.
38. Ibid., ch. 3.
39. Ibid., pp. 114, 252–4.
40. Ibid., p. 245.
41. Ibid., pp. 261, 250, 68, 247, 66, 90.
42. See Mrs. Philip Champion de Crespigny. *The Mind of a Woman* (Edward Arnold, 1922), p. 126.
43. Wollstonecraft. *Works*, vol. 5, pp. 140, 155.
44. Ibid., pp. 45–6.
45. William Godwin. *Memoirs of the Author of a Vindication of the Rights of Woman* (Penguin Books, 1987), p. 215.
46. Wollstonecraft. *Works*, vol. 5, p. 172, 181, 122, 75.
47. Ibid., pp. 51, 60.
48. Ibid., pp. 215, 133, 211, 65–6.
49. Ibid., p. 214.
50. Ibid., pp. 82, 106, 129, 136, 211, 263, 211. This can be seen as demonstrating further how far republican ideals, like some forms of socialism later, provided a straightjacket for early feminism.
51. Ibid., pp. 136, 145, 124.
52. Ibid., p. 122.
53. Ibid., pp. 201, 205.
54. Ibid., pp. 114, 129, 127.
55. Ibid., p. 209.
56. Ibid., pp. 208, 210, 215, 219, 264.
57. Ibid., pp. 114, 116, 119, 222–5, 113, 140.
58. Ursula Vogel. 'Rationalism and Romanticism: Two Strategies for Women's Emancipation', in Vogel et al. *Feminism and Political Theory* (Sage, 1986), p. 31.
59. Ursula Vogel. 'Rationalism and Romanticism: Two Strategies for Women's Emancipation', in Vogel et al., pp. 17–46.
60. Wollstonecraft. *Works*, vol. 5, p. 95.
61. Ibid., vol. 7, p. 396.
62. Thomas Paine *Rights of Man*, ed. G. Claeys (Indianapolis, Hackett Publishing Company, 1992), pp. 37–8.

63. *Political Writings of the 1790s* (8 vols, Pickering & Chatto, 1995), ed. G. Claeys, vol. 1, p. 245.
64. Ibid., vol. 2, pp. 294–5.
65. Wollstonecraft. *Works*, vol. 6, p. 6.
66. Ibid., pp. 223, 231–4.
67. Ibid., p. 235.
68. R. Thompson. *A Tribute to Liberty: or, A Collection of Select Songs* (1793), p. 1.
69. C. Kegan Paul. *William Godwin, His Friends and Contemporaries* (2 vols, 1876), vol. 1, p. 383. See William Godwin. *Memoirs of the Author of a Vindication of the Rights of Woman* (1798), reprinted as *Memoirs of Mary Wollstonecraft*, Constable & Co., 1928, for example, p. 97. See p. 70, respecting Gilbert Imlay, and pp. 100–1 on Godwin. See generally R.N. Janes. 'On the Reception of Mary Wollstonecraft's "A Vindication of the Rights of Woman",' *Journal of the History of Ideas*, 39 (1978), 293–302.
70. Anna Wheeler here chastised Wollstonecraft for her 'timidity and impotence of conclusion' (*Appeal of One Half the Human Race*, 1824, p. xxiii.)
71. *The Autobiography of Harriet Martineau* (3rd edn, 3 vols, 1877), vol. 1. p. 400.
72. Elizabeth Robins Pennell. *Mary Wollstonecraft Godwin* (1885), p. 2.
73. For example, Brougham Villiers, ed. *The Case for Women's Suffrage* (T. Fisher Unwin, 1907), p. 10.
74. For example, W. Lyon Blease. *The Emancipation of English Women* (Constable & Co., 1910), pp. 73–95.
75. Ethel Snowden. *The Feminist Movement* (The Nation's Library, 1913), p. 82.

Chapter Five: The Spectre of 'Levelling'

1. Thomas Copeland. *Our Eminent Friend Edmund Burke* (New Haven, Yale University Press, 1949), p. 148.
2. For example, William Hunt. *The History of England From the Accession of George III. to the Close of Pitt's Administration* (Longmans, Green, & Co., 1905), contrasting p. 156 to p. 339.
3. This is implied for Burke, for example, in George Sabine. *A History of Political Theory* (New York, Holt, Rinehart & Winston, 1966), p. 617. But both works are often taught and edited together, for

example, Robert Dishman, ed. *Burke and Paine. On Revolution and the Rights of Man* (New York, Charles Scribners, 1971).

4. My estimate. The most complete bibliography of the debate describes about 350 titles. See Gayle Pendleton 'Towards a Bibliography of the Reflections and Rights of Man Controversy', *Bulletin of Research in the Humanities*, vol. 85 (1982), pp. 65–103. The chief primary sources are reprinted in my *Political Writings of the 1790s* (8 vols, Pickering & Chatto, 1995). A convenient one-volume source collection is Iain Hampsher-Monk, ed. *The Impact of the French Revolution. Texts from Britain in the 1790s* (Cambridge, Cambridge University Press, 2005).

5. In this debate the 'liberal' side is represented by Joyce Appleby, for example, in 'Modernization Theory and the Formation of Modern Social Theories in England and America', *Comparative Studies in Society and History*, vol. 20 (1978), pp. 259–85, and Isaac Kramnick, for example, 'Religion and Radicalism. English Political Theory in the Age of Revolution', *Political Theory*, vol. 5 (1977), pp. 505–34, 'English Middle-Class Radicalism in the Eighteenth Century', *Literature of Liberty*, vol. 3 (1980), pp. 5–48, and 'Republican Revisionism Revisited', *American Political Science Review*, vol. 87 (1982), pp. 629–64. The republican side is defended by J.G.A. Pocock *The Machiavellian Moment. Florentine Political Thought and the Atlantic Republican Tradition* (Princeton, Princeton University Press, 1975), and *Virtue, Commerce and History* (Cambridge, Cambridge University Press, 1985). Notable accounts of this debate include R.R. Fennessy *Burke, Paine, and the Rights of Man* (The Hague, Martinus Nijhoff, 1963), James T. Boulton. *The Language of Politics in the Age of Wilkes and Burke* (Routledge & Kegan Paul, 1963), pp. 75–272. See also John Dinwiddy. 'Interpretations of Anti-Jacobinism', in Mark Philp, ed. *The French Revolution and British Popular Politics* (Cambridge, Cambridge University Press, 1991), pp. 18–37. A recent extensive study is Jenny Graham. *The Nation, The Law and the King, Reform Politics in England, 1789–1799* (2 vols, New York, University Press of America, 2000).

6. See especially the essay, 'Virtue, Rights and Manners', reprinted in J.G.A. Pocock. *Virtue, Commerce, and History* (Cambridge, Cambridge University Press, 1985), pp. 37–50.

7. For example, most prominently at the outset of the revolution debate in Richard Price *A Discourse on the Love of Our Country*, reprinted in *Political Writings of the 1790s*, vol. 3, pp. 3–22.

8. 'Anarchical Fallacies. Being an Examination of the Declaration of Rights Issued During the French Revolution', in Jeremy Bentham. *The Works of Jeremy Bentham* (11 vols, 1843), vol. 2, pp. 489–534, here p. 501.

9. *The Spirit of the Times*, no. 1 (1790), p. 11.

10. *The Correspondence of the Revolution Society* (1792), p. 233.

11. Some notable loyalist works in this period, especially Edward Tatham's *Letters to the Right Honourable Edmund Burke on Politics* (Oxford, 1791), attempted to provide a more secure political-philosophical foundation for Burke's views, drawing especially on Aristotle. The first compendium of responses to the revolution was published in 1793 as *A Comparative Display of the Different Opinions of the Most Distinguished British Writers on the Subject of the French Revolution* (2 vols).

12. Reprinted in *Political Writings of the 1790s*, vol. 1, pp. 11–58.

13. Ibid., pp. 121–54.

14. Ibid., vol. 2, pp. 2–29.

15. Published anonymously. Scott was Warren Hastings' political agent, and this work, among others, doubtless helped to cement in Burke's mind an association between the 'Revolution Society', and 'their allies, the Indian delinquents' (*The Correspondence of Edmund Burke*, Cambridge, Cambridge University Press, 1967, vol. 6, p. 140). The story is still more complex, however; some, like Cornwallis, thought that Hastings 'in a great measure owes his misfortunes to the mistaken zeal of his friend Major Scott, who bullied Burke into the persecution' (*Correspondence of Charles, First Marquis Cornwallis*, 1859, vol. 1 p. 376).

16. On British witnesses of the Revolution, see John G. Alger. *Englishmen in the French Revolution* (1889), J.M. Thompson, ed. *English Witnesses of the French Revolution* (Oxford, Blackwell, 1938), and David Erdman. *Commerce des Lumières. John Oswald and the British in Paris, 1790–1793* (Columbia, MO, University of Missouri Press, 1986).

17. *Political Writings of the 1790s*, vol. 1, pp. 182, 193, 157–8.

18. Reprinted in ibid., pp. 270–386. On Mackintosh see Patrick O'Leary. *Sir James Mackintosh. The Whig Cicero* (Aberdeen, Aberdeen University Press, 1989), and Lionel McKenzie. 'The French Revolution and English Parliamentary Reform: James Mackintosh and the *Vindiciae Gallicae*', *Eighteenth Century Studies*, 14 (1980), 264–82.

19. *The Speeches of the Right Honourable Charles James Fox* (6 vols, 1815), vol. 6, p. 366 (1796).

20. *The Correspondence of Edmund Burke*, vol. 6, p. 311.

21. Burke to Mackintosh, 23 December 1796, ibid., p. 193.

22. *Political Writings of the 1790s*, vol. 1, p. 309.

23. Bentham is in fact cited by Mackintosh.

24. Reprinted in *Political Writings of the 1790s*, vol. 1, p. 330.

25. He was principally reliant on Hume. See David Hume. *Essays Moral, Political, and Literary* (2 vols, 1882), vol. 1, p. 191.

26. J.G.A. Pocock, ed. Edmund Burke, *Reflections on the Revolution in France* (1987), pp. xxxii–iii, 69, J.G.A. Pocock. *Virtue, Commerce and History*, pp. 193–212, 280–1.

27. He noted that it was 'a work that has been more generally read than any publication in my time, and which has contributed more than any other to excite a spirit of party; the clergy almost universally approving it, and the low church party and Dissenters as generally condemning it' (Joseph Priestley. *An Appeal to the Public, on the Subject of the Riots in Birmingham*, Birmingham, 1791, p. 22). On Priestley's political ideas see Isaac Kramnick. 'Eighteenth Century Science and Radical Social Theory: The Case of Joseph Priestley's Scientific Liberalism', 25 (1986), 1–30,

28. Reprinted in *Political Writings of the 1790s*, vol. 2, 316–85, Jenny Graham. 'Revolutionary Philosopher: The Political Ideas of Joseph Priestley (1733–1804)', *Enlightenment and Dissent*, 8 (1989), 43–68, Margaret Canovan. 'Paternalistic Liberalism: Joseph Priestley on Rank and Inequality', *Enlightenment and Dissent*, 2 (1983), 23–39, and *Joseph Priestley. Political Writings*, ed. Peter Miller (Cambridge, Cambridge University Press, 1993).

29. [William Petty.] *Temperate Comments Upon Intemperate Reflections: or, A Review of Mr. Burke's Letter* (1791), p. 13.

30. *The Correspondence of William Augustus Miles on the French Revolution* (2 vols, 1890), vol. 1, p. 198.

31. *Speeches of the Late Right Honourable Richard Brinsley Sheridan* (5 vols, 1816), vol. 3, pp. 13–14 (April 1792).

32. *The Life of Sir Samuel Romilly* (1840), vol. 1, pp. 426–7.

33. It was reported that seven-eighths of the members of reformist clubs in Scotland were tradesmen (Home Office papers, HO102/6 f. 19).

34. See John Dinwiddy. 'Conceptions of Revolution in the English Radicalism of the 1790s', in Eckhart Hellmuth, ed. *The*

Transformation of Political Culture. England and Germany in the Late 18th Century (Oxford, Oxford University Press, 1990), pp. 535–60.

35. John Thelwall noted that 'it was not *Tom Paine* but *Edmund Burke* that made me so zealous a reformer, and convinced me of the necessity of annual Parliaments and universal suffrage' (*The Tribune*, 3 vols, 1795–6, vol. 3, p. 195). Another reformer, similarly, stated that Burke had 'set the higher orders against the lower, the rich against the poor' (*Considerations on the French War*, 1794, p. 14).

36. See especially *The London Corresponding Society's Addresses and Regulations* (1792) and *The Correspondence of the Corresponding Society* (1795). Many documents relating to the Society have been reprinted in Mary Thale, ed. *Selections from the Papers of the London Corresponding Society 1792–1799* (Cambridge, Cambridge University Press, 1983), and further in Michael Davis, ed. *London Corresponding Society 1792–1799* (6 vols, Pickering & Chatto, 2002), which includes additional valuable documentation about the organisation. The LCS had about 70 divisions by mid-1795, with a weekly attendance at meetings of over 2000.

37. See *An Abstract of the History and Proceedings of the Revolution Society* (1789).

38. On symbolism in the radicalism of this period see James A. Epstein. *Radical Expression: Political Language, Ritual and Symbol in England, 1790–1850* (Oxford, Oxford University Press, 1994).

39. See generally Mary Thale. 'London Debating Societies in the 1790s', *Historical Journal*, vol. 32 (1989), pp. 57–86.

40. John Butler. *The Political Fugitive: Being a Brief Disquisition into the Modern System of British Politics* (New York, 1794), p. 80. One radical noted that 'the people are quite sick of all those idle party names of Whig and Tory, Court and Country, Pittite and Foxite, which have been raised by the creatures of faction to cloak their knavery, and to perpetuate the slavery of the People' (Public Record Office, TS959/3505).

41. Pitt thus described this as meaning that 'French principles were inculcated as the true standard of political belief' (*The Speeches of the Right Honourable William Pitt in the House of Commons*, 4 vols, 1806, vol. 2, p. 147).

42. Herbert Butterfield. 'Charles James Fox and the Whig Opposition in 1792', *Cambridge Historical Journal*, vol. 9 (1949), p. 293.

43. For an explication of this view see Gwyn Williams. *Artisans and Sans-Culottes. Popular Movements in France and Britain during the French Revolution* (New York, W.W. Norton, 1969), p. 4.

44. See *An Account of the Proceedings of the British Convention* (1794). On some views expressed at the Edinburgh meeting, see Arthur Sheps. 'The Edinburgh Convention of 1793 and the American Revolution', *Scottish Tradition*, vol. 5 (1975), pp. 23–37.

45. See, for example, the list of demands in *The Derby Address, At a Meeting of the Society for Political Information* (1792), pp. 1–2.

46. *Address of the Bristol Constitutional Society For a Parliamentary Reform* (1794), p. 3.

47. See, for example, David Williams' *Lessons to a Young Prince* (*Political Writings of the 1790s*, vol. 3, pp. 23–110).

48. See, for example, *The Address Published by the London Corresponding Society, at the General Meeting Held at the Globe Tavern* (1794), p. 4. The Bill of Rights left no recourse to natural rights, but concentrated chiefly on limiting monarchical power, notably through sect. 1, which prevented the king from suspending laws without consent of parliament; sect. 4, which declared illegal the 'levying money for or to the use of the crown, by pretence or prerogative, without grant of parliament'; sect. 5, which upheld the right of subjects to petition the king; sect. 6, which made illegal the keeping of a standing army without consent of parliament; sect. 8, which declared 'That election of members of parliament ought to be free'; and sect. 13, which held that 'for redress of all grievances, and for the amending, strengthening, and preserving of the laws, Parliaments ought to be held frequently'.

49. Henry Yorke. *These are the Times That Try Men's Souls!* (1793), p. 21.

50. *A Letter to William Paley* (1793), p. 3, responding to Paley's *Reasons for Contentment* (1792) (*Political Writings of the 1790s*, vol. 7, pp. 219–26).

51. At Tooke's trial John Cartwright was asked whether he 'would get out with the Friends of the People at Hounslow, or stay in with the Society for Constitutional Information?' (F.D. Cartwright, ed. *The Life and Correspondence of Major Cartwright*, 2 vols, 1826, vol. 1, p. 218). Tooke himself opposed universal suffrage and tried to ensure that Cartwright's views did not dominate the SCI. 'Hounslow' was thus where universal suffrage commenced. As Hounslow Heath was a well-known haunt of highwaymen, going beyond Hounslow also probably implied lurching towards anarchy.

52. *Proceedings of the Society of Friends of the People; Associated for the Purpose of Obtaining a Parliamentary Reform* (1793), p. 50. The reason for this appears to have been John Cartwright's uncompromising adherence to universal male suffrage.

53. *Memoirs of Thomas Hardy* (1832), p. 15. He added that the LCS 'did more in the eight or nine years of its existence, to diffuse political knowledge among the people of Great Britain and Ireland than all that had ever been done before' (p. vii.). But Fox was happy to support such formulations, contending of the LCS that 'it was impossible to believe that, among the whole, there was a majority unfavourable to monarchy. They might, indeed, have professed to maintain the doctrine of annual parliaments, and universal suffrage. These principles, however, were not borrowed from the French; they had been inculcated in discourses and writings, by respectable characters in Great Britain many years since; and if they contained the evil imputed to them, the French might complain, with more justice, that they had been imported into France from this country' (*The Speeches of the Right Honourable Charles James Fox*, 6 vols, 1815, vol. 6, p. 39.)

54. *Address of the London Corresponding Society to the Other Societies of Great Britain, United for Obtaining a Reform in Parliament* (1792), in *Political Writings of the 1790s*, vol. 4, p. 57; *Address to the Nation, from the London Corresponding Society* (1793), ibid., p. 63.

55. *Address of the London Corresponding Society to the Inhabitants of Great Britain, on the Subject of a Parliamentary Reform* (1792), p. 5.

56. *The Report of the Committee of Constitution of the London Corresponding Society* (n.d.), pp. 3–4

57. *London Corresponding Society. Report of the Sub-Committee of Westminster, Appointed April 12, 1780* (1794), pp. 11–13. The precedent was in fact fairly widely accepted as established; see C.B. Roylance Kent. *The English Radicals* (1899), p. 97. The SFP would shortly take up the cause of payment of MPs; see *The Plan of Reform … Society of the Friends of the People* (1795).

58. *Address of the British Convention* (1793), in *Political Writings of the 1790s*, vol. 4, pp. 85–6, 89.

59. Henry Cockburn. *An Examination of the Trials for Sedition Which Have Hitherto Occurred in Scotland* (2 vols, 1888), vol. 1, p. 242.

60. *The Speeches of the Hon. Thomas Erskine* (4 vols, 1810), vol. 2, p. 49.

61. Quoted in G.M. Trevelyan. *Lord Grey of the Reform Bill* (Longmans, Green & Co., 1920), p. 63.

62. *The Speeches of the Right Honourable Edmund Burke* (4 vols, 1816), vol. 4, p. 47.

63. James Mackintosh presumed that the Royal Proclamation was Pitt's response to the new organisation. See *A Letter to the Right*

Honourable William Pitt, on his Apostacy from the Cause of Parliamentary Reform (2nd edn., 1793), p. 42. For the Society's attempt to distance itself from Paine, see *Proceedings of the Society of the Friends of the People* (1792), pp. 30–1.

64. *The Speeches of the Right Honourable William Pitt in the House of Commons* (4 vols, 1806), vol. 2, p. 91. A similar proposal by the Society to consider a petition for reform in 1793 was defeated by a wide margin.

65. *Political Writings of the 1790s*, vol. 7, pp. 121–2. For Paine's response see 'Letter Addressed to the Addressers on the Late Proclamation', *The Writings of Thomas Paine*, ed. Moncure Conway, 4 vols (New York, G.P. Putnam's Sons, 1902–8), vol. 3, pp. 45–96.

66. Plowden regarded the Proclamation as a turning point in Parliament, and 'the test, upon which Mr. Burke's proselytes read openly their recantation of their former opinions, and enlisted formally under the banner of his doctrines'. It was also used for other purposes, for instance to excuse the unprecedented search of Paine's papers, sealed and unsealed, when he left for France in September 1792 (*A Short History of the British Empire During the Last Twenty Months*, 1794, pp. 81, 145).

67. It was reported at Newcastle that the Proclamation 'has roused curiosity, and Payne's and other political pamphlets are anxiously enquired after by those who have no other name for them than the "books that are cried down"' (*Newcastle Chronicle*, no. 1460, 23 June 1792, p. 2). Similarly the *Annual Register* noted that 'far from preventing [the *Rights of Man*] from being read, the sale became more extensive and rapid than ever' (*The Annual Register ... for the Year 1792*, 1799, p. 165). The French Ambassador, Chauvelin, also complained that certain passages in the Proclamation gave the false impression of hostile French intentions towards Britain and a design of sowing sedition there. A response by Lord Grenville afterwards read to the National Assembly assured France of Britain's intent to maintain existing treaties of navigation and commerce between the two nations.

68. E.g., Samuel Romilly, who said that 'It is written in his own wild but forcible style; inaccurate in point of grammar, flat where he attempts wit, and often ridiculous when he indulges himself in metaphors; but, with all that, full of spirit and energy, and likely to produce a very great effect' (*The Life of Sir Samuel Romilly*, 1840, vol. 1, 415–16).

69. The chief account of loyalism generally is Robert Dozier. *For King, Constitution and Country. The English Loyalists and the French Revolution* (Lexington, University Press of Kentucky, 1983). See also Bernard Schilling. *Conservative England and the Case against Voltaire* (New York, Columbia University Press, 1950); Henry Winkler. 'The Pamphlet Campaign against Political Reform in Great Britain, 1790–1795', *The Historian*, vol. 15 (1952), pp. 23–40; Austin Mitchell. 'The Association Movement of 1792–3', *Historical Journal*, vol. 4 (1961), pp. 56–77; Eugene Black. *The Association. British Extraparliamentary Political Organization 1769–1793* (Cambridge, MA, Harvard University Press, 1963), pp. 233–74; Donald Ginter. 'The Loyalist Association Movement of 1792–3 and British Public Opinion', *Historical Journal*, vol. 9 (1966), pp. 179–90; Alan Booth. 'Popular Loyalism and Public Violence in the North-west of England, 1790–1800', *Social History*, vol. 8 (1983), pp. 295–313; Clive Emsley. 'Repression, "Terror" and the Rule of Law in England During the Decade of the French Revolution', *English Historical Review*, vol. 100 (1985), 801–25; Thomas Schofield. 'Conservative Political Thought in Britain in Response to the French Revolution', *Historical Journal*, vol. 29 (1986), pp. 601–22; H.T. Dickinson, 'Popular Conservatism and Militant Loyalism 1789–1815', in H.T. Dickinson, ed. *Britain and the French Revolution, 1789–1815* (Macmillan, 1989), pp. 103–27; H.T. Dickinson, 'Popular Loyalism in Britain in the 1790s', in Eckhart Helmuth, ed. *The Transformation of Political Culture. Britain and Germany in the Late Eighteenth-century* (Oxford, Oxford University Press, 1989), pp. 503–33; and David Eastwood. 'Patriotism and the English State in the 1790s', in Mark Philp, ed. *The French Revolution and British Popular Politics* (Cambridge, Cambridge University Press, 1991), pp. 146–68. Unpublished work includes Gayle Trusdel Pendleton. 'English Conservative Propaganda During the French Revolution', Emory University Ph.D. (1976), Thomas Schofield. 'English Conservative Thought 1789–1796', University of London Ph.D. (1984).

70. The Society's own proceedings were printed as *Liberty and Property Preserved against Republicans and Levellers. A Collection of Tracts … To Which is Prefixed the Proceedings of the Society* (10 pts, 1793). A useful if hostile account of its objects is [Joseph Towers.] *Remarks on the Conduct, Principles, and Publications, of the Association at the Crown and Anchor* (1793).

71. He was briefly Chief Justice of Newfoundland, then a commissioner of bankruptcy, standing counsel to the Mint, clerk and secretary to the Board of Trade, paymaster to the metropolitan police, High Steward of the Manor and Liberty of Savoy from 1793, and King's printer from 1800. It was claimed in 1792 that his offices were worth £1000 p.a.

72. For the offending tract, see *Political Writings of the 1790s*, vol. 8, pp. 220–52. The charge was led by Sheridan, and was widely regarded as a vendetta. Reeves's response to the issue of parliamentary corruption was that it was inevitable, but being proportionate to the power of the Commons, had to be allayed by ministerial power and monarchical power. This implied that 'An independent House of Commons is no part of the English Constitution' (*Association Papers*, Part Two, 1792, p. 4.)

73. As much as £5000 p.a. in secret service funds were expended securing correct opinions. On the press in this period, see A. Aspinall. *Politics and the Press* c.*1780–1850* (Home & Van Thal, 1949). On the development of Pitt's views see Jennifer Mori. *William Pitt and the French Revolution 1785–1795* (Keele, Keele University Press, 1997), chs. 4–5. Attitudes towards the war are treated in Emma Vincent Macleod. *A War of Ideas. British Attitudes to the Wars against Revolutionary France, 1792–1802* (Ashgate, 1998).

74. *De L'État de la France, Présent et à Venir* (1790), which appeared in November.

75. These Pitt defined as demanding 'the will of the majority, the will of the multitude' (*The Speeches of the Right Honourable William Pitt in the House of Commons*, 4 vols, 1806, vol. 2, p. 154).

76. It has been estimated that approximately 45% of loyalist pamphlets were written by persons directly employed, patronised or pensioned by the government (Gayle Trusdel Pendleton. 'English Conservative Propaganda During the French Revolution', Emory University Ph.D., 1976, p. 57).

77. 'NO JACOBINS ADMITTED HERE' was the sign witnessed at many Birmingham public houses by 1793 (*The Rights of the Devil*, Sheffield, 1793, p. 30). Magistrates typically posted notices requiring publicans 'to be particularly cautious not to suffer any Clubs or Societies tending towards a breach of the peace to be held in their respective houses, or any seditious doctrines or conversations to pass there, without immediately communicating the same to the Constable of such parish, and also to a Magistrate: And to

be watchful over strangers, whether foreigners or natives of this country, who carry any suspicious appearance, and to give the like notice thereof' (*Notice to the Publicans in Blything Hundred*, 1793).

78. Plowden stated baldly of Reeves's association that 'The extermination of the Dissenters was their aim' (*A Short History of the British Empire During the Last Twenty Months*, 1794, p. 195).

79. Catherine Hutton. *Memoirs of a Gentlewoman of the Last Century* (1891), p. 70. See generally R.B. Rose. 'The Priestley Riots of 1791'. *Past and Present*, 18 (1960), 68–88.

80. [James Mackintosh]. *A Letter to the Right Honourable William Pitt, on his Apostacy from the Cause of Parliamentary Reform* (2nd edn., 1793), p. 39. See generally David Eastwood. 'Patriotism and the British State in the 1790s', in Mark Philp, ed. *The French Revolution and British Popular Politics* (Cambridge, Cambridge University Press, 1991), p. 146–68.

81. *Political Writings of the 1790s*, vol. 7, pp. 215–18. The corporation of Blandford alone distributed 5000 copies of the *Charge*.

82. Only one notable member of Reeves' Association, Thomas Law, resigned in disgust at its methods. See Thomas Law. *A Letter to Mr. Reeves and his Associates, for Preserving Liberty and Property* (1793).

83. John Young. *Essays on the Following Interesting Subjects* (Glasgow, 1797), p. 97.

84. *Vindiciae Britannicae: Being Strictures on a Late Pamphlet by G. Wakefield* (1794), p. 28.

85. Many of the Scottish trials were reprinted in Henry Cockburn. *An Examination of the Trials for Sedition Which Have Hitherto Occurred in Scotland* (2 vols, Edinburgh, David Douglas, 1888).

86. *Constitutional Letters in Answer to Mr. Paine's Rights of Man* (1792), p. 18; Alexander Dalrymple. *The Poor Man's Friend: An Address to the Industrious and Manufacturing Part of Great Britain* (Edinburgh, 1793), p. 13; *Fragment of a Prophecy Lately Discovered in the Cell of a French Hermit. By a Convert from the 'Society for Revolutions'* (1791), p. 27; *The Interests of Man in Opposition to the Rights of Man* (Edinburgh, 1793), pp. 46–8; *An Humble Address to the Most High, Most Mighty, and Most Puissant the Sovereign People* (1793), p. 15. On these arguments see especially H.T. Dickinson. *Liberty and Property. Political Ideology in Eighteenth Century Britain* (Weidenfeld & Nicolson, 1977), pp. 270–318 and Janice Lee. 'Political Antiquarianism Unmasked: the Conservative Attack on the Myth of the Ancient Constitution', *Bulletin of the Institute of Historical Research*, vol. 54 (1981), pp. 166–79.

87. Frederick Hervey. *A New Friend on an Old Subject* (1791), p. 18; John Jones. *The Reason of Man: With Strictures on Paine's Rights of Man* (Canterbury, 1793), p. 15.

88. Precise examinations of the economic proposals of the *Rights of Man* were comparatively rare. One Lt. Col. Chalmers defended Adam Smith against Paine's criticisms of his treatment of the Bank of England, but also claimed that Smith had been called 'the high priest of democracy' because he seemed to oppose many existing taxes. A long tract published in Germany accused Paine of corrupting Smith's principles 'by associating them with the temerity of language and inaccuracy of assertion which passion has inspired him with', and of mistakenly defining wealth as specie rather than labour. Another critic invoked the free trade principles of Arthur Young, Hume and Smith, and then curiously condemned Paine's supposed claim 'that we have no right to limit the wages of the labourer' (Lt. Col. Chalmers. *Strictures on a Pamphlet Written by Thomas Paine on the English System of Finance* (1796); R. Dinmore, Jr. *An Exposition of the Principles of the English Jacobins* (Norwich, 1796), pp. 20, 32; S.A. Joersson. *Adam Smith, Author of an Inquiry into the Wealth of Nations and Thomas Paine Author of the Decline and Fall of the English System of Finance* ('Germany', 1796), pp. 4, 11; *Rights and Remedies, or the Theory and Practice of True Politics* (1795), part 2, p. 161).

89. *An Humble Address to the Most High, Most Mighty, and Most Puissant the Sovereign People* (1793), p. 10; *Resolutions of Common Sense, for the Preventing of Popular Delusion from Political Orators* (n.d.), p. 1; *The True Briton's Catechism* (1793), p. 32; William Keate. *A Free Examination of Dr. Price's and Dr. Priestley's Sermons* (1790), p. 53; Rev. C.E. de Coetlogon. *The Peculiar Advantages of the English Nation* (1792), p. vi; Alexander Dalrymple. *The Poor Man's Friend* (1793), p. 4; *A Whipper for Levelling Tommy* (1793), p. 24; *Britannia's Address to the People* (n.d.), pp. 6–7; [Frederick Hervey]. *An Answer to the Second Part of the Rights of Man* (1792), pp. 4–5, 9–10; *Philosophical Sketches* (1793), pp. 1–8.

90. William Agutter. *Christian Politics; or, The Origin of Power and the Grounds of Subordination* (1792), pp. 6–7; Samuel Cooper. *The First Principles of Civil and Ecclesiastical Government Delineated* (Yarmouth, 1791), p. 63; *A Letter from a Magistrate to Mr. William Rose* (1791), pp. 19–20; Edward Tatham. *Letters to the Rt. Hon. Edmund Burke on Politics* (1791), p. 39; Rev. R. Nares. *Principles of Government Deduced From Reason* (1792), p. xi.

91. *A New Dialogue between Monsieur François and John English on the French Revolution* (n.d.), p. 12; *Remarks on the Proceedings of the Society of the 'Friends of the People'* (1792), p. 85; *A Comparative Display of the Different Opinions of the Most Distinguished British Writers on the Subject of the French Revolution* (3 vols, 1811) (reprint edn., New York, AMS Press, 1970), vol. 2, pp. 360–1; *Facts, Reflections, and Queries, Submitted to … the Associated Friends of the People* (Edinburgh, 1792), p. 20; Hannah More. *Village Politics. Addressed to All Mechanics, Journeymen, and Day Labourers* (Durham, 1793), pp. 3, 12. More continued:

TOM: 'What, then, dost take French liberty to be?'
JACK: 'To murder more men in one night than their poor king did in all his life.'
TOM: 'And what dost thou take a democrat to be?'
JACK: 'One who likes to be governed by a thousand tyrants and yet can't bear a king.'
TOM: 'What is equality?'
JACK: 'For every man to put down everyone that is above him.'
TOM: 'What are the rights of man?'
JACK: 'Battle, murder, and sudden death.'
TOM: 'What is it to be an enlightened people?'
JACK: 'To put out the light of the Gospel, confound right and wrong, and grope about in pitch darkness.'

92. Francis Plowden. *Jura Anglorum. The Rights of Englishmen* (1792), pp. 14–32; John Wilde. *An Address to the Lately Formed Society of the Friends of the People* (1793), pp. 575–8.

93. *The Interests of Man* (1793), pp. 6, 8–11; *Rights Upon Rights with Observations Upon Observations* (1791), p. 5; *Letters to Thomas Paine; in Answer to His Late Publication on the Rights of Man* (1791), pp. 62, 15–16; Tobias Molloy. *An Appeal from Man in a State of Civil Society, to Man in a State of Nature* (1792), pp. 77–9, 82, 88.

94. Rev. Robert Thomas. *The Cause of Truth, Containing … A Refutation of Errors in the Political Works of Thomas Paine* (Dundee, 1797), pp. 1, 25–8, 33, 37, 73–5. Rev. James Brown. *The Importance of Preserving Unviolated the System of Civil Government in Every State* (1794), pp. 14, 50, 108–44, 171–211, 305; William Brown. *An Essay on the Natural Equality of Man* (1st American edn, Philadelphia, 1793, esp. pp. 78–102.

95. For example, Samuel Bradburn. *Equality: A Sermon* (Bristol, 1794), p. 25. See also *Equality No Liberty; or, Subordination the Order*

of God (Edinburgh, 1793), Richard Watson. *The Wisdom and Goodness of God in Having Made Both Rich and Poor* (1793); William Agutter. *Christian Politics; Or, The Origin of Power, and the Grounds of Subordination* (1792).

96. James Scott. *A Sermon Preached at Park-Street Chapel* (1793), p. 9. Dissenters throughout this period corresponding accused the Church of England of being 'infected by doctrines of passive obedience and non-resistance' ([Samuel Heywood.] *High Church Politics ... Against the Practices and Principles of High Churchmen*, 1792, pp. 73–103).

97. *Liberty and Equality; A Dialogue between a Clergyman and His Parishioner* (1794), p. 11. Another noteworthy dialogue on this subject is *Liberty and Equality; Treated of in a Short History Addresssed from a Poor Man to His Equals* (1792).

98. T.B. Howell, ed. *A Complete Collection of State Trials* (1817), vol. 22, col. 870; *The Origin of Duty* (1796), p. 25; Alexander Dalrymple *The Poor Man's Friend*, p. 22; *Defence of the Rights of Man* (1791), p. 11; *Remarks on Mr. Paine's Pamphlet, Called the Rights of Man* (Dublin, 1791), pp. 16–17.

99. *Principles of Order and Happiness Under the British Constitution* (1792), p. 13; *The Interests of Man* (1793), pp. 13, 16; *A Candid Inquiry into the Nature of Government, and the Right of Representation* (1792), p. 9; *An Humble Address to the Most High, Most Mighty, and Most Puissant the Sovereign People* (1793), p. 10.

100. Adam Smith. *An Inquiry into the Nature and Causes of the Wealth of Nations* (2 vols, 1869), vol. 1, p. 14.

101. Andrew Burnaby. *The Blessings Enjoyed by Englishmen, A Motive for their Repentance* (1793), p. 14.

102. *Political Writings of the 1790s,* vol. 8, p. 4.

103. John Somers Cocks. *A Short Treatise on the Dreadful Tendency of Levelling Principles* (1793), p. 10; *The Address of a Buckinghamshire Farmer* (1792); *Ten Minutes' Caution from a Plain Man to His Fellow Citizens* (1792), p. 6; Hannah More. *Village Politics. Addressed to All Mechanics, Journeymen, and Day Labourers* (Durham, 1793), p. 14; *Free Communing; or a Last Attempt to Cure the Lunatics, Now Labouring Under That Dreadful Malady, Commonly Called the French Disease* (Edinburgh, 1793), p. 30.

104. *Analytical Review,* vol. 9 (1791), 303; *The Speeches of the Right Honourable William Pitt in the House of Commons* (4 vols, 1806), vol. 2, p. 47.

105. Francis Plowden. *A Short History of the British Empire During the Last Twenty Months* (1794), p. 49.

106. See Edmund Burke. *An Appeal from the New to the Old Whigs* (1791), in which the 'New Whigs' are accused of supporting the doctrine of popular sovereignty by contrast with the 'Old Whig' ideal of a contract between ruler and ruled.

107. William Black. *Reasons for Preventing the French, Under the Mask of Liberty, From Trampling Upon Europe* (1793), p. 40; *An Exposure of the Domestic and Foreign Attempts to Destroy the British Constitution* (1793), pp. 59–60; James Scott. *Equality Considered and Recommended, in a Sermon* (1794), p. 10; [Arthur Young.] *A Plain and Earnest Address to Britons* (Ipswich, 1792), pp. 4–7.

108. *A Trip to the Island of Equality* (n.d.); *Buff; or a Dissertation on Nakedness: A Parody on Paine's Rights of Man* (1792), p. 27.

109. *A Caution against the Levellers* (1793), p. 13.

110. [Thomas Atkinson.] *A Concise Sketch of the Intended Revolution in England* (1794). Robert Thomas argued similarly that Paine had 'insinuated' the idea of equality of property (*The Cause of Truth, Containing … A Refutation of Errors in the Political Works of Thomas Paine*, Dundee, 1797, p. 49).

111. *Political Writings of the 1790s*, vol. 7, p. 216; Philodiceus. *A Letter on Equality: Addressed to the Public* (1794), p. 22.

112. See *Principles of Order and Happiness under the British Constitution* (1792), pp. 9–13.

113. John Jones. *The Reason of Man: Part Second. Containing Strictures on Rights of Man* (Canterbury, 1793), pp. 4–5; *Facts, Reflections, and Queries, Submitted to … the Associated Friends of the People* (Edinburgh, 1792), p. 7; *A Few Minutes' Advice to the People of Great Britain on Republics* (Bristol, 1792); J. Courtenay. *Philosophical Reflections on the Late Revolution in France* (1790), p. 40; Charles Patton. *The Effects of Property upon Society and Government Investigated* (1797); Sir Brooke Boothby. *Observations on the Appeal from the New to the Old Whigs* (1792), p. 178; Peter White. *Rational Freedom: Being a Defence of the National Character of Britons, and of Their Form of Government* (Edinburgh, 1792), p. 107; Thomas Hearn. *A Short View of the Rise and Progress of Freedom in Modern Europe* (1793), p. 59.

114. John Gifford. *A Plain Address to the Common Sense of the People of England* (1792), p. 48.

115. *Liberty and Equality; A Dialogue between a Clergyman and His Parishioner* (1794), p. 1.

116. *A Plain and Earnest Address to Britons, Especially Farmers* (6th edn., Newark, 1792), p. 7.

117. *A Serious Caution to the Poor* (1792); William Black. *Reasons for Preventing the French, Under the Mask of Liberty, From Trampling Upon Europe* (1793), p. 39; [A. Young.] *A Plain and Earnest Address* (Ipswich, 1792), p. 9; *The Patriot* (1793), pp. 73–5; British Library Add. MS. 16920 f. 17.

118. John Gifford. *A Plain Address to the Common Sense of the People of England, Containing an Interesting Abstract of Pain's Life and Writings* (1792), p. 32; *A Country Curate's Advice to Manufacturers* (n.d.); British Library Add. MS. 16927 f. 47; Public Record Office Papers, HO102/6; HO102/60; John Young. *Essays on the Following Interesting Subjects* (Edinburgh, 1794), p. 112; R. and S. Wilberforce. *The Life of William Wilberforce* (5 vols, 1838), vol. 2, p. 2; William Fox. *An Examination of Mr. Paine's Writings* (1793), p. 12.

119. *The Duties of Man* (1793), p. 25; Rev. Robert Thomas. *The Cause of Truth, Containing ... A Refutation of Errors in the Political Works of Thomas Paine* (Dundee, 1797), p. 37; *A Few Plain Questions* (1793), p. 10.

120. *Facts, Reflections, and Queries, Addressed to the Consideration of the Associated Friends of the People* (Edinburgh, 1792), p. 20; *Six Essays on Natural Rights, Liberty and Slavery, Consent of the People, Equality, Religious Establishments, the French Revolution* (1792), p. 5.

121. *To the Gentry, Clergy, and Loyal Inhabitants of the Hundred of Blything, in Suffolk* (1792), p. 2.

122. Thomas Hardy. *The Patriot* (2nd edn., Edinburgh, 1793), p. 10.

123. James Scott. *Equality Considered and Recommended, in a Sermon* (1794), pp. 6–7. Still useful on this issue is H.V.S. Ogden. 'The State of Nature and the Decline of Lockean Political Theory in England, 1760–1800', *American Historical Review*, vol. 46 (1940–1), pp. 21–44.

124. Arthur Young. *The Example of France a Warning to Britain* (Bury St Edmunds, 1793), pp. 2, 56; *An Appeal to the Common Sense of the British People on the Subjects of Sedition and Revolution* (1793), p. 21; *A Letter to a Friend in the Country: Wherein Mr. Paine's Letter to Mr. Dundas is Particularly Considered* (1792), p. 15; *The Antigallican* (1793), pp. 30–34; John Somers Cocks. *A Short Treatise on the*

Dreadful Tendency of Levelling Principles (1793), p. 20; W. Miles. *The Correspondence of William Augustus Miles on the French Revolution 1789–1817* (2 vols., 1890), vol. 1, p. 364. On Young's reaction to the revolution see Arthur Young. *The Autobiography of Arthur Young*, ed. M. Betham-Edwards (1898), pp. 198–206. On the use of the American model by Paine's opponents see David Wilson. *Paine and Cobbett. The Transatlantic Connection* (Montreal, McGill-Queen's University Press, 1988), pp. 89–95.

125. Booksellers were still prosecuted for the offence: see *Speeches of the Late Right Honourable Richard Brinsley Sheridan* (5 vols, 1816), vol. 3, p. 93. See generally J. Ann Hone. 'Radicalism in London, 1796–1802: Convergencies and Continuities', in John Stevenson, ed. *London in the Age of Reform* (Oxford, Basil Blackwell, 1977), pp. 79–101.

126. Henry Redhead Yorke. *These are the Times That Try Men's Souls!* (1793), p. 34.

127. Quoted in T.W. Moody. 'The Political Ideas of the United Irishmen', *Ireland Today*, 3 (1936), 23.

128. *The Correspondence of the London Corresponding Society* (1795), p. 82; *A Narrative of the Proceedings at the General Meeting of the London Corresponding Society Held on Monday, July 31, 1797* (1797), p. 13; *Newcastle Chronicle*, no. 1484 (8 December 1792), p. 2; *Considerations on the French War* (1794), p. 18.

129. During the debates on the suspension of Habeas Corpus in 1794, in *The Speeches of the Right Honourable William Pitt in the House of Commons* (4 vols, 1806), vol. 2, p. 207.

130. *The Speech of the Hon. Thomas Erskine, at a Meeting of the Friends to the Liberty of the Press* (1792), p. 6.

131. Pitt's views are addressed in [James Mackintosh.] *A Letter to the Right Honourable William Pitt, on his Apostacy from the Cause of Parliamentary Reform* (2nd edn., 1793). Richmond's letter to Lieutenant-Colonel Sharman proposing universal suffrage, written in 1783, was often referred to by reformers and was reprinted in 1792, 1795, 1797, 1813, and 1817. A good collection of reformist literature from 1775–83 is *Sound Reason and Sound Argument For a Reform in Parliament* (n.d., *c.* 1794), edited by Daniel Isaac Eaton. See generally Clive Emsley. 'Repression, "Terror" and the Rule of Law in England During the Decade of the French Revolution', *English Historical Review*, 100 (1985), 801–25.

132. On the trials see Clive Emsley. 'An Aspect of Pitt's "Terror": Prosecutions for Sedition during the 1790s', *Social History*, vol. 6 (1981), pp. 155–84; Albert Goodwin. *The Friends of Liberty. The English Democratic Movement in the Age of the French Revolution* (Hutchinson, 1979), pp. 307–58; Alan Wharam. *The Treason Trials, 1794* (Leicester, Leicester University Press, 1992); John Barrell. 'Imaginary Treason, Imaginary Law. The State Trials of 1794', in Barrell. *The Birth of Pandora and the Division of Knowledge* (Macmillan, 1992), pp. 119–42, and in particular, John Barrell. *Imagining the King's Death. Figurative Treason, Fantasies of Regicide 1793–1796* (Oxford, Oxford University Press, 2000).

133. For example, *Political Correspondence; Or, Letters to a Country Gentleman* (1793), p. i.

134. A good account of the difficulties the events of 1792–3 posed to former sympathisers with the revolution is Thomas Somerville. *The Effects of the French Revolution* (Edinburgh, 1793).

135. George Skene Keith. *Tracts on the Reform of the British Constitution* (1793), Postscript, p. iii. Some directly blamed Louis' fate and the war on Burke and those who upheld his views. See, for example, William Fox. *The Interest of Great Britain, Respecting the French War* (3rd edn., 1793), pp. 2–3.

136. Francis Basset. *The Crimes of Democracy* (1798), p. 8.

137. *War with France the Only Security of Britain* (1794), p. 10.

138. On loyalism and views of the war, see J.E. Cookson. *The Friends of Peace. Anti-War Liberalism in England, 1793–1815* (Cambridge, Cambridge University Press, 1982), ch. 5.

139. Fox confessed that 'their successive rulers have been as bad and as execrable … as any of the most despotic and unprincipled governments that the world ever saw', adding that 'Men bred in the school of the house of Bourbon could not be expected to act otherwise' (*The Speeches of the Right Honourable Charles James Fox*, 6 vols, 1815, vol. 5, p. 391). Sheridan's view was similar: 'a long established despotism so far degraded human nature, as to render its subjects, on the first recovery of their rights, unfit for the exercise of them' (*Speeches of the Late Right Honourable Richard Brinsley Sheridan*, vol. 3, p. 185).

140. William Playfair. *Inevitable Consequences of a Reform in Parliament* (1792), p. 6.

141. The London Corresponding Society grew by some eight hundred members in one month alone during mid-1795.

142. Plowden, for example, concluded that 'a vast federative combination of the great powers against France ... must have been formed' at Pilnitz (*A Short History of the British Empire During the Last Twenty Months*, 1794, p. 104).

143. *Political Correspondence; or, Letters to a Country Gentleman* (1793), pp. 104–5.

144. Sheridan commented that 'In his own conviction, however, none of these dangers had any actual existence', with the parliamentary report on treason itself being 'merely a political artifice' (*Speeches of the Late Right Honourable Richard Brinsley Sheridan*, vol. 3, p. 362). One account of the crucial events leading to the bills was *Truth and Treason! Or a Narrative of the Royal Procession to the House of Peers, October the 29th, 1795* (1795).

145. For critical reactions to the bills, see, for example, *The Proceedings and Speeches at the Meeting ... to Petition Parliament against Lord Grenville's and Mr. Pitt's Treason and Sedition Bills* (Norwich, 1795), and generally, *The History of Two Acts* (1796).

146. The Acts were 'An Act for the Safety and Preservation of His Majesty's Person and Government against Treasonable and Seditious Practices and Attempts', and 'An Act for the more Effectually Preventing Seditious Meetings and Assemblies'.

147. *An Appeal to the People on the Two Despotic Bills, Now Depending in Parliament* (1795), p. 15.

148. See Richard Twomey. 'Jacobins and Jeffersonians: Anglo-American Radical Ideology, 1790–1810', in Margaret Jacob and James Jacob, eds. *The Origins of Anglo-American Radicalism* (George Allen & Unwin, 1984), pp. 284–99.

149. An interesting case is examined in Melvin Lasky. 'The Recantation of Henry Redhead Yorke', *Encounter*, vol. 41 (1973), pp. 67–85.

150. One instance from a later period is William Dickson. *Hints to the People of the United Kingdom ... On the Present Important Crisis* (Edinburgh, 1803). An excellent register of the political mood of the south-east in this period is John Gale Jones. *Sketch of a Political Tour Through Rochester, Chatham, Maidstone, Gravesend, & c.* (1796). There were of course also extensive comments on French developments in this period and later, such as George Skene Keith. *Particular Examination of the New French Constitution* (Aberdeen, 1801).

151. Richard Watson. *An Address to the People of Great Britain* (1798), p. 11. On the role of the clergy in the counter-revolutionary debate see Richard A. Soloway. *Prelates and People: Ecclesiastical Social Thought in England, 1783–1852* (Routledge & Kegan Paul, 1962), and Robert Hole. *Pulpits, Politics and Public Order in England 1760–1832* (Cambridge, Cambridge University Press, 1989), pp. 95–174. Unpublished work includes Nancy U. Murray. 'The Influence of the French Revolution on the Church of England and Its Rivals, 1789–1802', Oxford University D.Phil. (1975).

152. For example, Edmund Burke. *Reflections on the Revolution in France* (1790), p. 132. In Parliament in early 1790, Burke noted that atheism 'seems in France, for a long time, to have been embodied into a faction, accredited, and almost avowed', and also insisted, on the basis of the recent writings of Price, Priestley and others, that 'our establishment appeared to be in much more serious danger than the church of France was in a year or two ago' (*The Speeches of the Right Honourable Edmund Burke*, 4 vols, 1816, vol. 3, pp. 458, 480). One defence of the Dissenters was Robert Jacomb. *A Letter Vindicating Dissenters from the Charge of Disloyalty* (1793).

153. See also, for example, *Political Correspondence; or, Letters to a Country Gentleman* (1793), pp. 80–4. Some aspects of the conspiracy theory are developed in Seamus Deane. *The French Revolution and Enlightenment in England 1789–1832* (Cambridge, MA, Harvard University Press, 1988).

154. See, for example, Robert Nares' claim that those supporting the Revolution were essentially 'men without Religion' (*Man's Best Right; A Solemn Appeal in the Name of Religion*, 1793, p. 9).

155. See, for example, Elizabeth Hamilton. *Memoirs of Modern Philosophers* (1800).

156. The starting-point for understanding this transformation remains Ford K. Brown. *Fathers of the Victorians. The Age of Wilberforce* (Cambridge, Cambridge University Press, 1961).

157. But some would also explicitly defend the new sense of equality. See, for example, James Pilkington. *The Doctrine of Equality of Rank and Condition Examined and Supported on the Authority of the New Testament and on the Principles of Reason and Benevolence* (1795), which contends that 'Jesus Christ intended, that the worldly

circumstances of mankind should be nearly, if not entirely equal'
(p. 9). See also *Political Dialogues upon the Subject of Equality* (1792).

158. *Resolutions of the Society Associated for the Purpose of Obtaining a Parliamentary Reform* (1792), p. 6.

159. George Dyer. *The Complaints of the Poor People of England* (1793), p. 13.

160. Charles Pigott. *The Rights of Princes* (1795), p. 2.

161. Rare praise accorded to schemes for equality of landed property included in this collection, in John Oswald's *Review of the Constitution of Great–Britain*, was printed in France. See *Political Writings of the 1790s*, vol. 3, pp. 411–46. On the continuity of the Spartan, Roman agrarian law and Christian collectivist traditions in eighteenth-century Britain, see my edition of *Utopias of the British Enlightenment* (Cambridge, Cambridge University Press, 1994), pp. xxv–viii.

162. The standard nineteenth-century account is Allen Davenport's *The Life and Principles of Thomas Spence* (1836). For recent work on Spence and his followers, see Malcolm Chase. *The People's Farm. English Agrarian Radicalism 1775–1840* (Oxford, Clarendon Press, 1988), and Iain McCalman. *Radical Underworld: Prophets, Revolutionaries and Pornographers in London, 1795–1840* (Cambridge, Cambridge University Press, 1988). There have also been two modern editions of his writings: Thomas Spence. *The Political Works of Thomas Spence* (1776–1800), ed. H.T. Dickinson (Avero Publications, 1982), and Geoffrey Gallop, ed. *Pigs' Meat: The Selected Writings of Thomas Spence* (Spokesman Books, 1982).

163. Thomas Spence. *The Rights of Man* (4th edn., 1793), p. 8.

164. Thomas Spence. *The End of Oppression* (2nd edn., n.d.), p. 5; Spence. *The Meridian Sun of Liberty* (1796), p. 2.

165. Thomas Spence. *The End of Oppression* (2nd edn., n.d.), pp. 11–12; Thomas Spence. *The Important Trial of Thomas Spence* (2nd edn., 1803), pp. 12, 36.

166. Thomas Spence. *The Important Trial of Thomas Spence*, pp. 21, 37, 43.

167. Thomas Spence. *The Constitution of a Perfect Commonwealth* (1798), p. v; Thomas Spence. *The Important Trial of Thomas Spence*, p. 73. Even a decade later his followers similarly insisted that 'Landlords, and landlords only! are the oppressors of the people, the drones of the hive', and like Spence believed that after his Plan had been implemented, 'Commerce and trade, freed from taxes, will immediately revive and extend itself'

(*Address and Regulations of the Society of Spencean Philanthropists* (1815), p. 3; Thomas Evans. *Christian Policy the Salvation of the Empire* (1816), p. 31.)

168. See Thomas Spence. *The Political Works of Thomas Spence*, ed. H.T. Dickinson (Newcastle upon Tyne: Avero Publications, 1982), pp. xii–xv.

169. John Reeves. *Thoughts on the English Government* (1795), p. 13; William Paley. *Equality as Consistent with the British Constitution* (1793) in *Political Writings of the 1790s*, vol. 7, pp. 227–32; *A Letter of Condolence and Congratulation from Antichrist to John Bull* (1795), pp. 5–6; *A Rejoinder to Mr. Paine's Pamphlet, Entitled, Rights of Man; or, An Answer to Mr. Burke's Attack on the French Revolution* (n.d.), pp. 51, 55; Robert Dozier. *For King, Constitution, and Country* (1983), pp. 82–3. On the few High Tories of the 1790s see J.G.A. Gunn. *Beyond Liberty and Property. The Process of Self-Recognition in Eighteenth-Century Political Thought* (Montreal, McGill-Queen's University Press, 1983), pp. 164–85.

170. For example, *English Chartist Circular*, vol. 2, no. 58 (1842), p. 22. See generally John Dinwiddy. 'English Radicals and the French Revolution', in Dinwiddy. *Radicalism and Reform in Britain 1780–1850* (Hambledon Press, 1992), pp. 207–28.

Chapter Six: Varieties of Whiggism

1. Specifically on Fox's support for the Prince of Wales, during the Regency debate, quoted in W.E.H. Lecky. *History of England in the Eighteenth Century* (7 vols, 1892), vol. 5, p. 389. The word is apparently a neologism when used by Pitt. There is a pun here on 'wigging', in the sense of being critical; un-'wigging' would imply removing someone's capacity to be critical. This is doubly amusing because Fox, assuming the Prince's prerogative to rule as regent, could be seen as taking a Tory line on the issue.

2. The standard studies are Frank O'Gorman. *The Whig Party and the French Revolution* (Macmillan, 1967), and L.G. Mitchell. *Charles James Fox and the Disintegration of the Whig Party* (Oxford, Oxford University Press, 1971). See also John Derry. 'The Opposition Whigs and the French Revolution, 1789–1815', in H.T. Dickinson, ed. *Britain and the French Revolution* (Macmillan, 1989), pp. 39–60. Herbert Butterfield. 'Charles James Fox and the Whig Opposition in 1792',

Cambridge Historical Journal, vol. 9 (1949), pp. 293–330; and J.G.A. Pocock. 'Radical Criticisms of the Whig Order in the Age of Revolutions', in Margaret Jacob and James Jacob, eds. *The Origins of Anglo-American Radicalism* (George Allen & Unwin, 1984), pp. 33–53.

3. O'Gorman seems to accept at face value the view that 'some members of the opposition had set on foot a dangerous campaign which had for its aim the adoption of Paine's principles', for which, I will argue below, there is scant evidence. See *The Whig Party and the French Revolution* (Macmillan, 1967), p. 74.

4. Cf. T.E. Kebbel: 'Before the French Revolution, Toryism was not regarded as a purely defensive organisation. Before 1793 the institutions of the country were not threatened. The Whigs were just as good Conservatives, as the Tories, and they had reason to be. When they quitted this position, and, following the lead of Mr. Fox, joined hands with the Jacobins, the Tories were compelled to change their ground, too. As the Whigs became destructives, the Tories became Conservatives' (*Lord Beaconsfield and Other Tory Memories*, Cassell & Co., 1907, pp. 344–5).

5. W.E.H. Lecky. *History of England in the Eighteenth Century* (7 vols, 1892), vol. 5, p. 377; J.L. Le B. Hammond. *Charles James Fox. A Political Study* (Methuen, 1903), p. 253.

6. Mitchell describes Fox as 'obsessed with his struggle with George III' throughout this period (*Charles James Fox and the Disintegration of the Whig Party*, Oxford, Oxford University Press, 1971, p. 192).

7. *The Speeches of the Right Honourable Charles James Fox* (6 vols, 1815), vol. 4, p. 52.

8. Ibid.

9. Ibid., p. 53.

10. See *The Speeches of the Right Honourable Edmund Burke* (4 vols, 1816), vol. 3, p. 470.

11. *The Speeches of the Right Honourable Charles James Fox*, vol. 4, p. 56.

12. Ibid., p. 68.

13. Ibid., pp. 221–2.

14. For Burke's own response to the charge, see Burke. *Speeches* (4 vols, 1816), vol. 4, pp. 15–28.

15. *The Speeches of the Right Honourable Charles James Fox*, vol. 4, pp. 199–200.

16. On another account, however, given in the *Public Advertiser*, Fox said 'he for one admired the new constitution, considered altogether,

as the most glorious fabrick ever raised by human integrity since the creation of man', which does not as directly invoke such a comparison. (When Burke repeated the phrase, he used the words 'a most stupendous and glorious fabric of human integrity' at one point, and 'the most stupendous and glorious edifice of liberty' in another.) Edmund Burke. *The Works of the Right Honourable Edmund Burke* (12 vols, 1899), vol. 4, p. 77; cf. *The Speeches of the Right Honourable Charles James Fox*, vol. 4, 227. But the 'liberty' quote is often assumed to be correct; for example, in Edward Lascelles. *The Life of Charles James Fox* (Oxford, Oxford University Press, 1936), p. 225, and William Windham. *Correspondence of Edmund Burke and William Windham* (1910), p. 24.

17. Earl Russell. *The Life and Times of Charles James Fox* (2 vols, 1866), vol. 2, p. 252.
18. Ibid., p. 254.
19. Ibid., pp. 260–1.
20. *The Speeches of the Right Honourable Charles James Fox*, vol. 4, p. 216.
21. Ibid., p. 222.
22. Ibid., p. 224.
23. Ibid., p. 228.
24. Earl Russell. *The Life and Times of Charles James Fox* (2 vols, 1866), vol. 2, p. 270.
25. *The Speeches of the Right Honourable Charles James Fox*, vol. 4, p. 232. Privately Fox still insisted (in early 1793), in Auckland's account, 'that the sovereignty was absolutely in the people, that the monarchy was elective, otherwise the dynasty of Brunswick had no right' (*The Journal and Correspondence of William, Lord Auckland*, vol. 2, p. 496).
26. 'His reason was, that though he saw great and enormous grievances, he did not see the remedy' ... 'he had not said that a parliamentary reform could be no remedy to existing grievances, but that he had heard of no specific mode of reform that he was convinced would be a proper remedy' (*The Speeches of the Right Honourable Charles James Fox*, vol. 4, pp 411–12).
27. *Life and Letters of Gilbert Elliot, First Earl of Minto* (3 vols, 1874), vol. 2, p. 104. It was reported by Thomas Pelham, in a letter to Lady Webster, dated June 15, 1792, that Fox had told him '(what I knew to be the truth, notwithstanding what is now said) that he had never been consulted about it, and that, on the contrary, the Associators seemed determined not to have any advice, and

particularly not to have his. This I know to be true, for
Lauderdale told me that they were determined not to consult Fox
until they saw the probability of success, in order that he might
not be involved if they failed' (Earl of Ilchester, ed. *The Journal of
Elizabeth Lady Holland*, 2 vols, Longmans Green & Co., 1908, vol. 1,
p. 15).

28. *The Speeches of the Right Honourable Charles James Fox*, vol. 4, p. 409.
29. Ibid., p. 440.
30. Ibid., pp. 447–9: 'The honourable gentleman who seconded the
motion thought proper to say, as a proof that there existed a
dangerous spirit in this country, that it was manifested "by the
drooping and dejected aspect of many persons, when the tidings
of Dumourier's surrender arrived in England". What, Sir, is this to
be considered as a sign of discontent, and of a preference
to republican doctrines? ... But, am I to be told that my sorrow was
an evident proof of *my* being connected with the French nation,
or with any persons in that nation, for the purpose of aiding them
in creating discontents in England, or in making any attempt to
destroy the British constitution? If such a conclusion were to be
drawn from the dejection of those who are hostile to the maxims
of tyranny, upon which the invasion of France was founded, what
must we say of those men who acknowledge that they are sorry
the invasion did not prosper? Am I to believe that the honourable
gentleman, and all others, who confess their sorrow at the failure
of Prussia and Austria, were connected with the courts in concert,
and that a considerable body of persons in this country were actually in the horrid league formed against human liberty? Are we
taught to bring this heavy charge against all those, whose spirits
drooped on the reverse of the news, and when it turned out that
it was not Dumourier, but the Duke of Brunswick who had
retreated? No; he would not charge them with being confederates
with the invaders of France; nor did they believe, nor could they
believe, that the really constitutional men of England, who
rejoiced at the overthrow of that horrid and profligate scheme,
wished to draw therefrom any thing hostile to the established
government of England.

But what, Sir, are the doctrines that they desire to set up by this
insinuation of gloom and dejection? That Englishmen are not to
dare to have any genuine feelings of their own; that they must not

rejoice but by rule; that they must not think but by order; that no man shall dare to exercise his faculties in contemplating the objects that surround him ... but according to the instructions that he shall receive. That, in observing the events that happen to surrounding and neutral nations, he shall not dare to think whether they are favourable to the principles that contribute to the happiness of man, or the contrary ...

31. *The Speeches of the Right Honourable Charles James Fox*, vol. 4, p. 452.
32. *The Correspondence of Edmund Burke*, vol. 7, p. 315.
33. Earl Russell. *The Life and Times of Charles James Fox*, vol. 2, pp. 312–13.
34. See ibid., vol. 3, p. 11.
35. *The Speeches of the Right Honourable Charles James Fox*, vol. 5, p. 7.
36. Ibid., p. 13.
37. John Derry. *Charles James Fox* (B.T. Batsford, 1972), p. 322.
38. *The Speeches of the Right Honourable Charles James Fox*, vol. 5, p. 66.
39. Ibid., p. 107. O'Gorman writes that in the debates on 7 May Fox's 'attitude was dramatically reversed', (O'Gorman, ibid., p. 135) and that his opposition to universal suffrage was now only to the practical means of organising it. But Fox states clearly that 'there was no practical mode of collecting such suffrage' at all (*Speeches*, vol. 5, p. 108), which makes him appear more consistent. Indeed, despite Pitt's lengthy assault on universal suffrage, Fox denied that it was in fact proposed by Grey as such (*Speeches*, vol. 5, p. 104).
40. Cf. Thomas Moore, who reported that Lord Holland told him much later that 'Mr. Fox was never a member of the Friends of the People; never a Reformer, in the sense of those who think the people have a right to change the representation' (*Memoir, Journal, and Correspondence of Thomas Moore*, 8 vols, 1853, vol. 4, p. 219).
41. *The Speeches of the Right Honourable Charles James Fox*, vol. 5, pp. 114–15.
42. Ibid., p. 118.
43. Ibid., p. 149.
44. Ibid., p. 156.
45. Ibid., p. 313, 317–18.
46. Ibid., p. 275. Pitt's view was that 'a plan had been formed, and was in forwardness, to assemble a convention of the people, which was to assume the character and powers of a national representation, and to supersede the authority of parliament. A mere parliamentary reform was not the real aim of these societies' (ibid, p. 273).

Elsewhere Pitt said of the period 1792–3 that 'Societies had been formed in this country, affiliated with the jacobin clubs in France; and though they had since assumed a different shape, were then employed for the purpose of spreading Jacobin principles. In this object they proceeded with a degree of boldness and confidence, proportioned to the success of the French arms. We thus beheld the scheme which we had anticipated as the result of the new constitutions in France, opening upon us. ... their instruments here always took care to connect the system of parliamentary reform with all those delusive doctrines, upon which was founded the newly-raised fabric of French freedom. Nothing less than a national convention was held out as a sufficient remedy for the abuses which prevailed in the representation, and the sole organ through which a more perfect form of government was to be obtained; namely, such a government as should acknowledge no other source of authority and no other rule of conduct, than the will of the majority. In short, French principles were inculcated as the true standard of political belief, and the example of the French government proposed as a worthy object of imitation' (*Speeches of the Right Honourable William Pitt*, 4 vols, 1806, vol. 2, p. 146).

47. For example, *Speeches of the Right Honourable William Pitt*, vol. 2, pp. 188–9, for comments in May 1794 on the LCS.

48. *The Speeches of the Right Honourable Charles James Fox*, vol. 5, p. 45.

49. *Speeches of the Right Honourable Richard Brinsley Sheridan* (5 vols, 1816), vol. 2, p. 242.

50. Ibid., pp. 242–6.

51. Ibid., vol. 3, p. 13.

52. Ibid., p. 39.

53. See W.E.H. Lecky, *A History of England in the Eighteenth Century* (7 vols, 1892), vol. 7, p. 124.

54. *Speeches of the Right Honourable Richard Brinsley Sheridan*, vol. 3, p. 82.

55. Ibid., p. 164.

56. Ibid., p. 362.

57. Ibid., pp. 196–7.

58. In Parliament he 'added some warm compliments to Mr. Burke's general principles; but said that he could not conceive how it was possible for a person of such principles, or for any man who valued our own constitution, and revered the Revolution that

obtained it for us, to unite with such feelings an indignant and unqualified abhorrence of all the proceedings of the patriotic party in France. He conceived their's to be as just a Revolution as ours, proceeding upon as sound a principle and a greater provocation. He vehemently defended the general views and conduct of the National Assembly' (ibid., p. 242, Feb 1790).

59. Earl Russell. *The Life and Times of Charles James Fox*, vol. 2, p. 249.

60. Porchester himself refused to join the Society because it was insufficiently republican: *The Journal of Elizabeth Lady Holland* (2 vols, Longmans, Green & Co., 1908), vol. 1, p. 14. A few months later he called the society seditious, and was raised to an earldom. Lord Holland was quoted as arguing that 'Lord Porchester was right in saying that the Association was not as Republican as he wished, otherwise he would probably have got a marquisate'. See generally Iain Hampsher-Monk. 'Civic Humanism and Parliamentary Reform: The Case of the Society of the Friends of the People', *Journal of British Studies*, 18 (1978), 70–88. The SFP aimed, according to James Mackintosh, 'by the liberality of their principles, to reclaim every thinking man who had been seduced into Republicanism, and by the moderation of their views, to attract every honest man who had for a moment been driven into Toryism' ([James Mackintosh.] *A Letter to the Right Honourable William Pitt, on his Apostacy from the Cause of Parliamentary Reform*, 2nd edn., 1793, p. 42). Its members included Charles Grey, Samuel Whitbread, Richard Brinsley Sheridan, George Rous, the Earl of Lauderdale, Thomas Erskine, John Cartwright, Joseph Towers, James Mackintosh and some twenty-eight members of Parliament. See *Proceedings of the Society of Friends of the People; Associated for the Purpose of Obtaining a Parliamentary Reform, In the Year 1792* (1793).

61. G.M. Trevelyan. *Lord Grey of the Reform Bill* (Longmans, Green & Co., 1920), p. 43. O'Gorman notes that Fox wrote privately that he wished, with respect to the SFP, 'to put an end to a scheme so injurious to us as a party' (*The Whig Party and the French Revolution*, Macmillan, 1967, p. 84).

62. The description is accurate, since 23 out of 24 MP's who joined the SFP were to follow Fox rather than Portland in 1794.

63. *Proceedings of the Society of Friends of the People; Associated for the Purpose of Obtaining a Parliamentary Reform* (1793), p. 4, states these objects: 'To restore the Freedom of Election, and a more equal

representation of the People in Parliament'; 2. 'To secure to the People a more frequent exercise of their Right of electing their Representatives'.

64. Ibid., pp. 12, 14, 16. But to the opposition this was impossible: Windham said of the reformers (13 December 1792) that 'All they wanted was a perfect representation of the people. Such a constitution would no more be the constitution of England than the constitution of Venice; in short. their view was to destroy all hereditary right, and perhaps afterwards to attempt an equalization of property'; William Windham. *Speeches in Parliament* (3 vols, 1812), vol. 1, p. 222.

65. *Proceedings of the Society of Friends of the People; Associated for the Purpose of Obtaining a Parliamentary Reform* (1793), p. 31.

66. See my introduction to *Political Writings of the 1790s*, vol. 1, pp. xxx–xliii.

67. *Holborn Society of the Friends of the People* (1792), p. 4.

68. *Southwark Society of Friends of the People* (1792), p. 2. See Thomas Paine. *Address and Declaration of the Friends of Universal Peace and Liberty* (1792), p. 5: 'we admit of no maxims of government or policy, on the mere score of antiquity, or other men's authority, the *Old* Whigs, or the *New.*'

69. This is the principal charge of the pamphlet, *Remarks on the Proceedings of the Society, Who Style Themselves 'The Friends of the People'* (1792).

70. *Holborn Society of the Friends of the People* (1792), p. 3; *Southwark Society of Friends of the People* (1792).

71. 'If the Duke contents himself with asking if he means to apply the principles of the French Revolution to England, and to acquiesce in the negative answer, the explanation will be wholly nugatory. The point to be explained is not whether he means to introduce the French Revolution here, but why, if he does not, he extols and magnifies it in the language and sentiments of those who do; and how these two things are compatible. This is what wants explanation' (Fox in relation to Portland, June 1791), *Life and Letters of Sir Gilbert Elliot* (3 vols, 1874), vol. 1, pp. 377–8.

72. G.M. Trevelyan. *Lord Grey of the Reform Bill* (Longmans, Green & Co., 1920), p. 53.

73. Earl of Malmesbury. *Diary and Correspondence of James Harris, First Earl of Malmesbury* (3 vols, 1844), vol. 2, p. 460.

74. See 'Address to the Addressers', in *The Writings of Thomas Paine*, ed. Moncure Conway (4 vols, New York, G.P. Putnam's Sons, 1908), vol. 3, p. 94.

75. *The Correspondence of the Revolution Society in London, with the National Assembly* (1792), p. iv.

76. Ibid., p. 20.

77. Ibid., pp. 44, 62, 83–4, 100.

78. Ibid., pp. 110, 128.

79. For example, ibid., p. 217.

80. Ibid., p. 260. On the connection between such sentiments and anti-war feeling generally, see J.E. Cookson. *The Friends of Peace. Anti-War Liberalism in England 1793–1815* (Cambridge, Cambridge University Press, 1982), ch. 1.

81. *The Correspondence of the Revolution Society in London, with the National Assembly* (1792), pp. 203–4.

82. For example, *A Vindication of the Revolution Society against the Calumnies of Mr. Burke* (1792), in *Political Writings of the 1790s*, vol. 2, p. 395.

83. Usually as linked to 'radical reform', see, for example, the discussion in Arthur Young's *The Example of France a Warning to Britain*, in *Political Writings of the 1790s*, vol. 8, p. 122.

84. In the essay on Sir James Mackintosh; T.B. Macaulay. *The Complete Works of Lord Macaulay* (12 vols, Longmans, Green & Co., 1906), vol. 8, p. 431.

Chapter Seven: William Godwin

1. The case for the translation of these ideals into secular form in *Political Justice* is given in William Stafford. 'Dissenting Religion Translated into Politics: Godwin's *Political Justice*', *History of Political Thought*, 1 (1980), 279–99. The standard study of the text is Mark Philp. *Godwin's Political Justice* (Duckworth, 1986), esp. pp. 15–37. See also Martin Fitzpatrick. 'Heretical Religion and Radical Political Ideas in Late Eighteenth-Century England', in Eckhart Hellmuth, ed. *The Transformation of Political Culture. England and Germany in the Late 18th-Century* (Oxford, Oxford University Press, 1990), pp. 339–72.

2. I draw in this chapter upon arguments first presented in 'The Concept of Political Justice In Godwin's *Political Justice*: A Reconsideration', *Political Theory*, 11 (1983), 565–84; 'The Effects of Property on Godwin's Theory of Justice', *Journal of the History of Philosophy*, 22, (1984), 81–101; 'William Godwin's Critique of Democracy and Republicanism and Its Sources', *History of European*

Ideas, 7, (1986), 253–269, and 'From True Virtue to Benevolent Politeness: Godwin and Godwinism Revisited', in Gordon Schochet, ed. *Empire and Revolutions. Papers Presented at the Folger Institute Seminar 'Political Thought in the English-Speaking Atlantic, 1760–1800'* (Washington D.C., The Folger Library, 1993), pp. 187–226.

3. For a general account of these themes see Seamus Deane. *The French Revolution and Enlightenment in England 1789–1832* (Cambridge, MA, Harvard University Press, 1988).

4. William Godwin. *Enquiry Concerning Political Justice* (2 vols, 1842), vol. 1, p. 61.

5. Ibid., (2 vols, 1793) book 2, ch. 5. Francis Place, for instance, was disabused of the idea of 'abstract rights' by reading *Political Justice* (Graham Wallas. *The Life of Francis Place*, 4th edn, George Allen & Unwin, 1925, p. 29.)

6. William Godwin. *Enquiry Concerning Political Justice* (2 vols, 1842), vol. 1, p. 60. The example is scrutinised in D.H. Monro. 'Archbishop Fenelon versus My Mother,' *Australasian Journal of Philosophy* (1950), 154–73, reprinted in *Godwin's Moral Philosophy* (Oxford, Oxford University Press, 1953), pp. 9–35. In the first edition the choice is more refined: it is the Archbishop as opposed to a chambermaid who might be my wife or mother (*Enquiry Concerning Political Justice*, 2 vols, 1793, vol. 1, p. 83.)

7. The term 'anarchism' was first used in a positive sense by Pierre-Joseph Proudhon in *What is Property?* (1840). On Godwin's debt to Swift see James A. Preu. *The Dean and the Anarchist* (Tallahassee, Florida State University, 1959). Godwin uses it only negatively, as in 'the terror of general anarchy' (William Godwin. *Enquiry Concerning Political Justice*, 2 vols, 1842, vol. 1, p. 142).

8. William Godwin. *Enquiry Concerning Political Justice* (1793), vol. 1, p. 2.

9. Quoted in C. Kegan Paul. *William Godwin. His Friends and Contemporaries* (2 vols, 1876), vol. 1, p. 67.

10. William Godwin. *Enquiry Concerning Political Justice* (2 vols, 1842), vol. 1, p. 47.

11. Ibid., p. 3.

12. Ibid., p. v.

13. Abinger Collection, Bodleian Library, Dep. c. 200. Thanks to Lord Abinger for permission to quote from this collection.

14. Élie Halévy. *The Growth of Philosophic Radicalism* (Faber & Faber, 1972), p. 192.

15. Abinger Collection, Dep. b. 229/9.

16. William Godwin. *Enquiry Concerning Political Justice* (2 vols, 1842), vol. 2, p. 62.
17. J. J. Rousseau. *The Social Contract and Discourses*, ed. G. D. H. Cole (J.M. Dent, 1973), pp. 74, 78, 83.
18. J. J. Rousseau. 'Considerations on the Government of Poland,' in *Rousseau: Political Writings*, ed. F. Watkins (Nelson, 1953), p. 220.
19. Ibid., p. 295.
20. J. J. Rousseau. *The Social Contract and Discourses*, p. 20.
21. William Godwin. *Enquiry Concerning Political Justice* (2 vols, 1842), vol. 2, p. 62.
22. Ibid., p. 98.
23. Ibid., p. 240; see J.S. Mill, *On Liberty* (1859), ch. 3.
24. Ibid., p. 103.
25. See George Crowder. *Classical Anarchism: The Political Thought of Godwin, Proudhon, Bakunin and Kropotkin* (Oxford, Clarendon Press, 1991), pp. 39–73.
26. William Godwin. *Enquiry Concerning Political Justice* (2 vols, 1842), vol. 1, p. 162.
27. Ibid., vol. 2, p. 211.
28. 'Considerations on Lord Grenville's and Mr. Pitt's Bills,' in *Uncollected Writings* (1785–1822), ed. Jack W. Marken and Burton R. Pollin (Gainesville, Florida, Scholars' Facsimiles and Reprints, 1968), pp. 196–7.
29. William Godwin. *Enquiry Concerning Political Justice* (2 vols, 1842), vol. 2, p. 163.
30. Ibid., p. 163.
31. Ibid., p. 80.
32. Ibid., p. 58.
33. Ibid., vol. 1, p. 103.
34. Ibid., vol. 2, p. 89.
35. Ibid., p. 70.
36. It was reprinted separately in 1890 by H.S. Salt, who proclaimed Godwin to be 'a true prophet' of two leading later nineteenth-century movements, Socialism and Simplification (*Seventy Years Among Savages*, George Allen & Unwin, 1921, p. 73). I here summarise an argument first developed in my 'The Effects of Property on Godwin's Theory of Justice', *Journal of the History of Philosophy*, 22 (1984), 81–101.
37. On accounts of luxury in this period see generally Istvan Hont. *Jealousy of Trade. International Competition and the Nation-State in*

Historical Perspective (Cambridge, MA, Harvard University Press, 2005).

38. William Godwin. *Enquiry Concerning Political Justice* (1842), vol. 2, p. 223.
39. Ibid.
40. Ibid. (1793), vol. 1, pp. 88–9.
41. Ibid., vol. 2, p. 794.
42. Ibid. (2 vols, 1842), vol. 2, p. 230.
43. Ibid. (1793), vol. 2, pp. 789–90.
44. Ibid. (2 vols, 1842), vol. 2, p. 203.
45. Ibid., p. 211.
46. On these changes see Peter Marshall. *William Godwin* (New Haven, Yale University Press, 1984), pp. 155–71, and Mark Philp. *Godwin's Political Justice*, pp. 193–213.
47. He would write in his *Memoir of Mary Wollstonecraft* that 'moral reasoning is nothing but the awakening of certain feelings' (Constable & Co., 1928, p. 89).
48. William Godwin. *The Enquirer* (1797), p. x.
49. Ibid., p. 326.
50. He would indeed even defend Burke against Mary Wollstonecraft's 'too contemptuous and intemperate treatment' of the *Reflections* in the first *Vindication* (*Memoirs of Mary Wollstonecraft*, 1928, p. 50).
51. William Godwin. *The Enquirer* (1797), p. vi.
52. Abinger Collection, Dep. b. 228.
53. Ibid., 229/9.
54. William Godwin. *Enquiry Concerning Political Justice* (2 vols, 1793), vol. 1, p. 71.
55. Ibid., vol. 2, p. 816.
56. Ibid., p. 235.
57. Ibid., p. 236. This recalls Hume's distinction between innocent and vicious luxury, as being particularly where luxury 'leaves no ability for such acts of duty and generosity as are required by his situation and fortune' (*Essays Moral, Political and Literary*, 2 vols, 1882, vol. 1, p. 307).
58. William Godwin. *Enquiry Concerning Political Justice* (2 vols, 1842), vol. 2, pp. 236–7.
59. Ibid., p. 237.
60. Leslie Stephen's claim was for 'over four thousand' (*Studies of a Biographer*, 4 vols, Smith, Elder & Co.,1907, vol. 3, p. 120).
61. [Thomas Northmore.] *Memoirs of Planetes; or a Sketch of the Laws and Manners of Makar* (1795), reprinted in my *Utopias of the British*

Enlightenment (Cambridge, Cambridge University Press, 1994), pp. 137–98.

62. [John Fenwick.] *Public Characters of 1799–1800* (1801), pp. 373–4.
63. *Diary, Reminiscences, and Correspondence of Henry Crabb Robinson* (3 vols, 1869), vol. 1, pp. 31–2.
64. William Hazlitt. *Political Essays* (1819), p. 99.
65. *Anti-Jacobin Review*, 19 (1804), 53–5.
66. William Hazlitt. *The Spirit of the Age* (1915), p. 28.
67. *Public Characters of 1799–1800* (1800), p. 376.
68. John Thelwall. *The Tribune*, vol. 2, p. vii.
69. Treasury Solicitors Papers, 11/955/3500 (26 February 1794).
70. Ibid., 11/956/3501 (18 February 1794). It is usually argued that Thelwall did not follow Godwin this far down the road towards 'anarchism' (for example, B. Sprague Allen. 'William Godwin's Influence upon John Thelwall', *Publications of the Modern Language Association of America*, 37, 1922, 678).
71. William Belcher. *Holcroft's Folly* (n.d.), p. 8. See John Thelwall. *The Tribune*, vol. 1, p. 229.
72. *Considerations on Lord Grenville's and Mr. Pitt's Bills* (1795).
73. See J.R. MacGillvray. 'The Pantisocracy Scheme and Its Immediate Background', in Malcolm Wallace, ed. *Studies in Romanticism* (Toronto, University of Toronto Press, 1931), pp. 131–69.
74. William Hazlitt. *The Spirit of the Age* (4th edn, 1915), p. 24.
75. Leslie Stephen. *Studies in Biography* (4 vols, Smith, Elder & Co., 1907), vol. 1, p. 245. On the renunciation of Godwinism by Wordsworth and Coleridge see Alfred Cobban. *Edmund Burke and the Revolt Against the Eighteenth Century* (2nd edn., George Allen & Unwin, 1960).
76. S.T. Coleridge. *On the Constitution of the Church and State* (2nd edn, 1830), pp. 53–7.
77. S.T. Coleridge. The Watchman, *The Collected Works of S.T. Coleridge* (Princeton, Princeton University Press, 1970), vol. 2, pp. 43–44, 98–100.
78. *The Life and Correspondence of Robert Southey*, ed. C.C. Southey (2nd edn, 6 vols, 1849), vol. 1, p. 247.
79. Opposition to a secular version of utilitarianism is also apparent in the anti-Godwinian literature, notably in Thomas Green. *An Examination of the Leading Principle of the New System of Morals, as That Principle is Stated and Applied in Mr. Godwin's Enquiry Concerning Political Justice* (1799).

80. Charles Findlater. *Liberty and Equality: A Sermon* (Edinburgh, 1800), p. 25.
81. George Walker. *The Vagabond* (1799), pp. 112–14.

Chapter Eight: John Thelwall

1. An evaluation of his intellectual achievements is given in Iain Hampsher-Monk. 'John Thelwall and the Eighteenth-Century Radical Response to Political Economy', *Historical Journal*, 34 (1991), 1–20 and my edn., *The Politics of English Jacobinism. Writings of John Thelwall* (University Park, Pa., Pennsylvania State University Press, 1995), pp. xiii–lvi. Also useful is Geoffrey Gallop. 'Ideology and the English Jacobins: the Case of John Thelwall', *Enlightenment and Dissent*, 5 (1986), 3–20, Andrew McCann. *Cultural Politics in the 1790s. Literature, Radicalism and the Public Sphere* (Macmillan, 1999), ch. 3, and E.P. Thompson. 'Hunting the Jacobin Fox', *Past and Present*, 142 (1994), 94–140, and most recently, Michael Scrivener. *Seditious Allegories. John Thelwall and Jacobin Writing* (University Park, Pa., Pennsylvania State University Press, 2001).
2. John Thelwall. *Peaceful Discussion, and Not Tumultuary Violence, the Means of Redressing National Grievances* (1795), pp. 12–13. In 1795, he criticised the new French constitution for restricting the franchise.
3. Public Record Office. Treasury Solicitors Papers, TS11/956.
4. John Thelwall. *The Tribune* (3 vols, 1795–6), vol. 2, pp. 210–11; vol. 3, p. 196.
5. Ibid., vol. 1, p. 197; Walter Moyle. *Democracy Vindicated*, ed. John Thelwall (1796), p. 39–40.
6. Charles Cestre. *John Thelwall* (Swan Sonnenschein, 1906), p. 58.
7. On 'moral economy' debates in this period, see E.P. Thompson. 'The Moral Economy of the English Crowd in the 18th Century', *Past and Present*, 50 (1971), 76–136.
8. John Thelwall. *Poems Written in Close Confinement in the Tower and Newgate* (1795), p. 3.
9. John Thelwall. *The Peripatetic, or, Sketches of the Heart, of Nature and Society*, 3 vols, 1793, vol. 1, pp. 38–9, 134–5, 145–6, 173–4. Excerpts from the *Peripatetic* appeared in Daniel Isaac Eaton's *Politics for the People* (1794), 48–50, 73–6, 118–21, 212–17.
10. Reprinted in John Thelwall. *The Poetical Recreations of the Champion* (1822), pp. 169–70.

11. John Thelwall. *The Tribune*, vol. 1, p. 13.
12. *Moral and Political Magazine of the London Corresponding Society*, June 1796, p. 26.
13. John Thelwall. *The Tribune*, vol. 3, pp. 115–16.
14. Ibid., p. 5.
15. Ibid., vol. 2, p. 8, vol. 3, pp. 38, 44.
16. For example, ibid., vol. 1, pp. 36, 130. Some called Smith 'the high priest of democracy' at this time (R. Dinmore, Jr. *An Exposition of the Principles of the English Jacobins*, Norwich, 1796, p. 20).
17. John Thelwall. *The Tribune*, vol. 1, p. 13; vol. 2, pp. 38, 46, 59, 66–7, 150; vol. 3, pp. 38–9.
18. John Thelwall. *The Rights of Nature*, letter one, p. 65.
19. John Thelwall. *The Speech of John Thelwall at the General Meeting of the Friends of Parliamentary Reform, called by the London Corresponding Society, October 26, 1795* (1795), p. 14. But Thelwall praised as just and moderate the agrarian laws of ancient Rome (Walter Moyle. *Democracy Vindicated*, ed. John Thelwall, 1796, p. 20).
20. John Thelwall. *The Speech of John Thelwall at the General Meeting of the Friends of Parliamentary Reform, called by the London Corresponding Society, 26th October, 1795* (1795), p. 14.
21. John Thelwall. *The Tribune*, vol. 3, pp. 43, 46, 248; John Thelwall. *The Speech of John Thelwall at the General Meeting of the Friends of Parliamentary Reform, called by the London Corresponding Society, 26th October, 1795* (1795), pp. 9, 20. This vision of the best commerce being that which furnished the greatest employment to all, and nourished the health and strength of the inhabitants, as well as being 'most certain', was also shared by writers like Capel Lofft (*Elements of Universal Law*, 1779, pp. 120–1). But Lofft also opposed luxury and insisted that 'Luxury in a *commonwealth* is either extinct the instant it springs up, or the *commonwealth*' (Ibid., p. 106).
22. *Agrarian Justice* was written in the winter of 1795–6 and published in early 1796 in Paris. A London edition appeared in 1797. One copy of *The Tribune* survives (in the Cambridge University Library) which is inscribed to 'Citizen Thomas Paine, with the respect and sincere admiration of the author', though there is no way of knowing when or even if Paine received it.
23. John Thelwall. *The Rights of Nature* (1796), pt 1, p. 16.
24. Ibid., pt 2, p. 46. It ought, in short, actively to promote the ends of 'society' as writers like Pufendorf had used the term, and as Paine had also concluded at the end of his *Rights of Man*, Part

Two; or to follow the obligation to improve both body and soul, as Hutcheson phrased it, as well as the 'talents', as Sharp had insisted (Francis Hutcheson. *A System of Moral Philosophy*, 2 vols, 1755, vol. 2, pp. 111–12; Granville Sharp. *A Tract on the Law of Nature*, 1777, p. 23). Cestre thus misleads in asserting that Thelwall 'chiefly aimed at reducing the excessive consumption of luxuries by the few, in order to increase the share of necessaries for the many', and saw commerce as at best only a doubtful good. This was true for the early 1790s, but far less so after 1795 (*John Thelwall*, pp. 59, 61).

25. John Thelwall. *The Rights of Nature*, pt 2, pp. 39–42. Natural law writers agreed that the chief obligation of property was not hindering the rights of others to enjoy their own. On this obligation see, for example, Thomas Rutherforth. *Institutes of Natural Law* (2 vols, 1754), vol. 1, pp. 138–9.

26. John Thelwall. *The Rights of Nature*, pt 2, pp. 27, 38–9.

27. Thomas Paine. *Agrarian Justice* (1796), p. 6.

28. Adam Smith. *Wealth of Nations* (1776), Bk 3, ch. 1.

29. John Thelwall. *The Rights of Nature*, pt 2, pp. 54–55. Thelwall may here have followed Blackstone's account of the evolution of property (*Commentaries on the Laws of England*, 5th edn., 1773, vol. 2, pp. 1–9).

30. John Thelwall. *The Rights of Nature*, pt 2, p. 62.

31. He wrote that 'if *Polybius, Machiavel*, etc., have placed too much stress upon the moral causes, *Harrington, Moyle*, and other English writers have erred still more in referring everything to 'the balance of property', adding that 'The progress of intellect, the balance of property, and the insolence of oppression have their respective influences in the production of great revolutions' (Walter Moyle. *Democracy Vindicated*, ed. John Thelwall, 1796, p. 21).

32. John Thelwall. *The Rights of Nature*, pt 2, pp. 77–86.

33. Ibid., pp. 54–79. This extended the natural law view that contracts which tended to ruin the community were no longer binding (for example, Hugo Grotius. *De Jure Belli et Pacis*, 3 vols, Cambridge, Cambridge University Press, 1853, vol. 2, p. 125, Francis Hutcheson. *A Short Introduction to Moral Philosophy*, 2nd edn., 1753, p. 168). Thelwall later recalled having suffered under a 'surfeit … of the glossing and barbarous jargon of the law' during his studies of the subject. Here while mentioning Grotius and Pufendorf and quoting frequently from Blackstone, he disgustedly dismisses 'Sir W. Blackstone, and the fraternity of Lincoln's

Inn' for their slavish devotion to ancient custom (*The Rights of Nature*, pt 2, p. 24, pt 3, p. 110).

34. On the background to the concept of 'implied contract' see Peter Birks and Grant MacLeod. 'The Implied Contract Theory of Quasi-Contract: Civilian Opinion Current in the Century Before Blackstone', *Oxford Journal of Legal Studies*, 6 (1986), 46–85.

35. John Thelwall. *The Rights of Nature*, pt 2, pp. 80–2, 45, 76. For Blackstone on implied contracts see the *Commentaries*, vol. 3, pp. 159–67.

36. For example, Albert Goodwin. *The Friends of Liberty. The English Democratic Movement in the Age of the French Revolution* (Hutchinson, 1979), p. 473.

37. Hugo Grotius. *De Jure Belli et Pacis*, vol. 1, pp. 238–9; Samuel Pufendorf. *The Whole Duty of Man According to the Law of Nature* (5th edn., 1735), pp. 135–6; Francis Hutcheson. *A System of Moral Philosophy* (1755), vol. 1, p. 330; John Locke. *Locke's Two Treatises of Government* (Cambridge, Cambridge University Press, 1970), p. 317, and generally John Dunn. *The Political Thought of John Locke* (Cambridge, Cambridge University Press, 1969). Rutherforth follows the doctrine of tacit consent by occupation (*Institutes*, vol. 1, pp. 48, 81), emphasising that this would have been seen as 'for the convenience of all', while rejecting Locke's theory that labour contributed to property (p. 56).

38. See Istvan Hont. 'The Language of Sociability and Commerce: Samuel Pufendorf and the Theoretical Foundations of the "Four Stages Theory",' in *Jealousy of Trade. International Competition and the Nation-State in Historical Perspective* (Cambridge, MA, Harvard University Press, 2005), pp. 159–84. On Grotius and the introduction of a contract in the transition from common property see Richard Tuck. *Natural Rights Theories* (Cambridge, Cambridge University Press, 1979), p. 77.

39. Thomas Paine. *Agrarian Justice* (1796), pp. 5–8.

40. Ibid., p. 13.

41. John Thelwall. *The Rights of Nature*, pt 3, pp. 83–4.

42. Grotius, for example, distinguishes between societies of equals, such as brothers, and those of unequals, such as masters and servants (*De Jure Belli et Pacis*, vol. 1, p. 4).

43. Francis Hutcheson. *A System of Moral Philosophy* (1755), vol. 1, p. 288.

44. Adam Smith. *Wealth of Nations* (1776), Bk 1, ch. 2.

45. Edmund Burke. 'Thoughts and Details on Scarcity' (1795), *Works*, vol. 5 (1887), p. 139.

46. *The Tribune*, vol. 2 (1795), p. 113.

47. Hugo Grotius. *De Jure Belli et Pacis*, vol. 1, p. 237. The best contemporary account of partnership was William Watson. *A Treatise of the Law of Partnership* (1794). On partnerships between labour and capital, see pp. 135–7.

48. Thomas Rutherforth. *Institutes*, vol. 1, pp. 231, 214, 276, vol. 2, p. 255.

49. John Thelwall. *The Rights of Nature*, pt 3, p. 80.

50. Samuel Pufendorf. *The Whole Duty of Man* (5th edn., 1735), pp. 162–3, 169, 140–1.

51. A position followed by, for example, William Paley. 'Principles of Moral and Political Philosophy', *The Works of William Paley* (1831), p. 37.

52. This solved the Lockean problem of the right to the produce of others' labour outside of the common materials of nature. For Locke, though the mixing of labour with common property created private property in the natural state, 'my servant's turfs' belonged to me in later social stages, even if he or she had cut and stacked them, nay even presumably if they were cut on common land. For Thelwall no servant ought ever to labour at such a disadvantage. See John Locke. *Locke's Two Treatises of Government*, pp. 306–7. Blackstone merely acknowledged that in return for work a servant was entitled to wages (*Commentaries*, vol. 1, p. 428).

53. For Francis Hutcheson, for example, 'the indigent must be supported by the compensations they get' for their labour (*A System of Moral Philosophy*, vol. 2, p. 1). Grotius had insisted that the poor had the right to purchase necessities at a fair price (Hugo Grotius. *De Jure Belli et Pacis*, vol. 1, p. 252). Pufendorf reiterated cases where extreme necessity superseded existing rights (*The Whole Duty of Man*, pp. 87–8). Cumberland agreed that no right of dominion permitted the removal of necessities from the innocent (Richard Cumberland. *A Treatise of the Law of Nature*, 1727, p. 68). William Paley, too, recognised the imperfect right of the poor to relief by the rich on the basis of original divine intention ('Principles of Moral and Political Philosophy', pp. 20, 50). See also Thomas Horne. *Property Rights and Poverty. Political Argument in Britain, 1605–1834* (Chapel Hill, University of North Carolina Press, 1990), pp. 123–41.

54. William Ogilvie. *An Essay on the Right of Property in Land* (1781), p. 12. For treatments of partnership see, for example, Francis Hutcheson. *A System of Moral Philosophy*, vol. 2, p. 71, Samuel Pufendorf. *The Whole Duty of Man*, pp. 168–9.

55. But unlike the later Owenite socialist view, for which it clearly laid the foundations by concentrating on the contractual relationship between labourer and employer, Thelwall's theory did not enjoin the exact exchange of equal amounts of labour in contracts in order for justice to be fulfilled. In Grotian terms, Thelwall demanded beneficial contracts, with a limited degree of equality, Owenism commutational contracts, where complete equality was more substantial. See Hugo Grotius. *De Jure Belli et Pacis*, vol. 2, p. 65. On the relations between early British socialism and natural jurisprudence, and the notion of the ideal of partnership and 'co-operation' as a new form of sociability, see my *Citizens and Saints. Politics and Anti-Politics in Early British Socialism* (Cambridge, Cambridge University Press, 1989), pp. 23–62.

56. See my 'Justice, Independence and Industrial Democracy: the Development of John Stuart Mill's Views on Socialism', *Journal of Politics*, 49 (1987), 122–47. There is some evidence that Thelwall was interested in the development of consumer co-operation in the post-war period. In 1832, for example, he wrote proposing a visit to Dr William King of Brighton, who had established a well-known co-operative store (letter of 3 November 1832, Seligman Collection, Columbia University Library).

57. See my *Machinery, Money and the Millennium: From Moral Economy to Socialism, 1815–1860* (Princeton University Press, 1987), pp. 99–109.

58. John Thelwall. *The Rights of Nature*, letter four, p. 90; *The Tribune*, vol. 2, p. 67.

59. Quoted in Charles Cestre. *John Thelwall*, p. 164. In *The Rights of Nature*, Thelwall noted that 'every large workshop and manufactory is a sort of political society (Letter one, pp. 20–1). See also his comments on the dangers to common use rights of a 'pestilential manufactury' (Letter Two, p. 28).

60. Edmund Burke. *A Letter from the Right Hon. Edmund Burke to a Noble Lord* (1796), p. 35.

61. Robespierre's 'wanton and revengeful cruelties' and 'scenes of blood and cruelty' are condemned in *The Tribune*, vol. 1 (1795), pp. 155, 114. See also ibid., pp. 249–54, and the comparison of

Pitt's and Robespierre's characters at the end of this lecture (ibid., pp. 255–60). The so-called Jacobin element in Thelwall's thinking emerged most clearly in the letter introduced as evidence during his trial. But he also considered that at a critical period in the revolution the Jacobins were better equipped to govern than any other group. See *The Tribune*, vol. 1, 1795, p. 246). Given his attitude towards violence, Thelwall is despite such reservations perhaps best associated with the Girondins, whom Paine also supported.

Conclusion

1. On Irish radicalism, see Marianne Elliott. *Partners in Revolution. The United Irishmen and France* (New Haven, Yale University Press, 1982); Marianne Elliott. 'Ireland and the French Revolution', in H.T. Dickinson, ed. *Britain and the French Revolution, 1789–1815* (Macmillan, 1989), pp. 83–102; David Dickson, Daire Keogh, Keven Whelan, eds. *The United Irishmen* (Dubin, Lilliput Press, 1993), esp. David Dickson. 'Paine and Ireland', pp. 135–50; Nancy Curtin. *The United Irishmen* (Oxford, Clarendon Press, 1994), and most recently, Ultán Gillen. 'Monarchy, Republic and Empire: Irish Public Opinion and France, c. 1787–1804', D.Phil., Oxford, 2005. An excellent sourcebook for northern Irish radicalism in the early period is *Belfast Politics: Or, A Collection of the Debates, Resolutions, and Other Proceedings of That Town, in the Years MDCCXCII and MDCCXCIII* (1793).
2. *Memoirs of the Life of Sir Samuel Romilly* (3 vols, 1840), vol. 1, p. 427; Francis Plowden. *A Short History of the British Empire During the Last Twenty Months* (1794), p. 240.
3. See J.R. Western. 'The Volunteer Movement as an Anti-Revolutionary Force, 1793–1801', *English Historical Review*, vol. 71 (1956), pp. 603–14.
4. William Hamilton Reid. *The Rise and Dissolution of the Infidel Societies of This Metropolis* (1801), p. iii.
5. See also *Application of Barruel's Memoirs of Jacobinism to the Secret Societies of Ireland and Great Britain* (1798), *Jacobinism Displayed; In an Address to the People of England* (Birmingham, 1798); [Thomas Atkinson.] *An Oblique View of the Grand Conspiracy against Social Order* (1798); and W.H. Reid. *The Rise and Dissolution of the Infidel Societies in this Metropolis* (1800), which surveys the period from

1794–1800. On the reception of Barruel in Britain, see Bernard Schilling. *Conservative England and the Case against Voltaire* (New York, Columbia University Press, 1950), pp. 248–77; and on Robison, J.B. Morrell. 'Professors Robison and Playfair, and the *Theophobia Gallica*: Natural Philosophy, Religion and Politics in Edinburgh, 1789–1815', *Notes and Records of the Royal Society of London*, vol. 26 (1971), pp. 43–63.

6. For example, [G.W.E. Russell.] *Collections and Recollections* (1898), p. 77: ' "I have heard persons of great weight and authority", writes Mr. Gladstone, "ascribe the beginnings of a reviving seriousness in the upper classes of lay society to a reaction against the horrors and impieties of the first French Revolution in its later stages" '.

7. See generally Donald Winch. *Riches and Poverty: An Intellectual History of Political Economy in Britain, 1750–1834* (Cambridge, Cambridge University Press, 1996), pp. 230–80, and Donald Winch. *Malthus* (Oxford, Oxford University Press, 1987). pp. 24–35.

8. Quoted in C. Kegan Paul. *William Godwin, His Friends and Contemporories* (2 vols, 1876), vol. 1, pp. 323–4.

9. T.R. Malthus. *An Essay on the Principle of Population* (1798), p. 20.

10. Ibid., p. 13.

11. Quoted in Patricia James. *Population Malthus. His Life and Times* (Routledge & Kegan Paul, 1979), p. 69.

12. William Godwin. *The Enquirer* (1797), p. 168.

13. '… utility … is the surest foundation of all morality' (*An Essay on the Principle of Population*, 2nd edn, 1803, p. 560).

14. T.R. Malthus. *An Essay on the Principle of Population* (1798), pp. 79–80.

15. Ibid. (2nd edn, 1803), pp. 530–2.

16. Ibid., p. 531.

17. Ibid. (1798), pp. 176–7.

18. Robert Wallace. *Various Prospects of Mankind, Nature, and Providence* (1761).

19. T.R. Malthus. *An Essay on the Principle of Population* (1798), p. 204.

20. Ibid. (2nd edn, 1803), pp. 564–5.

21. *Thomas Poole and His Friends*, ed. Mrs. Henry Sandford (2 vols, 1888), vol. 2, p. 123.

22. William Smyth. *Lectures on History* (2nd series, 3 vols, 1842), vol. 3, p. 71.

23. Leonard Hobhouse. *Social Development. Its Nature and Conditions* (George Allen & Unwin, 1924), p. 328.

24. H.S. Foxwell (introduction to Menger. *The Whole Produce of Labour*, 1899, p. xxxiv) doubts that Hall knew Godwin's work because he did not cite him. J.R. Dinwiddy asserts that Hall probably had read Godwin ('Charles Hall, Early English Socialist', *International Review of Social History*, 21, 1976, 256–65, reprinted in Dinwiddy. *Radicalism and Reform in Britain, 1780–1850* (Hambledon Press, 1992). *The Effects of Civilization* is discussed at length in the first important socialist journal, *The Economist* (vol. 1, no. 4, 17 February 1821, 49–50). Hall's *Effects* was well known amongst the early socialists, being reprinted in 1814, 1820 and 1850. The third edition was brought out by Hall under the title, *An Enquiry into the Cause of the Present Distress of the People*. The fourth edition was reprinted by the Christian Owenite John Minter Morgan. Godwin had defined wealth as 'a power vested in certain individuals by the institutions of society, to compel others to labour for their benefit' (*The Enquirer*, p. 177.)

25. Hall's chief source for the history of the poor seems to have been F.M. Eden's *The State of the Poor* (3 vols, 1797). Eden agreed that the poor worked harder than a century earlier, but also thought they had more comforts 'if the comforts of labourers depend on the demand for labour' (vol. 1, pp. 406–7). Little is known of Hall's life. He was born about 1738, studied medicine at Leyden, and practised at Tavistock for much of his life. Imprisoned for a relatively small debt in 1816, he remained incarcerated largely on principle and probably died soon after being released in 1825.

26. See 'Four Letters between Thomas Spence and Charles Hall', *Notes and Queries*, NS 28, no. 4 (August 1981), 317–321.

27. A. Ferguson. *An Essay on the History of Civil Society* (1767) (Edinburgh, Edinburgh University Press, 1966), pp. 301–40. Thelwall had intended to deal with manufactures in later lectures which were not delivered.

28. Charles Hall. *The Effects of Civilization on the People in European States* (1805), p. 27. Hall criticised Spence for retaining 'all the individual property except ... that of land' (meaning stock, implements and the like), adding that 'this wealth ... being power [would] be exercised by the possessors over the non-possessors' (Hall to Spence, n.d., in *Notes and Queries*, 226, 1981, 318).

29. Adam Smith. *An Inquiry into the Nature and Cause of the Wealth of Nations* (2 vols, 1776), vol. 2, pp. 366–7. See generally Donald Winch. *Adam Smith's Politics* (Cambridge, Cambridge University

Press, 1978). See John Brown. *An Estimate of the Manners and Principles of the Times*, (2 vols, 1757–8), vol. 1, p. 192: 'the common Artificer, and still more the common labourers, gain little or nothing by the exhorbitant advance of trade'.

30. Charles Hall. *The Effects*, pp. 70–3, 84–6, 115, 131–4.

31. See my *Citizens and Saints. Politics and Anti-Politics in Early British Socialism* (Cambridge, Cambridge University Press, 1989), pp. 152–61.

32. With Godwin. Hall's is an early, important use of the word, though it is not of course exclusively associated with manufacturers. Godwin uses 'capitalist' in later editions of *Political Justice* (2 vols, 1842), vol. 2, p. 148. (The *Oxford English Dictionary* gives the first use of the word as mid-nineteenth century.) Eden had also juxtaposed 'monied capitalist' to 'landed proprietor' in 1797 (*A History*, vol. 1, p. 407).

33. See J.G.A. Pocock. *The Machiavellian Moment. Florentine Political Thought and the Atlantic Republican Tradition* (Princeton, Princeton University Press, 1975), pp. 462–505.

34. Charles Hall. *The Effects*, p. 72. Sir James Steuart had also tried to ascertain what minimal percentage of population was necessary to maintain agricultural production. See his *An Inquiry into the Principles of Political Oeconomy* (2 vols, 1767; repr. Oliver & Boyd, 1966), vol. 1, pp. 51–55.

35. Charles Hall. *The Effects*, pp. 318, 321.

36. See my *Citizens and Saints*, pp. 150–52.

37. See Asa Briggs. 'The Language of "Class" in Early Nineteenth-Century England', in Briggs and John Saville, eds. *Essays in Labour History* (Macmillan, 1960), pp. 43–73, and more generally, Gareth Stedman Jones. *Languages of Class* (Cambridge, Cambridge University Press, 1982).

38. Menger wrote that 'Hall may be regarded as the first socialist who saw in rent and interest unjust appropriations of the return of labour, and who explicitly claimed for the worker the undiminished product of his industry' (*The Whole Produce of Labour*, p. 48), and saw Hall as a 'socialist' in addition because the state was to possess all land and parcel it out, though without common production. The second point, however, is merely a republican agrarian law. The first does capture Hall's insights, except that it needs to be seen in terms of his definition of wealth as the power to command labour, without which his theory of unjust appropriation is

meaningless. Godwin, it might be added, saw the claim of 'the whole produce of labour' as morally 'a kind of usurpation' (*Political Justice*, pp. 710–11), given our duty to distribute property justly.

39. Thomas Spence. *The Important Trial of Thomas Spence* (2nd edn, 1803), p. 16.

40. Charles Hall. *The Effects*, pp. 75, 184–91, 248–59. Hall's source for his views of America appears primarily to have been J.P. Brissot de Warville's *New Travels in the United States of America. Performed in 1788* (English transl., 1792). But while Brissot emphasised that American virtue depended on most living in the country and remaining independent, and was worried only by the aristocracy of southern slave-holders, he expected slavery to be abolished (pp. xix–xxi, xxxi, 281).

41. Ogilvie, for example, had proposed a division of lands into plots of 40 acres (*An Essay on the Right of Property in Land*, Glasgow, 1781, pp. 92–100), and Burgh, 35–50 acres (*An Account of the First Settlement, Laws, Form of Government, and Police of the Cessares, A People in South America*, 1764, reprinted in my *Utopias of the British Enlightenment*, Cambridge, Cambridge University Press, 1994, p. 65).

42. Charles Hall. *The Effects*, pp. 65–8, 107, 214–16, 262–6, 283, 281, 307.

43. Leslie Stephen. *History of English Thought in the Eighteenth Century* (2 vols, 1881), vol. 2, p. 201.

Reading List: Major Figures

Burke

The standard modern critical edition of the *Reflections* is L.G. Mitchell, ed. *The Writings and Speeches of Edmund Burke*, vol. 8 (Oxford: Oxford University Press, 1989), pp. 53–293. The best accessible edition is edited by J.G.A. Pocock (Indianapolis: Hackett Publishing Company, 1987). Studies of Burke's political thought include Alfred Cobban. *Edmund Burke and the Revolt against the Eighteenth-century* (George Allen & Unwin, 1929), Carl Cone. *Burke and the Nature of Politics* (Lexington: University of Kentucky Press, 1957), Peter Stanlis. *Edmund Burke and the Natural Law* (Ann Arbor: University of Michigan Press, 1958), Francis Canavan. *The Political Reason of Edmund Burke* (Durham, NC: Duke University Press, 1960), Burleigh Wilkins. *The Problem of Burke's Political Philosophy* (Oxford: Clarendon Press, 1967), Frank O'Gorman. *Edmund Burke. His Political Philosophy* (George Allen and Unwin, 1973), Frederick Dreyer. *Burke's Politics. A Study in Whig Orthodoxy* (Waterloo, Ont.: Wilfred Laurier University Press, 1979), Michael Freeman. *Edmund Burke and the Critique of Political Radicalism* (Oxford: Blackwell, 1980), F.P. Lock. *Burke's Reflections on the Revolution in France* (George Allen and Unwin, 1985), Iain Hampsher-Monk. *The Political Philosophy of Edmund Burke* (Longman, 1987), Steven Blakemore. *Burke and the Fall of Language. The French Revolution as Linguistic Event* (Hanover, N.H., University Press of New England, 1988), and Tom Furniss. *Edmund Burke's Aesthetic Ideology: Language, Gender, and Political Economy in Revolution* (Cambridge, Cambridge University Press, 1933). Essay collections include Stephen Blakemore, ed. *Burke and the French Revolution: Bicentennial Essays* (Athens, GA: University of Georgia Press, 1992).

Recent biographies include Conor Cruise O'Brien's *The Great Melody. A Thematic Biography of Edmund Burke* (Sinclair-Stevenson, 1992), and, for Burke's early career, F.P. Lock. *Edmund Burke* (Oxford: Clarendon Press, 1998), vol. 1: 1730–84.

For bibliography see Leonard Cowrie. *Edmund Burke, 1729–97: A Bibliography* (Westview CT: Greenwood Press, 1994).

Paine

Paine scholarship, like that respecting Burke, has often been predictably and lamentably partisan. A hostile life of Paine commissioned by the government appeared as Francis Oldys [i.e. George Chalmers]. *The Life of Thomas Paine* (1791). It reached 10 editions by 1796, and was met by the reformers' *Impartial Memoirs of the Life of Thomas Paine* (1793). Later biographies by contemporaries include W.T. Sherwin. *Life of Thomas Paine* (1819) and Thomas Clio Rickman. *The Life of Thomas Paine* (1819). Modern Paine scholarship commences with Moncure Conway's two-volume biography, *The Life of Thomas Paine* (2 vols, 1892) and his edition of *The Writings of Thomas Paine* (4 vols, 1894–6). A later edition of his works is Thomas Paine. *Complete Writings*, ed. Philip Foner (New York, Citadel Press, 1945). Later biographies include A.O. Aldridge. *Man of Reason. The Life of Thomas Paine* (The Cresset Press, 1960) and John Keane. *Tom Paine. A Political Life* (Bloombury Books, 1995). Studies of his thought include A.J. Ayer. *Thomas Paine* (Faber & Faber, 1988), my *Thomas Paine: Social and Political Thought* (Unwin Hyman, 1989), Mark Philp. *Paine* (Oxford, Oxford University Press, 1989), Jack Fruchtman. Jr. *Thomas Paine: Apostle of Freedom* (Four Walls Eight Windows, 1994), and Edward Larkin. *Thomas Paine and the Literature of Revolution* (Cambridge, Cambridge University Press, 2005). An accessible edition of *Rights of Man* is published by Hackett publishing Company (1992).

Wollstonecraft

Biographies of Wollstonecraft include: Claire Tomalin. *The Life and Death of Mary Wollstonecraft* (1974), Janet Todd. *Mary Wollstonecraft. A Revolutionary Life* (Weidenfeld & Nicolson, 2000), Barbara Taylor.

Mary Wollstonecraft and the Feminist Imagination (Cambridge, Cambridge University Press, 2003), Caroline Franklin. *Mary Wollstonecraft: A Literary Life* (Palgrave, 2004), and Lyndall Gordon. *Vindication: A Life of Mary Wollstonecraft* (Virago, 2005). Studies of her ideas include Jennifer Lorch. *Mary Wollstonecraft: The Making of a Radical Feminist* (Oxford: Berg, 1990), Gary Kelly. *Revolutionary Feminism. The Mind and Career of Mary Wollstonecraft* (London, Macmillan, 1992), Virginia Sapiro. *A Vindication of Political Virtue: the Political Theory of Mary Wollstonecraft* (Chicago, University of Chicago Press, 1992), and Saba Bahar. *Mary Wollstonecraft's Social and Aesthetic Philosophy* (Basingstoke Palgrave, 2002). A useful collection of essays is Claudia Johnson, ed. *The Cambridge Companion to Mary Wollstonecraft* (Cambridge, Cambridge University Press, 2002).

Godwin

Godwin's main works are reprinted in Mark Philp, ed. *Political and Philosophical Writings of William Godwin* (7 vols, Pickering and Chatto, 1993). The *Enquiry Concerning Political Justice* has been reprinted as a Penguin classic (1976).

The standard nineteenth-century account of Godwin is Charles Kegan Paul. *William Godwin. His Friends and Contemporaries* (2 vols, 1876). Biographies include Peter H. Marshall. *William Godwin* (Yale University Press, 1984), and Don Locke. *A Fantasy of Reason. The Life and Thought of William Godwin* (Routledge and Kegan Paul, 1980). Studies of Godwin's thought include D.H. Monro. *Godwin's Moral Philosophy* (Oxford, Oxford University Press, 1953), Burton R. Pollin. *Education and Enlightenment in the Works of William Godwin* (New York, Las Americas Publishing Company, 1962), Frederick Rosen. *Progress and Democracy. William Godwin's Contribution to Political Philosophy* (Garland, 1987), Mark Philp. *Godwin's Political Justice* (Duckworth, 1986), and John P. Clark. *The Philosophical Anarchism of William Godwin* (Princeton University Press, 1977).

An exhaustive bibliography of Godwin and Godwiniana is provided in Burton R. Pollin. *Godwin Criticism. A Synoptic Bibliography* (Toronto, University of Toronto Press, 1967).

Thelwall

Thelwall's chief writings are reprinted in my edition *The Politics of English Jacobinism. Writings of John Thelwall* (University Park, Pa., Penn State University Press, 1995), Biographies include Mrs. J. Thelwall. *The Life of John Thelwall* (1837) and Charles Cestre. *John Thelwall. A Pioneer of Democracy and Social Reform in England During the French Revolution* (Swan Sonnenschein, 1906).

Index